Online Counseling: A Handbook for Mental Health Professionals

Online Counseling: A Handbook for Mental Health Professionals

Edited by:

Ron Kraus
OnlineClinics.com

Jason S. Zack
University of Miami

George Stricker
Derner Institute,
Adelphi University

ELSEVIER
ACADEMIC
PRESS

AMSTERDAM • BOSTON • HEIDELBERG • LONDON
NEW YORK • OXFORD • PARIS • SAN DIEGO
SAN FRANCISCO • SINGAPORE • SYDNEY • TOKYO
Academic Press is an imprint of Elsevier

Elsevier Academic Press
525 B Street, Suite 1900, San Diego, California 92101-4495, USA
84 Theobald's Road, London WC1X 8RR, UK

This book is printed on acid-free paper. ∞

Library of Congress Cataloging-in-Publication Data
Application submitted

British Library Cataloguing in Publication Data

A catalogue record for this book is available from the British Library

ISBN: 0-12-425955-3

For all information on all Academic Press publications
visit our website at www.academicpress.com

Printed in the United States of America
03 04 05 06 07 08   9 8 7 6 5 4 3 2 1

TABLE OF CONTENTS

PART I

THE NEW MEDIUM: HISTORY & RESEARCH

1

ONLINE BEHAVIOR, COMMUNICATION, AND EXPERIENCE

MICHAEL A. FENICHEL

2

THE PSYCHOLOGY OF TEXT RELATIONSHIPS

JOHN SULER

3

ONLINE COUNSELING: A HISTORICAL PERSPECTIVE

JOHN M. GROHOL

4

ONLINE COUNSELING RESEARCH

MICHAEL J. MALLEN

PART II

THE PRACTICAL ASPECTS OF ONLINE COUNSELING

5

TECHNOLOGY OF ONLINE COUNSELING

JASON S. ZACK

6

ETHICAL AND LEGAL CONSIDERATIONS FOR
PROVIDERS OF MENTAL HEALTH SERVICES ONLINE

RON KRAUS

7

THE BUSINESS ASPECTS OF ONLINE COUNSELING

RON KRAUS & JASON S. ZACK

PART III

Clinical Issues in Online Counseling

8

Online Counseling Skills Part I: Treatment Strategies and Skills for Conducting Counseling Online

Elizabeth Zelvin & Cedric M. Speyer

9

Online Counseling Skills Part II: In-Session Skills

Gary S. Stofle & Peter J. Chechele

10

ONLINE COUNSELING GROUPS

DONNA R. BELLAFIORE, YVETTE COLÓN & PAUL ROSENBERG

11

INTERNET-BASED PSYCHOLOGICAL TESTING
AND ASSESSMENT

AZY BARAK & TOM BUCHANAN

12

INTERNATIONAL AND MULTICULTURAL ISSUES IN ONLINE COUNSELING

ADRIAN E. G. SKINNER & GARY LATCHFORD

PART IV

A LOOK TO THE FUTURE OF ONLINE COUNSELING

13

THE FUTURE OF ONLINE COUNSELING

LEONARD HOLMES & MARTHA AINSWORTH

Contributors

Numbers in parentheses indicate the pages on which the authors' contributions begin.

Martha Ainsworth (255) Metanoia.org and Beliefnet.com, Princeton, New Jersey 08540.

Azy Barak (217) University of Haifa, Haifa 31905, Israel.

Donna R. Bellafiore (197) DRB Alternatives, Inc., Naperville, Illinois 60540.

Tom Buchanan (217) Department of Psychology, University of Westminster, London, W1B 2UW, United Kingdom.

Peter J. Chechele (181) Conscious Choices, Concord, California 94521.

Yvette Colón (197) American Pain Foundation, Baltimore, Maryland 21201-4111.

Patrick H. DeLeon (xxi) United States Senate, Washington, D.C. 20510.

Michael A. Fenichel (1) PsychServices.com and *Current Topics in Psychology*, New York, New York 10023.

John M. Grohol (51) PsychCentral.com, Bradford, Massachusetts 01835.

Leonard Holmes (255) Veterans Affairs Medical Center, Hampton, Virginia, 23667.

Ron Kraus (xxxvi, 123, 145) OnlineClinics.com, Teaneck, New Jersey 07666; American & International Association of Online Psychotherapists, 07666; EthicsCode.com, Teaneck, New Jersey 07666; International Society for Mental Health Online, Miami, Florida 33233; Fairleigh Dickinson University, metropolitan campus, Teaneck, New Jersey 07666.

Gary Latchford (241) Academic Unit of Psychiatry, University of Leeds, Leeds, LS2 9LT, United Kingdom.

Michael J. Mallen (69) Iowa State University, Department of Psychology, Ames, Iowa 50011.

Paul Rosenberg (197) eGetgoing, San Jose, California 95128; Department of Psychiatry and Biobehavioral Sciences, UCLA School of Medicine, San Jose, California 95128.

Morgan T. Sammons (xxi) U.S. Navy Bureau of Medicine and Surgery, Washington, D.C. 20372.

Adrian E. G. Skinner (241) Department of Psychology, Craven and Harrogate Primary Care NHS Trust, Harrogate, North Yorkshire, HG2 7RY, United Kingdom.

Cedric M. Speyer (161) Warren Shepell Consultants, Corp., Toronto, Ontario, M5S 1N5, Canada.

Gary S. Stofle (181) Columbus Area, Inc., Columbus, Ohio 43205.

George Stricker (xxxvii) The Derner Institute, Adelphi University, Garden City, New York 11530.

John Suler (19) Department of Psychology, Rider University, Lawrenceville, New Jersey 08648.

Jason Zack (xxxvii, 91, 145) University of Miami, Coral Gables, Florida 33146.

Elizabeth Zelvin (161) Lzcybershrink.com, New York, New York 10024.

ABOUT THE CONTRIBUTORS

Martha Ainsworth is president emerita of the International Society of Mental Health Online (2002), founder and director of Metanoia.org, community producer of the multifaith spirituality website Beliefnet.com, and is a professional musician.
(http://www.Metanoia.org, www.Beliefnet.com)

Azy Barak, Ph.D., is a professor of psychology at the University of Haifa, Haifa, Israel. He earned his bachelor's degree and master's degree at Tel Aviv University, and his doctorate degree at Ohio State University, where he majored in counseling psychology. Since 1995 he has specialized in the psychology of the Internet and is involved in research, development, and teaching in this area.
(http://construct.haifa.ac.il/~azy/azy.htm)

Donna R. Bellafiore, L.C.S.W., C.A.D.C., is president of DRB Alternatives, Inc. She is in private practice in Naperville, Illinois. Donna is a published author of a popular self-help guide, *Straight Talk About Betrayal: A Self-Help Guide For Couples.* She has also been featured in the *Chicago Tribune* and the *Naperville Sun.* Her current experience includes research on communications and the development of online infidelity support groups since 1998. (http://www.drbalternatives.com)

Tom Buchanan, Ph.D., is a senior lecturer in psychology at the University of Westminster, London, United Kingdom. He teaches mainly in the areas of personality and social psychology. His research work currently focuses on use of the Internet for assessment of personality, and on development of online research techniques and their application to research questions difficult to address by other means (e.g., self-reported effects of recreational drug use on memory).

Peter J. Chechele, M.A., is a Licensed Marriage and Family Therapist practicing in the Bay Area specializing in clinical work with individuals, couples, and families. He has provided online counseling since 1997 and is a member of the International Society of Mental Health Online (ISMHO). (http://www.cybertherapy.com)

Yvette Colón, M.S.W., A.C.S.W., B.C.D., is the director of Education and Internet Services at the American Pain Foundation. She has been facilitating online support and psychotherapy groups since 1993. She was a recipient in 2001 of a Project on Death in America Social Work Leadership Award to create a new interactive teaching forum that used the Internet to provide focused, intensive training on end-of-life social work practice. She has published and lectured widely on technology-based social work services and clinical aspects of online group therapy (http://www.painfoundation.org).

Patrick H. DeLeon, Ph.D., J.D., M.P.H., is president emeritus of the American Psychological Association and has served as administrative assistant for U.S. Senator Daniel K. Inouye (D-HI) since 1973.

Michael A. Fenichel, Ph.D., is a clinical psychologist whose 20 years of research and practice activities have spanned across the areas of psychotherapy, individual and group dynamics, intelligence, cognitive processing, and the phenomenology of online experience. A founding member of International Society for Mental Health Online (ISMHO), he was also a coleader of the first and longest-running online clinical case study group—a multidisciplinary, international group of mental health professionals. Aside from peer supervision activities online, he has supervised both clinical and school psychology interns for several New York area graduate programs and has published numerous articles in both print journals and on his award-winning website, "Current Topics in Psychology." (http://www.fenichel.com)

John M. Grohol, Psy.D., is a Boston-area author, researcher, and expert in the area of online psychology and mental health. He has been involved in psychology online since 1991 and has built some of the Internet's best-known mental health resources. Presently he advises HelpHorizons.com, an e-therapy services portal, and runs his own behavioral Internet company, Liviant. (http://www.psychcentral.com)

Leonard Holmes, Ph.D., is a clinical psychologist currently working at the Department of Veterans Affairs Medical Center in Hampton, Virginia. He also works online and is the Guide to Mental Health Resources for About.com. In the summer he teaches Health Psychology at the College of William and Mary. (http://www.leonardholmes.com)

Ron Kraus, Ph.D., C.S.W., is a clinical and child psychologist practicing in New York City and northern New Jersey. Ron has taught traditional as well as online courses at the metropolitan campus of Fairleigh Dickinson University since 1998. He founded the American and International Association of Online Psychotherapists (AAOP.com) and OnlineClinics.com in 1999, and served as the 2003 President of the International Society for Mental Health Online (ISMHO). Ron's projects online include www.EthicsCode.com and the memorial site www.StillRemember.com. He is married to a health care professional and is the father of two.
(http://www.RonKraus.com)

Gary Latchford is a research tutor in clinical psychology at the University of Leeds, Leeds, United Kingdom. He is also a clinical health psychologist at St. James University Hospital, Leeds. He has written about trauma and eating disorders. His clinical interests include coronary heart disease and diabetes.

Michael J. Mallen, M.A., is currently a doctoral student in counseling psychology at Iowa State University. He received his master's degree from the University of Minnesota in Educational Psychology. Currently, he is working on a dissertation investigating counselor reactions to delivering treatment through synchronous chat. He has also published work on the differences between face-to-face and online discourse.

Paul Rosenberg, M.D., Chief Medical Officer of eGetgoing.com, is also an assistant clinical professor in the Department of Psychiatry and Biobehavioral Sciences at the UCLA School of Medicine in San Jose, California. In 2000, he and his team at eGetgoing developed the first online live group treatment program for substance abuse. eGetgoing has treated people on five continents through the Internet. The clients can interact verbally and see the therapist throughout the group session. A teen treatment program and a new online teen assessment program have also been established. (http://www.eGetgoing.org)

Morgan T. Sammons, Ph.D., is head of the Mental Health Department at the Naval Medical Clinic, U.S. Naval Academy, Annapolis, Maryland; a commander in the U.S. Navy; and president emeritus of the Maryland Psychological Association (2001–2002). He is a prescribing psychologist and a graduate of the Department of Defense Psychopharmacology Demonstration Project.

Adrian E. G. Skinner is director of Clinical Psychology Services for Harrogate, North Yorkshire, United Kingdom. He has been practicing as a clinical psychologist for 30 years and is chair emeritus of the U.K. Division of Clinical Psychology. He has published in a variety of areas including psychotherapy and neuropsychology.

Cedric M. Speyer is clinical manager of E-Counseling for Warren Shepell Consultants, based in Toronto, Canada. He has master's degrees in creative writing, counseling psychology, and education, and is creative director for Hearing Heart Publications. As a pioneer of e-counseling in an Employee Assistant Program (EAP) setting, he developed the "four-session model" currently used in Canada and Japan. (https://www.warrenshepell.com/ecounseling/profile.html)

Gary S. Stofle, L.I.S.W., CCDCIIIE, is program manager with Columbus Area, Inc. Gary has been involved in online therapy since 1997 and feels committed to exploring the potential of the Internet to help and heal others. He lives in central Ohio with his wife and two daughters. (http://www.stofle.com)

George Stricker, Ph.D., is Distinguished Research Professor of Psychology and former dean of the Derner Institute, Adelphi University. He has received the American Psychological Association Award for Distinguished Contribution to Applied Psychology, the American Psychological Association Award for Distinguished Career Contributions to Education and Training in Psychology, and numerous other awards. His most recent books include the *Comprehensive Handbook of Psychotherapy Integration* with Jerry Gold, and *The Scientific Practice of Professional Psychology* with Steven Trierweiler.

John Suler, Ph.D., is a clinical psychologist and professor of psychology at Rider University who specializes in Internet research. He publishes all of his work in his online hypertext book "The Psychology of Cyberspace" and also maintains several other large websites, including "Teaching Clinical Psychology" and "Zen Stories to Tell Your Neighbors." (http://www.rider.edu/users/suler/psycyber/psycyber.html)

Jason S. Zack, Ph.D., is a behavioral science consultant based in Coral Gables, Florida. He is an adjunct assistant professor in the Department of Education and Psychological Studies at the University of Miami, and is president-elect of the International Society for Mental Health Online (ISMHO). (http://www.technopsychology.com)

Elizabeth Zelvin, CSW-R, is a New York City psychotherapist who has directed addictions programs and has written and lectured widely on online practice. Her publications include *Gender and Addictions: Men and Women in Treatment* and two books of poetry. Liz hosts a weekly chat on the AOL Social Work Forum. (http://www.lzcybershrink.com)

FOREWORD

WHITHER ONLINE COUNSELING: CONCEPTUALIZING THE CHALLENGES AND PROMISES OF DISTANCE MENTAL HEALTH SERVICE PROVISION

MORGAN T. SAMMONS, PH.D.

U.S. Navy Bureau of Medicine and Surgery[1]

PATRICK H. DELEON, PH.D., J.D., M.P.H.

President Emeritus, American Psychological Association

INTRODUCTION

As we enter the 21st century, it is intriguing to predict what our nation's health care delivery system will look like in the coming decades. There are many potential focal points for such speculation. Perhaps the most useful for readers of this volume is the reality that the number of nonphysician health care providers in the United States is projected to approximate the number of physicians providing primary care within only a few years (Cooper, Laud, & Detrich, 1998). With these increasing numbers will come an entirely different health care environment, including the gradual adoption of a different terminology, as well as a fundamentally different perspective as to what constitutes quality care. Counseling and the provision of mental health services, for example, will clearly be deemed in the very near future to be essential health services that are relevant to a wide range of human conditions and disease entities. A data-driven orientation and decision-making style, which is already fundamental to the behavioral sciences, will become increasingly incorporated into both clinical service delivery and health care systems planning. Accountability, regardless of which profession provides the service, will be one of the hallmarks of 21st-century health care service provision.

[1]The opinions expressed by the first author are his alone and do not represent the official policies or positions of the U.S. Navy or Department of Defense.

Providers and recipients of counseling services will be directly affected by the unprecedented and fundamental changes that are evolving both within and outside of the U.S. health care system. Within the health care arena, the historically silo-oriented (i.e., professionally isolated) training and clinical perspective of the various professional disciplines providing counseling or psychotherapy will, in all probability, gradually disappear. Interdisciplinary care will become the norm. Broader societal changes will also spur the shift to interdisciplinary care. Among these, technological changes will play a major role in shaping health care delivery.

Four out of ten U.S. households had Internet access as of August 2000, and it is predicted that 90 percent will have access by 2010 or before. As of this writing, between 70 million and 100 million Americans seek health information online (Institute of Medicine, 2001). The quality of information obtained online is highly variable, but the easy accessibility of medical information has affected the patient–provider relationship perhaps more than any other single factor in recent years. Patients, armed with knowledge that had not long ago been easily available only to highly educated professionals, are questioning diagnoses, treatments, and outcomes to a far greater extent than ever before. In addition, the volume of information and the rapidity with which it is disseminated will in all likelihood accelerate the pace at which medical innovations are implemented in clinical practice. The Institute of Medicine (IOM) reports that the lag between the discovery of more efficacious forms of treatment and their incorporation into routine patient care is unnecessarily long, in the range of about 15 to 20 years. This situation will perforce change as governmental entities expand the information infrastructure that will allow extensive treatment comparisons among patients, providers, institutions, and disease entities.

Economic forces in the health care market will also drive significant change in service delivery mechanisms. The costs of providing health care in the United States, which already boasts the most expensive health care in the world, are expected to continue to rise at rates far outpacing inflation. Americans in 2002 spent approximately 14% of the gross domestic product on health care. By the year 2012, this figure is estimated to approach 18%, driven largely by two factors—the cost of prescription drugs and the cost of physicians' services (Heffler et al., 2003). Unfortunately, it has become clear that high costs have not necessarily meant high quality. Variations in the quality of care received by most Americans are so extreme that they have been labeled "serious threats to the health of the U.S. public" (McGlynn et al., 2003, p. 2644). Thus, despite several decades of efforts to systematically improve quality, we have not made significant strides toward an overall improvement in the quality of care offered to our citizenry.

It is clear that a number of highly complex issues surround the delivery of online counseling services. More will undoubtedly evolve over time as professionals of all disciplines (and their clients) obtain firsthand experience with clinical services being provided in a virtual reality.

Projections indicate that health care will rapidly become more and more unaffordable to more and more Americans. It is axiomatic that those who will most keenly feel the adverse effects of this are those who can least afford to: the poor and the underserved. Furthermore, many Americans who are not economically disadvantaged will be increasingly unable to afford access to comprehensive health care. In this context, the distance provision of psychological services deserves close scrutiny as a mechanism for enhancing mental health service delivery. It is incumbent upon mental health professionals, in our manyfold roles as researchers, educators, administrators, policymakers, and clinicians, to devise and implement programs that will expand quality and accessibility of health care services to all sectors of society. Particularly in rural areas, or designated health professional shortage areas, we should be attuned to opportunities provided by distance service provision.[1] It is equally necessary for us to remain well-versed in state and federal regulations establishing standards and practice parameters for this emerging technology.

The subject of this book, online counseling, is but one example of distance service provision that may have particular applications in mental health. Telephone counseling and video teleconferencing (VTC) also provide approximations of the face-to-face (f2f) encounter, and these forms of intervention have a more established history in mental health. Distance service provision of mental health services has existed in embryonic or experimental form since 1959, when a long-running project to conduct group psychotherapy in different sites in the rural Midwest was initiated (Perednia & Allen, 1995). Much has happened technologically in the intervening years, making telehealth an increasingly attractive economic option. Evidence supporting the efficacy, as well as the cost-effectiveness, of telehealth and other distance modalities is slowly accruing, and distance mental health service provision, though largely in the form of telepsychiatry, is one of the most popular applications of telehealth today. But telehealth applications are still limited, and telehealth (by which we mean the provision of services using video links) and telephone counseling both differ significantly from online counseling. The absence of visual and aural cues presents unique challenges to online counseling. These limitations, as well as other technological and economic obstacles, must be satisfactorily addressed before online counseling, or any distance service provision, becomes a significant portion of the health care market.

---

[1]For the purposes of this chapter, distance service provision means the provision of psychotherapy, consultation or other psychological services between a provider or providers and a geographically separate recipient via videoteleconference, email, telephone, or similar modality.

CAN PSYCHOTHERAPY PROCESS SURVIVE
IN CYBERSPACE?

Whether online counseling or other mechanisms of distance service provision will enter the mainstream of mental health practice is still uncertain. Provision of distance services such as teaching, supervision, and professional-to-professional consultation have a more clearly defined place in psychological service delivery. But if direct online service delivery is to become accepted, two key issues must be resolved: *patient satisfaction* and *provider comfort* in an electronic, rather than f2f, environment. Numerous secondary issues also must be resolved; these are by no means minor nor are their solutions readily apparent. But if the first two conditions are unmet, distance provision of psychological services will not succeed.

The psychotherapeutic relationship rests largely on the patient's belief that she or he is able to effectively communicate the set of problems at hand, and that those problems are understood by the therapist. It seems clear that humans can communicate affect and establish an online consistency of emotional and intellectual communication to a sufficient degree that this may serve as an electronic shadow of that person's character, although, as Suler (see Chapter 2) notes, this may in large part be dependent on the skills of the writer in emotional self-expression. Studies of interrater[1] reliability of online communication of emotion may result in good concordance rates, although this may not be the case when the writer attempts to convey more subtle meanings. Also, as Suler observes, the ability to express oneself in writing varies widely between individuals, and although innovative written cues (punctuation used as shorthand for emotional states; use of bolded, colored, or italicized text; or the insertion of animated figures into text) may help convey meaning and affect, textual communication will always differ from f2f or VTC communication. This is because in the absence of visual and aural stimuli, the receiver—not the deliverer—perforce becomes the referent through which the intentions of the deliverer are interpreted.

Without visual or aural road maps, the receiver is forced to rely exclusively on his or her emotional referents to interpret the meaning of the text communicated. We believe this is an extension of what Suler (see Chapter 2) calls "solipsistic introjection," and this may prove to be the most important process limitation of online counseling. Consider that although a novelist may be skilled at elucidating the emotional structure of his or her characters, his or her words must pass through the internal filters of the reader and, for this reason, will never receive an identical interpretation. Broad emotional constructs are easy to convey via the written word;

---

[1]Interrater means the degree of concordance achieved when two observers independently rate the same process.

nuanced emotions are excruciatingly difficult, even to the most practiced writer. This, combined with the absence of visual and aural cues, makes the online communication of subtle emotional states enduringly problematic.

As Fenichel and colleagues (see Chapter 1) observe, Internet technology has become increasingly "transparent" to most Americans. We have, as a society, been particularly conditioned to respond to therapy provided in an electronic environment. In addition, the Internet may be a particularly comfortable nexus of therapy for patients who are shy or have other social phobias or inhibitions, perhaps as severe as agoraphobia. The obvious objection, of course, is that provision of services in a manner that perpetuates psychopathology may reinforce rather than assist dysfunctional behavior. Fenichel also points out the challenge that distance service may present to theories of psychopathology and for highly theory-based interventions.

What psychodynamic constructs can be applied to electronic behavior? How do concepts of resistance or object relations translate in the electronic age? Some degree of emotion can be easily communicated in online transactions, but can the deep, sustained sharing of emotion deemed necessary for many forms of psychotherapy be effectively maintained in an electronic environment? Does transference develop in cyberspace?

Are the *process* obstacles to forming a therapeutic alliance in distance counseling so great that they cannot be overcome? Only the brave—or foolhardy—would be likely to answer this in the affirmative at the present time. Just as cost obstacles and technological access issues, once considered prohibitive, are becoming less problematic, so it may be that psychological barriers to electronic therapies may dissipate as well. But process as well as numerous legal and regulatory issues must be resolved before this modality is adopted on a wide scale. We now turn to an analysis of these issues.

AN ORGANIZATIONAL HEURISTIC FOR INVESTIGATING DISTANCE PROVISION OF PSYCHOLOGICAL SERVICES

Most of the potential advantages of distance service provision have yet to be realized; indeed, its acceptability remains unknown. In considering the future of distance service provision, a focus on sociopolitics, as Lehoux and Blume (2000) suggested, rather than a focus on technological factors (which change rapidly and unpredictably), provides a more compelling framework for analysis. Lehoux and Blume (2000) recommended that the potential effects of distance service be analyzed across four broad constructs: the *actors* involved (i.e., providers, patients, families, manufacturers, administrators, and third party payers); the *flow of resources* (i.e., reimbursement strategies for providers, funding for development, placement, and maintenance of networks); *knowledge* (i.e., who establishes the rules for desired distance interventions, and how); and *power* (i.e., who controls this new technology—patients, providers, third party payers, or others, and to what end?). On a more pragmatic level, Lehoux, Battista, & Lance (2000) also suggested four primary goals that Internet service provision would have to meet to be effective: reducing need for transportation of patients and providers, improving service to underserved populations, enhancing knowledge of both providers and patients, and reducing rural isolation.

Attention to these factors, rather than technological or economic details, may help us develop a better picture of the future of distance mental health service provision. On the other hand, it is clear that unless we pay equal attention to the regulatory environment, providers will lose a voice in governance of this new medium. The National Academy of Science has suggested a focus on the following key areas: enhanced security, stronger forms of authentication, effective tools for protecting anonymity, and the use of federal agencies as models for demonstration projects (National Academy of Science, 2000). Such issues are of undeniable importance. In the following sections of this Forward, we will address these key areas, but we will primarily use Lehoux and Blume's model to delineate anticipated challenges to distance service provision.

ACTORS

Satisfaction: Patients, Providers, and Third Party Payers

Earlier studies examining patient satisfaction in distance service provision report generally good, but not universal, levels of patient and provider satisfaction. Many express satisfaction with distance services but also note that they prefer f2f interventions. Most such studies are in the context of VTC; patient and provider satisfaction tends to be high, though not universally so. Often, if the option of f2f consultation is present, patients state that they might prefer this option. Providers, on the whole, express high levels of satisfaction, particularly when the modality allows for time savings or expansion of provider roles. (See, among others, Brodey et al., 2000; Kennedy and Yellowlees, 2000; Simpson et al., 2001; Watanabe, Jennett, & Watson, 1999.)

Demographic characteristics (e.g., age, sex, and income) may be important covariates in patient satisfaction. Will younger patients, both more proficient in computer skills and more inured to electronic intrusions in daily life than older generations, embrace electronic services with greater avidity, or will they be more likely to find solace in the intimacy of interpersonal contact? Gender factors greatly in Internet usage, with young men more likely to use the Internet for recreation and satisfaction of libidinous urges and women more likely to use the Internet to seek information or to communicate. Will these gender differences influence whether, as well as how, men and women seek electronic consultation?

Outcomes

Few good outcomes studies exist yet for distance mental health service provision. Most published reports apply to VTC and are in the form of case studies or short-term pilots and are of variable quality (Roine, Ohinmaa, & Hailey, 2001). Of the studies those authors reviewed, however, the majority demonstrated that distance service provision was as least as effective as f2f, although most interventions did not result in cost savings. One large mental health pilot in a rural setting, however, demonstrated significant cost saving accruing from a reduced need for patient transfer. Another study that incorporated a one-year follow-up and the use of standardized outcomes measures also found that both patients and providers found distance provision of mental health services to be as effective as f2f care (Kennedy & Yellowlees, 2003).

Of the remaining few controlled outcomes studies available, two studies of online counseling for posttraumatic stress found significant improvement in treated patients. Lange et al. (2000) and Lange et al. (2001) reported that an online protocol of treatments for posttraumatic stress disorder and grief resulted in significantly improved symptoms and in general functioning as compared to wait-list controls. An investigation of reliability of distance neuropsychological evaluation of patients with alcohol abuse suggested comparable outcomes to f2f consultation with patient satisfaction listed as "good" (Kirkwood, Peck, & Bennie, 2000). A retrospective analysis of 49 patients found similar reductions in Global Assessment of Functioning scale scores between those treated with interactive television and those treated f2f. It was noted that those treated with distance methods had a higher attendance rate and that follow-up visits were shorter than in f2f encounters (Zaylor, 1999). Other uncontrolled studies (e.g., Ermer, 1999) also suggest similar outcomes for teleconferenced as opposed to f2f interviews but, again, methodology and small subject size hampers generalizability. Thus, controlled outcomes studies are few (Capner, 2000), and although initial results are encouraging, a firm foundation on which to proceed is still lacking.

FLOW OF RESOURCES

Cost

As in other applications of the Internet, any cost benefits accruing through the use of distance mental health service provision have yet to be realized. Most programs are small in scope and, like in any other area of service provision, there are economies of scale that are as yet unobtained. Greater numbers of patients than currently exist will be required to achieve savings, which may largely be through reduced transportation costs and paperwork (Lamminen et al., 2001). Savings to patients can be significant, particularly if the patient has to travel, both in terms of dollars and time.

Nevertheless, how much potential savings will offset costs of such services remains largely an unknown factor. Cost savings are at this point therefore questionable. An Irish study conducted over two years found that costs for teledermatology were higher than for standard care, largely due to fixed equipment costs, but when other factors (e.g., travel time, etc.) were factored in, telehealth, at least in the rural setting, represented some savings over conventional care (Loane et al., 2000).

It should be noted that most cost efficacy studies have been carried out in European Union countries and generally do not address mental health care. Few cost comparison studies are available for mental health services. An Alberta, Canada study found the breakeven point for use of teleprovision of psychiatric services to be over 300 teleconsultations per annum; however, this was considerably lower when distance media were used for administrative functions (Simpson et al., 2001). A study of child psychiatric service provision in Newfoundland revealed that even with significant travel costs factored in for patients (more than $400 per consultation), telehealth service was only marginally less expensive (Elford et al., 2000).

Liability

Practitioner liability is another issue that professionals and regulators must address. Reassuringly, there have been few lawsuits on the issue of telemedicine, and thus by extension of other forms of distance service provision; most, if not all, have involved allegations of misdiagnosis that were unaffected by the medium in which the service was provided (Rice, 1997). How this situation will change when the traditionally low risk enterprise of providing psychological counseling becomes more widespread in cyberspace is unknown.

Aside from tort concerns, insurers will have to determine risks to practitioners associated with patient abandonment, suboptimal outcomes, patient dissatisfaction, and other legal issues that are peculiar to distance service provision. Accountability has yet to be established for issues such as misdirected emails, surreptitious collection of personal data (e.g., email addresses, credit card payments), or communications between therapist and client. How accurate is the distance assessment of dangerousness, and how well do duty-to-warn statutes translate to the electronic environment? Client or patient dissimulation in online counseling is likely to be a larger issue than in f2f communication, where nonverbal cues or behavioral evidence may alert the practitioner to the existence of false information. This will have substantial ramifications when dealing with such populations as sex offenders, substance abusers, or others with compulsive behavioral disorders.

Other liability issues that continue to be unresolved relate to the vagaries of providing care in two locations. This is perhaps the largest of all legal impediments to be overcome. If a breach in the standard of care occurs, under which community's standards is that breach judged and in which jurisdiction are such breaches adjudicated? As Kaar (1998) observed, the jurisdiction having the greatest interest is not certain. The burden may fall either on the patient, to find counsel and file suit in the provider's state of licensure, or on the provider, to find counsel and defend his or her actions in the patient's state of residence. Rice (1997) noted that for medical practitioners the basic liability issues for distance service provision (i.e., the existence of a doctor–patient relationship, whether a standard of care was breached, and whether the patient suffered harm as a result) are identical to those for traditional practitioners. He noted, however, that the traditional definition of doctor–patient relationships may not seem applicable in this modality, where there is no physical contact or interaction. Also, standards of care for distance service provision have not been firmly established. Additionally, responsibility for the electronic loss or diversion of confidential information, and who bears ultimate responsibility (the referral source or the consultant) have yet to be delineated (Rice, 1997).

Reimbursement

Positive regulatory action (e.g., expansion of telehealth service provision under Medicare) and reimbursement by nongovernmental third party payers will be necessary before distance mental health service provision is fully utilized (Charles, 2000). In a survey of 29 Canadian university-based telehealth programs, Aires and Finley (2000) reported that 70% of respondents listed funding as a major factor affecting (negatively) the growth of their programs.

As the federal government and other third party payers become involved in reimbursement for online services, accountability to payers must be considered. Although recent federal regulations concerning the practice of telehealth have been interpreted as favorable to practitioners (e.g., the fact that a telehealth network was owned by a consultant was not found to be a violation of antikickback statutes; Stewart, 2000), regulation in this area is in its infancy. The Center For Medicare and Medicaid Services Health Care Financing Agency regulations pertaining to the reimbursement of telehealth services in authorized rural areas are developmental (Stewart, 2000), and the ability of mental health providers to submit for Medicare reimbursement is unsettled.

Will managed care act as a stimulus or an impediment to the growth of online counseling or other distance service provision? The ability to expand access and use a large panel of providers may prove alluring to behavioral health care entities. If costs can approximate or be less expensive than f2f care, distance services may become quite attractive to managed care entities. There is some evidence that insurers are reexamining compensation for services provided online. New Jersey Blue Cross/Blue Shield has begun paying physicians for online consultations with patients with whom the physicians had a previously existing relationship (Chin, 2003).

POWER AND KNOWLEDGE

Federal Regulations and Legislation

At the federal level, increasing attention is being given to ensuring that the providers of each of the traditionally deemed "core mental health" disciplines are appropriately recognized under the Title VII (health professions training and service delivery) legislation, as well as in Medicare and Medicaid. The professional associations representing psychologists, advance practice nursing, clinical social workers, marriage and family therapists, physicians' assistants, and clinical pharmacists have each become increasingly successful in convincing Congress and the administration that their members can contribute significantly to addressing, if not ultimately resolving, issues of access to care and affordability of insurance for the 41 million Americans who lack health care coverage (Institute of Medicine, 2002). Health policy experts' growing awareness of the critical importance of being sensitive to the cultural-psychosocial-economic gradient of health care has facilitated these legislative efforts and may assist in opening new marketplaces for those providing counseling services (Anderson & Anderson, 2003).

An understanding of the complex issues surrounding the determination of the profession's scope of practice is absolutely central to the delivery of online counseling. It is important to recognize that professional certification and licensure are state issues, and scope of practice issues are increasingly being addressed in state legislatures. In 1995 alone, more than 800 such bills were considered and approximately 300 laws were enacted. Two years later, 1600 bills were introduced and approximately 300 enacted into public law (Finocchio et al., 1998). These authors correctly noted that such legislation was often the result of interprofessional turf battles and that consumer protection—supposedly the very purpose of such legislation—was often lost in the fight. The intensity of many of these battles has led some national health policy experts to call for national standards for licensure and scope of practice, inasmuch as the 1990s are likely to be only a prelude to more vigorous activity in the future (O'Neil, 1998).

As Finocchio et al. (1998) noted, state-to-state differences in legislation relating to practice acts of the health professions no longer make sense. This is particularly true when services can be offered by a single provider to a clientele that may span a continent or exist beyond national boundaries. Of particular importance to distance service provision are the Pew Healthcare Commission's recommendations that:

> Congress should establish a national policy advisory body that will research, develop and publish national scopes of practice and continuing competency standards for state legislatures to implement . . . The national policy advisory board . . . should develop standards, including model legislative language, for uniform scopes of practice authority for the health professions. These standards and models would

be based on a wide range of evidence regarding the competence of the professions to provide safe and effective health care … States should require that their regulated health care practitioners demonstrate their competence in the knowledge, judgment, technical skills and interpersonal skills relevant to their jobs throughout their careers. (Finocchio et al., 1998, pp. v–vii)

Though such plans would do much to standardize many aspects of practice, a preliminary attempt at model legislation suggesting a special license to provide distance services (Federation of State Medical Boards, 1996) has not been widely accepted. Indeed, the trend appears to be toward a more restrictive posture (i.e., requiring separate licensure in each jurisdiction where the practitioner might provide services), rather than a more blanket or easily transportable license.

Those interested in the future of online counseling services know that as a practical reality medicine is the only profession possessing state practice acts that cover *all* of health care services. With this exclusivity, little or nothing exists that can be added to the medical act and medicine has no incentive to delete anything. Accordingly, medicine can (and frequently does) see every request for regulatory change from any other profession as a challenge requiring confrontation. History has shown that organized medicine has no institutional incentive to compromise. And, with all-inclusive practice authority, physicians possess the credentials, expertise, and political influence to comment on how any proposed modification of scope of practice laws would affect patients (DeLeon et al., 2003).

Regulatory and Ownership Concerns

The use of telemedicine technology to enter and purchase prescriptions is growing rapidly. Portable computers or palm-held digital devices with wireless Internet connections are being promoted to physicians as mechanisms for entering prescriptions. Drug compendiums that note interactions, dose forms, contraindications, and price structures are made available to providers with the suggestion that this information, combined with the ability to cross-check prescriptions in a central data bank, will enhance safety. Critics of such devices note, however, that use of these systems in clinical settings not only makes patient information available to unknown parties but also provides drug distributors with valuable information regarding the prescribing habits of the provider. Patient use of the Internet to purchase drugs is also growing significantly, and legal issues associated with this (e.g., purchase of cheaper drugs abroad that are then illegally imported into the United States, or purchase of drugs without adequate medical examination) are receiving increasing legal attention.

Regarding psychological services, much remains unknown. The development of specific regulatory models and implementation of adequate practice standards for mental health, as well as for other disciplines involved in distance provision, remains embryonic (Picot, 2000). This is particularly the case when the international provision of distance services is considered. Although the Internet is in many respects a great equalizer, users in different settings will apply their own prevailing sets of mores and expectations to its use. The expectation of candor and openness in many Western countries may not be matched in others. Legal, regulatory, and transnational quality assurance mechanisms have yet to be implemented in standardized ways, and the transnational measurement of cost efficacy and outcomes transnationally is problematic (Lacroix, 1999).

Guilds and Professional Associations

The financial component of regulations affecting the practice of online counseling is perhaps the least interesting of the problems that must be solved before distance technologies establish a foothold in the mental health arena. Any reflection on the mechanisms of health care reimbursement in this country leads to the recognition that payers will attempt to restrict reimbursement for online counseling until either or both of the following circumstances occurs. First, payers will not be willing to compensate providers until it becomes evident that treating a patient via the Internet offers cost savings over traditional counseling that are not offset by increased liability risks. Second, payers will reimburse providers only if there is a public perception that a desired service is being withheld from those seeking treatment, and patient, client, or provider groups are able to arouse sufficient political interest to compel payers to do so.

More interesting problems lie in the realm of ethics and policymaking within professional societies. That is, how will the providers of online services devise new professional and ethical codes to regulate the conduct of online counseling? A preeminent determinant of these standards will be *safety*, in the form of adequate protection of the patient's well-being, rights, and confidentiality. *Efficacy*, in the form of measurable improved outcome for distance service provision, will also remain, as in traditional mental health service provision, a benchmark for judging professional behavior. Finally, *self-interest*, in the form of a professional society's continued ability to limit membership to that society and maintain a monopoly on establishment of standards and sanctions governing members of that society, will determine the alacrity with which professional guilds embrace online and other forms of distance service provision.

These are but a few of the practice issues that await resolutions. Among others are establishment of informed consent for distance service provision, licensure and credentialing, confidentiality of information stored on systems that may not be owned by a practitioner, ownership of intellectual property rights on such systems, and, conceivably, antitrust issues, in that a network of online or telehealth resources might allow a single practice to establish dominance over a large geographic area (Edelstein, 1999).

CONCLUSION

The future of distance service provision depends not only on the ability of mental health professionals to establish standards for quality and ethical service provision, but also on how the Internet (and other forms of distance provision) affects multiple political, economic, and cultural factors around the globe (Kun, 2001). In regard to mental health services in particular, it is essential that better outcomes data and analyses of cost-effectiveness exist (Frueh et al., 2001). Patient acceptance and provider satisfaction are two additional key variables that must be positively answered for online counseling and other electronic therapy provision to become established modalities that policymakers and third party payers are willing to adopt. Finally, numerous jurisdictional, tort, and ethical considerations must be resolved in order for e-therapy to become an accepted modality.

When considering the future of this medium, two additional factors deserve recognition. The first is that online therapy provision is likely a transient phenomenon. Technical innovations and economies of scale will make desktop VTC rapidly more accessible and affordable. We have already entered into an era where desktop VTC capability is within the reach of most practitioners and greater and greater numbers of patients. The first author of this Foreword provides services via VTC every week to a clinic 50 miles away to an area, though urban, that would otherwise be without such services. This results in a significant cost benefit to patients, in that they need not drive substantial distances for f2f encounters, and they can continue to receive combined psychological and pharmacological services without referral to a third provider. Reported satisfaction of patients treated via this modality has been high, and most have adapted without hesitation to a VTC arrangement.

Though it should be obvious, we should also recognize that, even with reliable low cost devices available to most patients and providers, electronic modes of therapy are unlikely to entirely supplant f2f encounters. It is far safer to assume that online or VTC services will supplement, but not supercede, traditional services. Online therapy, however, may provide an acceptable augmentation of f2f services once a therapeutic relationship has been established, or when factors such as distance or compromised patient mobility (due to physical disability, confinement, or other factors) make regular patient–provider meetings problematic. One can easily imagine a scenario wherein a rural-based clinician, who visits a particular area only once in several weeks, could use online counseling or other forms of distance communication to provide greater continuity of care to patients in those areas.

Much remains to be settled, and much remains unknowable at present. As just mentioned, it is doubtful that electronic modes of therapy will ever completely replace traditional f2f service provision (see Jenkins & White,

2001), save perhaps in extremely remote areas or with patients whose mobility is constrained. It is equally clear that electronic therapy has great potential to augment currently available services and, quite feasibly, serve to improve access and reduce the cost of traditional mental health care.

In one of those brief supervisory episodes that do so much to shape the identity of a developing psychotherapist, a wise mentor of one of the current authors once observed that it is not the process of psychotherapy that counts, it's the *moment*—that instant in which the work of the patient and the therapist converges to create a catharsis or a new understanding of a problem leading to more adaptive behavior. In the final analysis, then, the fate of e-therapy rests not on how quickly we resolve legal, ethical, and financial obstacles to distance practice but on how well this medium can effectively capture that *moment* to effectuate individual growth and change.

REFERENCES

Aas, I. H. M. (2001). A qualitative study of the organizational consequences of telemedicine. *Journal of Telemedicine and Telecare, 7*:18–26.

Aires, L. M., & Finley, J. P. (2000). Telemedicine activity at a Canadian university medical school and its teaching hospitals. *Journal of Telemedicine and Telecare, 6*:31–35.

Anderson, N. B., & Anderson, P. E. (2003). *Emotional longevity: What really determines how long you live.* New York: Viking, The Penguin Group.

Brodey, B. B., Claypoole, K. H., Motto, J., et al. (2000). Satisfaction of forensic psychiatric patients with remote telepsychiatric evaluation. *Psychiatric Services, 51*:1305–1307.

Capner, M. (2000). Videoconferencing in the provision of psychological services at a distance. *Journal of Telemedicine and Telecare, 6*:311–319.

Charles, B. L. (2000). Telemedicine can lower costs and improve access. *Healthcare Financial Management, 54*(4):66–69.

Chin, T. (2003). New Jersey Blues launches online consultation at physician urging, *American Medical News*, February 3, 2003. Retrieved July 6, 2003, from http://www.ama-assn.org/sci-pubs/amnews/pick_03/bisc0203.htm.

Cooper, R. A., Laud, P., & Dietrich, C. L. (1998). Current and projected workforce of non-physician clinicians. *Journal of the American Medical Association, 280*:799–794.

DeLeon, P. H., Hagglund, K. J., Ragusea, S. A., et al. (2003). Expanding roles for psychologists in the 21st century. In G. Stricker & T. A. Widiger (Eds.), *Clinical psychology.* Volume 8 of the *Handbook of Psychology*, I. B. Weiner (Editor-in-chief) (pp. 551–568). New York: John Wiley & Sons.

Edelstein, S. A. (1999). Careful telemedicine planning limits costly liability exposure. *Health-care Financial Management*, December 1999:63–69.

Elford, R., White. H., Bowering, R., et al. (2000). A randomized, controlled trial of child psychiatric assessments conducted using videoconferencing. *Journal of Telemedicine and Telecare, 6*(2):73–82.

Ermer, D. J. (1999). Experience with a rural telepsychiatry clinic for children and adolescents. *Psychiatric Services, 50*:260–261.

Federation of State Medical Boards (1996). A Model Act to Regulate the Practice of Medicine Across State Lines. Retrieved July 6, 2003, from http://www.fsmb.org.

Finocchio, L. J., Dower, C. M., Blick, N. T., et al. (October, 1998). *Strengthening consumer protection: Priorities for health care workforce regulation.* San Francisco: Pew Health Professions Commission.

Frueh, B. C., Deitsch, S. E., Santos, A. B., et al. (2000). Procedural and Methodological Issues in Telepsychiatry Research and Program Development. *Psychiatric Services, 51*:1522–1527.

Heffler, S., Smith, S., Keehan, S., et al. (2003). Health spending projections for 2002–2012. Health Affairs. Retrieved July 6, 2003, from http://www.healthaffairs.org/WebExclusives/Heffler_Web_Excl_020703.htm.

Hilty, D. M., Sison, J. I., Nesbitt, T. S., et al. (2000). Telepsychiatric consultation for ADHD in the primary care setting. *Journal of the American Academy of Child and Adolescent Psychiatry, 39*:15–16.

Institute of Medicine (2001). *Crossing the quality chasm: A new health system for the 21st century*. Washington, DC: National Academy Press.

Jenkins, R. L., & White, P. (2001). Telehealth advancing nursing practice. *Nursing Outlook, 49*(2):100–105.

Kennedy, C., & Yellowlees, P. (2000). A community-based approach to evaluation of health outcomes and costs for telepsychiatry in a rural population: preliminary results. *Journal of Telemedicine and Telecare, 6*(Suppl 1):S155–157.

Kennedy, C., & Yellowlees, P. (2003). The effectiveness of telepsychiatry measured using the Health of the Nation Outcome Scale and the Mental Health Inventory. *Journal of Telemedicine and Telecare, 9*:12–16.

Kirkwood, K. T., Peck, D. F., & Bennie, L. (2000). The consistency of neuropsychological assessments performed via telecommunication and face to face. *Journal of Telemedicine and Telecare, 6*:147–151.

Kopel, H., Nunn, K., & Dossetor, D. (2001). Evaluating satisfaction with a child and adolescent psychological telemedicine outreach service. *Journal of Telemedicine and Telecare, 7*(Suppl 2):35–40.

Kun, L. G. (2001). Telehealth and the global health network in the 21st century: From homecare to public health informatics. *Computerized Methods and Programs in Biomedicine, 64*:155–167.

Lacroix, A. (1999). International concerted action on collaboration in telemedicine: G8 subproject 4. *Studies in Health Technology and Informatics, 64*:12–19.

Lamminen, H., Lamminen, J., Ruohonen, K., et al. A cost study of teleconsultation for primary-care ophthalmology and dermatology. *Journal of Telemedicine and Telecare, 7*:167–173.

Lange, A., van de Ven, P., Schrieken, B. A., et al. (2000). Internet-mediated, protocol-driven treatment of psychological dysfunction. *Journal of Telemedicine and Telecare, 6*:15–21.

Lange, A., van de Ven, P., Schrieken, B. A., et al. (2001). Interapy, treatment of posttraumatic stress through the Internet: a controlled trial. *Journal of Behavioral Therapy and Experimental Psychiatry, 32*:73–90.

Lehoux, P., Battista, R. N., & Lance, J. M. (2000). Telehealth: passing fad or lasting benefits? *Canadian Journal of Public Health, 91*:277–280.

Lehoux, P., & Blume, S. (2000). Technology assessment and the sociopolitics of health technologies. *Journal of Health Politics, Policy, and Law, 25*:1083–1120.

Loane, M. A., Bloomer, S. E., Corbett, R., et al. (2001). A randomized controlled trial assessing the health economics of realtime teledermatology compared with conventional care: an urban versus rural perspective. *Journal of Telemedicine and Telecare, 7*:108–118.

McGlynn, E. A., Asch, S. M., Adams, J., et al. (2003). The quality of health care delivered to adults in the United States. *New England Journal of Medicine, 348*:2635–2645.

Perednia, D., & Allen, A. (1995). Telemedicine technology and clinical applications. *Journal of the American Medical Association, 273*:483–488.

Picot, J. (2000). Meeting the need for educational standards in the practice of telemedicine and telehealth. *Journal of Telemedicine and Telecare, 6*(Suppl 2):S59–62.

Roine, R., Ohinmaa, A., & Hailey, D. (2001). Assessing telemedicine: a systematic review of the literature. *Canadian Medical Association Journal, 165*:765–771.

Simpson, J., Doze, S., Urness, D., et al. (2001). Telepsychiatry as a routine service—the perspective of the patient. *Journal of Telemedicine and Telecare, 7*:155–160.

Stewart, E. E. (2000). OIG offers guidance on the legality of telemedicine arrangements. *Healthcare Financial Management*, June 2000:71–72.

Watanabe, M., Jennett, P., & Watson, M. (1999). The effect of information technology on the physician workforce and health care in isolated communities: the Canadian picture. *Journal of Telemedicine and Telecare*, 5(Suppl 2):S11–19.

Zaylor, C. (1999). Clinical outcomes in telepsychiatry. *Journal of Telemedicine and Telecare*, 5(Suppl 1):S59–60.

INTRODUCTION

THE COMMUNICATION REVOLUTION AND ONLINE MENTAL HEALTH

A communications revolution began changing our world toward the end of the last millennium. With the introduction of public access to the Internet, an interconnected global community was formed for the first time in the history of mankind.

Among the many millions who logged on and began using the new, instant, always-available communications medium were mental health professionals and consumers of mental health services. The ability of the Internet to benefit the community of clinicians and clients is almost self-evident. With the Internet, people have immediate access to vast amounts of information and resources, services and even professional service providers from anywhere and at anytime. More and more providers and consumers of mental health services are making use of the net to engage in information gathering, professional consultations, and psychotherapy.

ABOUT THE BOOK, OUR READERS, AND THE DYNAMIC NEW FIELD

Who should read this book? We have assumed that most readers will have had at least some basic exposure to the principles and techniques of mental health counseling. That being said, the chapters have been written to also appeal to experienced professionals who are curious about online counseling and are considering the possibility of bringing their practice online.

Although every book that has anything to do with technology is doomed to be outdated as soon as it hits the shelves, we believe that this book will provide some lasting insights into the basics of how mental health counseling can be effectively translated to the online medium. From a practical standpoint, we believe this book, possibly coupled with supervised practice and training, will provide practitioners the fundamental tools needed to be competent online mental health professionals. Above all, we hope that this book will serve to mark the beginning of a new era for standardized, professional mental health counseling online.

ADDRESSING THE NEED FOR A COMPREHENSIVE GUIDE IN THE NEW FIELD

Until now, consumers and providers had few comprehensive sources of information from which they could learn how to locate, evaluate and/or deliver services online. Numerous articles have been published in scholarly journals along with the occasional chapter in books on new media and on innovative trends in mental health. This handbook for online professionals, among the very first of its kind, was designed to serve as a guide in the new field. Our aim was to collect, in a single place, everything that mental health professionals would need to know about online counseling. Is online counseling going to replace traditional face-to-face counseling methods? Well, probably not. However, many believe that online counseling will allow countless individuals the ability to access services they otherwise would never or could not reach. We believe it is critical that all mental health professionals learn about online counseling as part of their training, because their clients will be considering it, and they may be called upon to provide it.

Online counseling is a new modality. Experience shows that it usually takes some time before new modalities are established and then integrated. Years ago, some mental health professionals considered the idea of placing a telephone in the office. Today, most practitioners are available on the phone or through an answering service of some sort, and telephone hotline operations continue to save people's lives. The penetration of the Internet into our homes, workplaces, and our practices is already a reality. Millions of clients are looking for service online, and an overwhelming majority of clinicians use the Internet for some form of professional activity and email. The question we have tried to address in this manual is: Are clinicians prepared to practice online?

Often, the introduction of a general textbook marks the birth of a new field, much as the field of psychology is associated with the publication of

William James' 1890 book, *The Principles of Psychology*. Although we did not quite reinvent the field of psychology with this handbook, we do hope that this manual will lay the foundations to professional online counseling, education, and training. This book was made to guide and educate practitioners about use of the online medium and to make recommendations for effective, professional practice strategies.

SOME WORDS OF CAUTION

It is important for readers to recognize that online counseling—although here to stay—is a relatively new discipline. As is often the case with new modalities, the field is still dynamic and forming. Readers should not mistake this book to be a source of legal advice on the subject of online counseling, especially because standards are still changing and often differ from one jurisdiction to another. It is also important to remember that online counseling is not always the best treatment modality for all mental health conditions, particularly when face-to-face sessions may be required or if issues of safety to self or others are involved. We cannot hope to provide a completely consistent "how to" manual about the "right way" to do online counseling or address every possible situation. Such ideal methods and accepted theories have not yet been solidly established. However, we do hope that this book is the next best thing, which is to synthesize the collective wisdom of some of the most respected people in the field and establish the basics of online counseling.

Ron Kraus, Ph.D., C.S.W.—Teaneck, NJ
Jason S. Zack, Ph.D.—Coral Gables, FL
George Stricker, Ph.D.—Garden City, NY

ACKNOWLEDGMENTS

We are honored to have had the participation of our chapter authors. All contributors have graciously given of their time and expertise to this project. A quick glance at the table of contents will generate immediate recognition for those readers who have previously read anything about the online therapy field, or attended symposia at professional conferences where conversations about this new modality have grown louder and louder during the past years. It has been a privilege to work with the people who are collectively shaping the future of mental health.

We'd like to thank all of those who helped with the production of this work. Especially we appreciate the contribution of our colleagues from the International Society for Mental Health Online (ISMHO), as well as the people and research team at OnlineClinics.com. We also wish to thank those who read early drafts of this work and/or helped with the general editing process, including Judith Allen, Evgeny Chumak, Orna Hevron-Kraus, Bruce V. Hillowe, Dita Kraus, Michael Robinson, and Cedric M. Speyer. Finally, we'd like to express special thanks to our wives and others in our lives who love us, who endured the journey this project was, for their support, love, and understanding.

Ron Kraus, Ph.D., C.S.W.—Teaneck, NJ
Jason S. Zack, Ph.D.—Coral Gables, FL
George Stricker, Ph.D.—Garden City, NY

PART

I

THE NEW MEDIUM

HISTORY AND RESEARCH

1

ONLINE BEHAVIOR, COMMUNICATION, AND EXPERIENCE

MICHAEL A. FENICHEL

Editors' Note: In this chapter, the author lays the foundation for beginning to explore online counseling. He reviews general notions about the nature of the Internet and how consumers and professionals interact online. Finally, he presents a framework for understanding the role and importance of online counseling in the 21st century.

In graduate school many of us learned that the single most important factor in effective counseling and psychotherapy is the clinician. The ability to understand human nature, relationships, and communication styles has long been an underpinning to our conceptualization of key therapeutic ingredients, along with what clients experience as the "nonspecific factors" such as warmth, empathy, and genuineness. Add to the therapeutic relationship the goals and expectations of both client and counselor, the process and tools that are brought to bear in attaining a course of treatment that is experienced as helpful, and this fortuitous combination of an effective working relationship and appropriate clinical interventions is thought to be key to "success."[1]

With the advent of the Internet, communication has been revolutionized and basic tenets of human relationships have been broadened, intensified,

---

[1]Notwithstanding the interest and novelty attached to such classic software programs as *ELIZA,* where in effect the "therapist" is the computer itself, without direct human intervention but providing a simple feedback loop stimulating "client-centered therapy."

and challenged.[2] Opportunities now exist for socially shy, isolated, or physically challenged individuals to reach out for connectedness or support: they can use the Web to seek information, companionship, positive or negative means of "acting out," and increasingly to find advice or professional mental health services such as counseling or psychotherapy.[3] Although "What is therapy?" is still the subject of great debate, there is little doubt that many online clinicians, support communities, and self-help websites are offering therapeutic services and experiences. Counseling is available online as both an open-ended process and for a wide range of goal-directed ends, ranging from vocational decision making to bolstering social confidence and building self-help skills, self-esteem, and a sense of interpersonal competency. Online mental health practitioners serve also as a bridge to referrals in the face-to-face (f2f) community, or for online specialists with expertise in a given area of interest for the person seeking help.

The majority of Americans' lives are now touched by, and daily experience has been revolutionized by, having access to everybody else on earth with a computer and Internet connection. The society built on mobility via cars and highways has now solidly embraced the new technology, and the most promising means of getting where and what one wants is now, in many minds, "the information superhighway." The potential for interactive communication and for widening our understanding of human behavior across contexts and cultures is profound. An entire generation in the United States has integrated the Internet and the computer into their lives as easily as their parents embraced the telephone and television. Often the first solution in seeking help, support, or information today is to "go online." Certainly teens in particular are now as at ease with "IM'ing" (instant messaging) or "meeting" a group of friends in a chat room as they are with picking up the telephone.

It is the very *transparency* of using the computer in daily life, without being encumbered by thoughts of the wires, routers, and so forth (the Internet), that leads to the inevitable conclusion that an increasing number of people will turn to the Internet as quickly as they might turn to a telephone directory to find answers and services that respond to their need for information, support, or help. Add to this the populations already benefiting from telehealth services, such as the geographically isolated, physically challenged, vocationally mobile, or socially inhibited, and there is clearly a huge need that can be filled by online practitioners who are familiar with these problems, whether they entail interpersonal relationships, addictions, work-

---

[2]For example, according to a Harris Poll, by year 2000, 56% of all U.S. adults were online at home or at work and, of this group, 86% had sought information on health care or specific diseases via the Internet, up from 71% of users in 1998.

[3]The *Wall Street Journal* (June 4, 2002) went so far as to announce that "Online Therapy Goes Mainstream."

related stress, or anxiety. Working online, however, carries unique challenges and opportunities, which in turn demand additional skills (Fenichel et al., 2002; Fenichel, 2000). It is also incumbent upon the Internet-based mental health professional to understand and accept that not every situation or potential client is appropriate for online treatment (Suler et al., 2001).

Returning to the generally accepted model that assumes a counseling or therapy relationship to be the sum of its parts—the client, counselor, and intervention, in combination with the presenting situation, treatment goal, and several nonspecific factors—it becomes quite clear that the clinician who works entirely online is going to have to develop a new skill-set that includes safeguards for the client, methods to assess and refine accuracy of communication (absent verbal and visual cues), a framework that is both tangible and flexible, and processes that allow for a means of validating the results of both individual and cumulative work with the procedures being used.

Although this is a new frontier, it is already being embraced internationally in a variety of ways—from Japanese support for short-message "texting"-based counseling provided through Employee Assistance Plans (EAPs), to American experience with telehealth provision for unserved and underserved populations, to an innovative Internet-based suicide-prevention hotline being used with great success in Israel (Barak, 2001). Both individuals and the health care industry may be looking at online services as being the latest and most efficient means of delivering short-term services, as both prevention and intervention for a variety of problems.

LIFE IN CYBERSPACE

Much has been written about the phenomenology of life in cyberspace. Sometimes people take on new personas consistent with being in a "virtual" world, where one can feel anonymous while at the same time being instantly disinhibited about "opening up" to total strangers (Suler, 2002). Similarly, relationships online may be infused with fantasy, or may reflect a well-established pattern of realistic and rich communication between individuals or within groups. It is easy to reach out and make new "cyber buddies" in a chat room or community, and easy to walk away, too. It is easy to deceive and easy to be brutally truthful. Often those who are comfortable both online and offline with interpersonal relationships can integrate both types of experience into an overall "web" of online and offline social support, but many individuals develop preferences for one modality or the other. Not everybody loves computers or can use them without frustration, although for many people the Internet spells liberation and a world of opportunity. As has been widely discussed, the nature of text-based relationships lends itself not only to rapid disinhibition, but also to distortions, miscommunication, and the development of strong transference/counter-transference dynamics.

Freud *might* well have said, were he here to take this all in: "It's very easy to find websites, groups, and online activities and objects to which cathexis can be bound (and through which libido can be sublimated), and the Internet allows for a great deal of ease in free-association, transference, and projection." Freud also might well have wondered about "the psychopathology of everyday [online] life," while object relations aficionados might have good cause to wonder about how multitasking and message boards may impact on or invite "splitting," or help to evolve an inner world of part-objects and toxic/nontoxic object relations facilitated by the computer. Forget dreams. Just think of "The Interpretation of Web Experience"! For some, it may in fact be dreamlike. For some it can be "addictive" too (Fenichel, 1997). No doubt many dreams these days include Web-based content and "day residue" from online interpersonal relationships.

Meanwhile, back in the material world, it is impossible to ignore the myriad counselors, therapists, consultants, coaches, and advisers who are poised and ready to respond—online—to the anticipated groundswell of requests for help, for referral, for advice, and for counseling or psychotherapy. Many critical questions arise for which there is an urgent need for better understanding through research, experience, and professional dialogue. Who would one go to for the best possible treatment or counseling/advice? Where are the best-trained online counselors found? How are "best practice" skills being developed and taught? What traits should be looked for in the therapist or counselors when one cannot see the diplomas on the wall, the warm smile, or the books on the shelf that reveal one's therapeutic orientation? From the would-be provider's point of view, which strategies have shown the greatest potential? Does a combination of bibliotherapy, online journals, and f2f work best? What works best for whom, with whom, for what purpose? Studies to further our clinical understanding of online relationships are clearly warranted, along with a clarion call for further research by social scientists in response to the need. A great opportunity exists for groundbreaking empirical studies of how people are using Internet technologies to facilitate both intellectual/goal-directed pursuits as well as social/communicative endeavors, across daily life activities.

COMMUNICATING ACCURATELY AND EFFECTIVELY

One of the great challenges confronting online mental health professionals is being able to accurately perceive meaning and tone along with the context of text-based communication. Concurrently, the client is likely to benefit most when feeling consistently understood and believing the counselor or therapist to be concerned, empathic, and expert in helping with his or her particular problem.

A substantial body of information describes the various technical and practical challenges to effective online communication (e.g., Fenichel, 2000; Fenichel, 2002) and gives detailed analysis of the ways in which nuance, meaning, pacing, and emphasis can be finessed through text-based communication, either through email or during the course of chat-based communication (Suler, 2000).

And is not communicating and synthesizing experience and beliefs a basic premise for therapy? Is not the communication of goals and needs a basic premise in counseling?

John Suler and the members of the International Society for Mental Health Online (ISMHO) Clinical Case Study Group observed and described some of the many ways in which clients and counselors evolved "natural" communication styles that facilitated transparent, meaningful dialogue. For example:

> Experienced e-mail users have developed a variety of keyboard techniques to overcome some of the limitations of typed text—techniques that almost lend a vocal and kinesthetic quality to the message. They attempt to make e-mail conversations less like postal letters and more like a face-to-face encounter. Some of these strategies include the use of emoticons, parenthetical expressions that convey body language or "sub vocal" thoughts and feelings (sigh), voice accentuation via the use of CAPS and *asterisks*, and trailers. . . . to indicate a transition in thought or speech. Use of "smileys" and other commonly used symbols can convey not only facial expression but also a variety of emotional nuances. (Fenichel et al., 2002)

PHENOMENOLOGY OF 21st-CENTURY DAILY LIFE

Despite the assertion that it is possible and desirable to integrate online experience into one's daily life in a positive and effortless manner (e.g., Fenichel, 2002), it is apparent that for many people "cyberspace" offers an alternative, or "virtual," reality that can be dissociated from other aspects of daily life. Some relish the opportunities for anonymity, to be creative, to try on new personas and new behaviors, or to find supportive environments as an alternative to "real-life" situations that may be dysfunctional, stressful, or simply boring. Others see the Internet and computers merely as tools: to find information, send announcements, or make travel reservations. Still others use the Internet the same way they use a telephone, or television, or automobile: to reach a destination, communicate, or access a desired service. As all these approaches become more mainstream, with an increasing majority of American households having the means for both instrumental and social uses of technology through going online, society is poised for a blurring of boundaries and distinctions between means of accessing each other and the things we need. Already, many among us—particularly the younger and more pragmatic—do not think twice about turning to the Net to contact a friend, shop for a car, find medical information, or (gasp!) even to seek help in one way or another for psychological distress.

Increasingly, the mental health expert is not only easy to find online, but willing to respond to requests for help.

Much has already been written about the psychological dynamics of "online life" and about the denizens of the Internet (Netizens) who spend time conversing through email, list-servs, virtual communities, and message boards. Aside from the well-known disinhibition effect that derives from the empowerment that anonymity and lack of visual cues provide, opportunities to benefit from social support and opportunities for acting-out abound online. Until we know more about which are the most salient therapeutic factors, we can speculate that a combination of nonspecifics (e.g., warmth, empathy, and genuineness) can be powerful, and often *new,* experiences for the newly online individual who first discovers the ease of sharing personal experience with others over the Internet. Add to this a mental health professional's skill and experience (online as well as off), and it is easy to see why forming an initial therapeutic alliance seems inherently easy, certainly for the purposes of developing a treatment plan or well-circumscribed goals such as are the hallmark of short-term, goal-focused psychotherapies (e.g., Bellak & Small, 1978; Malan, 1976). Yet what we do know from experience suggests that despite the potential for forming a therapeutic relationship, and despite the growing reality of having many competent, professional, and ethical online clinicians, not *every* presenting problem is ideally suited for this modality (see e.g., Suler et al., 2001). There is also the risk of exacerbating a situation by providing opportunities for dissociative experience online, and this would argue for online counselors being sensitized to the way in which both guided and unguided dissociation can occur online. The phenomenon of "flaming" is one example of how the online experience can negatively affect relationships; stalking behavior can also thrive online. Two ways in which the Web's dissociative potential could be discouraged include activities such as role-playing or use of a Web page for creative and expressive pursuits. Counselors need to know about these aspects of online behavior and relationships because they can be very real and powerful, even if "only online." Not only can there clearly be depth and poignancy in the relationship between people online, but as Suler, King, and others have noted, tremendous potential exists for transference to quickly develop and deepen, as well as potential for developing and clarifying distortions, which for some is a key ingredient of psychotherapy. Paradoxically, although the absence of direct f2f contact might be seen as an obstacle to establishing a structured therapeutic framework, the online milieu may actually offer some clients greater structure and consistency than would otherwise be available, and attention is paid to limit-setting and boundaries as the therapist and client develop a routine of communication. In addition, the therapist and client will have easy access to a written record of dialogue, journal entries, a web log, a record of homework assignments, and a listing of the session appointments that were missed or kept.

One can truly wonder at the phenomenological aspects of online communication and Web-based interpersonal relationships. Such basic questions arise as, "Where and what is the 'here and now' in cyberspace?" (Fenichel, 2002). When does an email correspondence provide an appropriate "therapeutic frame"? What modality provides the right amount of structure, or the optimal therapeutic "holding environment"? When is a message board (MB) an appropriate supplement for f2f counseling, psychotherapy, or experiential classroom learning activities? When is an online community or MB effectively a self-contained "therapeutic milieu"? When might real-time chat be a powerful supplement to asynchronous email exchanges, or a treatment of choice in response to a given client's need for immediacy and an online therapist's willingness to "be there"? When might specific combinations of modality provide the best of all worlds, with f2f components and/or email journals, homework, or creative expression shared with a therapist to provide a longitudinal and multidimensional picture of the client's full range of daily functioning?

For the Net-savvy and skillful therapist or counselor amazing new opportunities exist for effective yet unconventional types of treatment using various modalities, separate or in combination. A number of situations and clientele have been identified for which Internet-facilitated mental health services have been clearly invaluable, often providing much-needed support (and sometimes treatment or referral) for a wide variety of people who have reached out through the Internet for assistance that they might not accept or find otherwise.

ONLINE BEHAVIOR IN CLINICAL PRACTICE

In 1999 the fledgling ISMHO established the Online Clinical Case Study Group (CSG), composed of mental health professionals from the fields of psychology, psychiatry, social work, nursing, family therapy, and community counseling. Now in its fourth year, this group has provided ongoing peer supervision while working toward formulating basic principles and strategies across a wide range of clinical work undertaken online, either exclusively or in combination with f2f practice. After initially focusing on ethical and practical considerations that needed to be at the forefront of any clinical practice online, the CSG learned firsthand the power of peer support, shared resources (including Web pages), case presentations, and skill-building in initial intake assessment, referrals, and working with the unique aspects of the Internet, both positive and negative. One profound benefit was the ability to seek collegial input in the event of a crisis or even for help with responding to an initial request for help or information. Being online and having colleagues across the globe, in different time zones, engaged in numerous specialties, and with knowledge of local health care systems and a huge network of colleagues and Web resources to draw on provided a *human* web of resources on which to draw, at any hour of the day or night, 365 days a year. Every member felt this to be a powerful and empowering experience.

The ISMHO Case Study Group confronted a number of situations that were thought to be impossible to address or manage online, given how difficult such clients and presenting problems can be f2f. In fact, what was discovered was that an online treatment frame sometimes worked exceptionally well.

As a result of three years of work and study, ISMHO's Case Study Group was able to highlight and clarify many of the challenges as well as the enormous potential of online clinical work. Along the way it was recognized that there exists an obvious need for online practitioners to have access to training and supervision that combines experiential and informational approaches, and that employs a means of studying outcome as well as process. After three years, a number of myths and realities about online clinical work had emerged rather clearly, and they were described in a third-year report (Fenichel et al., 2002). Perhaps one of the most powerful outcomes reported by group members was the realization that some endeavors thought to be impossible are clearly not (e.g., crisis intervention online and work with some types of serious psychopathology). For example:

> An advantage of online work with severely disturbed clients is that clients can choose to use e-mails, chat scripts, and other online exchanges (that can be saved) to rehearse, review, and reinforce therapeutic messages in a way that can be grounding, affirming, and increase reality testing. Also, the therapist's empathic words can function as a transitional object that can be internalized over time at the client's pace. Additionally, having access to an international group of online colleagues has proven very useful in making rapid, appropriate referrals, sometimes in single-session correspondence or very short-term consultation. (Fenichel et al., 2002)

It may be surprising to learn that, unlike using the telephone, going online is subjectively a very different experience across situations and modalities. One can use the vast array of hardware and software known collectively as "the Internet" to interact with others through a variety of channels: chat, email, video (or still-photo) enhanced communication, message boards, list-servs, and instant messaging via text are some of the most popular activities. One can insert photographs, poems, cartoons, journal articles, or brochures, and one can creatively and expressively use color, emoticons, and "text talk" (Suler, 1997) for emphasis or to help with accurate conveyance of nuance and emotional tone. The combined use of the Internet and the personal computer is far more multidimensional than simply picking up one's telephone to talking: People—particularly younger people who know no world without it—are using the Internet in ways that span from instant casual communication to information-seeking and sharing to profoundly creative activities and deeply meaningful personal dialogue and interaction.

In fact, the Pew Internet Report (2002) describes the findings of a longitudinal study that found that there is a slight drop-off of time spent online simply "surfing" the Net, as users become more focused and efficient in seeking what they really want and need. Interestingly, a growing number of people are reporting that in personal and professional activities, the Internet is increasingly being used to seek advice on matters of great importance.

SOCIAL CONNECTEDNESS: LIFE IN THE 21ST CENTURY

Life in our 21st-century world involves choosing from a menu of activities that combine the technology we have integrated into our daily lives to facilitate communication—television, radio, telephone, and the Internet. All of these resources can be used—some passively, some interactively—to reach out to friends and family, pursue hobbies, shop, and find information of importance to us. In this world, where f2f contacts compete with fax machines, company email, cell phones, and instant messaging, life has grown complex and tangled with options, obligations, and obstacles.

Research and debate continue regarding the benefits and risks to allocating interpersonal time to a computer screen rather than using the telephone or interacting f2f with friends and family. Yet nobody has challenged the concept of, say, shopping online, and any teenager will likely tell you that the time spent in chat and casual IM'ing is simply *additive* to time on the phone or playing video games or watching television. Recent evidence (LaRose, Eastin, & Gregg, 2001) suggests that despite initial theories of online time "paradoxically" leading to feelings of social isolation and depression, in fact the original studies may have been reflecting feelings of poor self-efficacy among people with little computer or Internet experience. It thus follows, particularly in light of the very large-scale, longitudinal studies of the Pew project, that with increased efficacy in using the Internet and feelings of self-efficacy and self-confidence in response to positive reinforcement from finding help and information more quickly and efficiently online, a shift in our relationships with (and on) the World Wide Web is widespread, and important to acknowledge and understand.

We are increasingly living in a world that is interconnected, which brings both incredible opportunities and new and unique challenges. One may well argue that much of the debate over the Internet reflects individual comfort levels with the medium and the people's ability to integrate Internet-facilitated communication tools into their lives in a transparent manner. In this light the computer is in fact but a tool that allows access to diverse mediums and to everybody on earth who has access to a computer and an Internet connection.

If we accept that for many people daily life involves Internet-facilitated communication—which it increasingly does, at least for the majority of

Americans, and a growing number of people around the planet—it seems reasonable to assume that the type of experience one shares in counseling or therapy sessions is likely going to reflect relationships, which exist, at least in part, in the "here and now" of cyberspace (Fenichel, 2002). This notion of the here and now has been central in many concepts of psychotherapy, ranging from Freud's transference-countertransference model to the Gestalt therapy process and the use of the here and now in group therapy. Why? One common thread appears to be that the here and now reflects a grounded reference point for "reality," by which a group or therapist can point out distortions, active processes and dynamics, and deeper beliefs and associative pathways of which the here and now behaviors appear to be derivations.

Another aspect of traditional therapies is that they may be "state dependent," in that the analytical session may entail the couch and a style of minimally directive therapy, whereas the psychiatric session may involve a prescription pad and the short-term behavior therapy environment may be a setting where notes are taken on homework assignments and diaries or logs. A Rational Emotive Behavior Therapy (REBT) environment entails f2f sessions that may feel like wrestling matches with self-defeating beliefs, and dialectical behavior treatments now extend far into intellectual and didactic realms that underlie cognition.

The online counselor is in a unique position of being able to benefit from discussion of offline (f2f) trials and tribulations while at the same time being in the same "state" as the client, reading the other's words in a private and self-selected environment, using a means most comfortable to both counselor and client, and guided by a treatment plan that recognizes realistic goals and expectations combined with the ability of the clinician to *truly* be empathic when hearing about online experiences of the client, as the clinician is living in this same new world as the client. The *new* nonspecifics of effective online counseling might well be demonstrated through client reports of "online warmth," "online genuiness," and "online empathy." Clinicians are now at a historical juncture where such online skills and functioning in an environment ripe for both written text and limitless fantasy require whole new perspectives and the development of new skills and theoretical frameworks as well.

The online practitioner clearly needs to be knowledgeable about mental health and the type of services being offered, and to be trained and supervised in the profession one is practicing. Yet one needs also to know about the various aspects and dimensions of 21st-century interpersonal relationships, which one did not study (until now) in psychology textbooks. Only if one can understand how a client may feel after being "flamed" in a chat room, or how easy it is to miscommunicate online, or what is meant by various emoticons and shorthand means of texting thoughts, can one truly be experienced by an online client as understanding and empathic. Beyond minimal competency at understanding online interpersonal life, which perhaps should now be a basic requirement in all f2f training practica (where it is needed), the online therapist should have the ability to address important events in a client's life as they occur both online and off. The savvy counselor can employ such strategies as mirroring a client's words (in writing), encouraging use of creative expression (e.g., using font color and graphics), employing a combination of modalities during a course of treatment (e.g., email and chat, or f2f and MB, or even virtual reality), and sharing self-help and informational resources that are abundantly available online. For the clinician to have so many tools available to assist in the client's self-discovery, self-healing, goal attainment, or facilitated "therapy" online is quite exciting and clearly has the potential to revolutionize the mental health care delivery systems that we now know and love so dearly.

CONCLUSION

Counseling and psychotherapy are traditionally offered in many ways, in many contexts. Such endeavors have increasingly been under the scrutiny of scientific study as to efficacy and professional consensus about ethics. In this new dawn where communication is possible between anyone on earth with the skills, desire, and technology to reach across barriers and boundaries, we confront both tremendous challenges and opportunities to do the right thing as practitioners and mental health professionals—using ourselves as the primary tool of good practice and judgment, and relying on our professional training, experience, skills, and tool-set, bringing forth the potential promise of access and alternative mental health care activities, such as could not or would not have been envisioned in the primordial days of the 20th century.

You, the reader of this book, will be the pioneers in counseling, peer supervision, training, and research utilizing the Internet. This is hopefully only the first of many systematic endeavors to present the breadth and depth of the issues involved, with the key concepts illuminated by pioneers in the field of online mental health, providing both practical and technical information that the evolving 21st-century mental health professional can use on a daily basis as a comprehensive reference.

KEY TERMS

Chat: Popularized in the 1990s by AOL and other large Internet service providers (ISPs) and online communities, text- and graphic-based "chatting" occurs in real-time between individuals or within a group, and may be entirely social or part of a professional or organizational forum. The most well-known forum may be the public chat room, but smaller, private chat environments are also widely used.

Counseling: Counseling is an activity as old as human history, regulated in some places and not others. For the purposes of discussion here, counseling refers to the provision of guidance, assistance with self-help or coping skills, and/or advice in response to client concerns about relationships or other daily life situations. Counseling may focus on vocational, behavioral, educational, spiritual, interpersonal, or emotional issues and counselors may employ a variety of theoretical frameworks.

Cyberspace: Cyberspace is a psychological construct that we as an online society invent, individually and collectively, to describe where experience takes place when people interact via computer. Some experience and conceptualize cyberspace in visual/spatial terms, whereas others think of it in terms of technological or interpersonal experience that is found "there" as part of daily life activities.

Disinhibition: This term is usually associated with learning theory, behavior study, and physiological assessment. Experience suggests a common tendency online to quickly open up and be very self-revealing, even to relative strangers or new acquaintances. Clinical practice and study suggest that the combination of a sense of freedom (through relative or complete anonymity) and an excitement about the ease of reaching out to others may provide feelings of both validation and empowerment, which in turn reinforce the surge of self-disclosure.

Email: Electronic mail, or email, remains the single most popular means of two-way communication via the Internet. It allows both individual and group mailings (e.g., using a list-serv or announcement list) and a wide variety of correspondence ranging from business letters, "post cards," and traditional "letters" between friends and family, to commercial applications, political mobilization, and professional relationships.

Emoticons: Emoticons are an essential tool for accurately communicating "tone of voice," whereby combinations of text symbols and/or graphics elaborate the nuance of affect and intonation that the sender wishes to convey. The most commonly used emoticon is the "smiley" [☺], which varies across cultures but is almost universally interpreted as an effort to be friendly, happy, or humorous. Other commonly used emoticons and acronyms express sadness, laughter, and other reflections of the user's "feeling tone."

Here and Now: This phrase was popularized by the Gestalt therapy movement as well as psychoanalytic and group therapy literature. Because online experience offers both synchronous and asynchronous components—often during a single sitting—it is important to recognize that one's subjective experience of "here" and "now" online may be state-dependent and reflect individual processing skills and personality styles.

IM'ing: Instant messaging, or IM'ing, is a hugely popular phenomenon around the world and, though used in business environments, is especially popular with children and teens. Instant messages are sent, through such programs as AOL's AIM or ICQ or MSN's Messenger, and allow individuals and groups to instantly communicate as well as to monitor when "buddies" indicate they have logged on to the Internet or are available to engage in online communication.

Internet: Historically begun as a governmental computer infrastructure to ensure reliable communication, the Internet is now embraced by millions around the world as a communication channel that offers easy access to other people and computers for both information and interpersonal communication.

MB: Sometimes referred to as a *forum*, a message board allows for the posting of messages and responses to particular topics, opinions, or queries, displayed graphically so that "threaded" discussions can be followed by topic.

Nonspecifics: The well-known and often-replicated findings within psychotherapy process and outcome research suggest that clients benefit not only from specific orientations or techniques employed in therapy, but also from nonspecific aspects of the relationship with the therapist. For example, Carl Rogers's pioneering studies identified warmth, genuineness, and empathy as three nonspecific factors of perceived value, as reported by the clients themselves.

Texting: This phenomenon, popular worldwide, is a form of instant messaging that is typically sent and received between people using cell phones, PDAs, pagers, and other portable devices. As the name implies, it is limited to text. The word *texting* is often used as a verb to describe the immediate communication.

Therapy: Therapy is another term with a long history but wide diversity of definition. Psychotherapy is an interpersonal process, widely regulated in the United States. A large number of theoretical frameworks have led to a number of specialized treatment models. Typically, therapy practitioners are required to undergo several years of training and supervised experience before being granted licensure or certification within a profession acknowledged by credentialing agencies (and the general public) as qualified to practice.

Therapeutic Alliance: This is a term used to denote the cognitive and interpersonal phenomena that "mesh" between client and therapist, allowing productive and harmonious work toward the same goals in a meaningful way, with a congruence of expectations and "fit."

Treatment: Often, *treatment* is used as a term to underscore the professional and/or healing relationship in a counseling or psychotherapy relationship, as opposed to circumscribed advice, guidance, or lay counseling. (See also *counseling* and *therapy.*)

STUDY QUESTIONS

1. How must we reframe the perpetual question of "What is therapy?" and how can counseling and other goal-oriented mental health services best be conceptualized given the new age of interpersonal communication?

2. In Japan, counseling occurs via "texting," and office workers "text" the person next to them rather than establish eye contact. Although cultural factors may not be as obvious to Americans surfing the Net, what does the American online therapist or counselor need to know about lifestyle in *this* country, among children, teens, and young adults who were "raised on the Internet"? What do established offline clinicians need to know about online life?

3. Although several excellent conceptual models and how-to guides are presented in the following pages, what are some ideas you have about the very first questions that need to be systematically studied? Some possible ideas involve goals and outcomes of online work, risks and benefits as a function of distance and reliance on text communication, and evaluating the state of readiness among traditional sources of training (graduate schools, continuing education, specialized training). What do you think?

4. How would *you* train somebody in the basics of effective online communication? Could the well-experienced therapist who is limited in online skills be an effective online counselor? Can the offline therapist benefit from being more familiar with the culturally prevalent online life that so many have? Conversely, do online therapists need any less training in traditional f2f psychotherapy techniques?

5. How should our society facilitate or obstruct licensed mental health professionals from providing consultation, treatment, counseling, or psychotherapy using the Internet? Should online counseling be used as a basis or a supplement to professional practice? Should it be used if the client is distant from the provider, rather than residing in the provider's state of licensure? Is licensure relevant to online clinical work? For whom? Should there be specialty licensing for online practitioners?

6. What is *your* vision of online therapy or counseling? What is the potential? What are the risks? Given that it is blossoming in popularity and providers are already meeting the growing demand, what is "best practice" for *your* profession were you to engage clients using the Internet, either as an adjunct to existing practice or as the channel whereby all interaction occurs?

7. What questions would you ask an online counselor about his or her theoretical orientation and services? Which would you want to be asked?

8. After reading this book, what questions arise, and what sorts of research and practice issues would you like to see systematically explored and presented to students and practitioners?

9. Extra credit: Some may describe online therapy as just one collective placebo effect. How would you respond to this, and how might we explore

the effectiveness of online services in ways similar to, or different from, other types of traditional psychotherapy online research?

SUGGESTED READINGS

Bai, Y. M., Lin, C. C., Chen, J. Y., et al. (2001). Virtual psychiatric clinics. *The American Journal of Psychiatry, 158*:1160–1161.

Barak, A. (2002). Psychological applications on the Internet: A discipline on the threshold of a new millennium. Retrieved October 19, 2002, from http://construct.haifa.ac.il/~azy/app-r.htm.

Bouchard, S., Payeur, R., Rivard, V., et al. (2000). Cognitive behavior therapy for panic disorder with agoraphobia in videoconference: Preliminary results. *CyberPsychology & Behavior, 3*:999–1007.

Fenichel, M. (1996). Current topics in psychology. Retrieved October 19, 2002, from http://www.fenichel.com/Current.shtml.

Fenichel, M. (2002). Online therapy. Retrieved October 19, 2002, from http://fenichel.com/OnlineTherapy.shtml.

Grohol, J. M. (1998). Future clinical directions: Professional development, pathology, and psychotherapy on-line. In J. Gackenbach (Ed.), *Psychology and the Internet: Intrapersonal, interpersonal, and transpersonal implications* (pp. 111–140). San Diego: Academic Press.

Holmes, L. G. (1998). Delivering mental health services on-line: Current issues. *CyberPsychology & Behavior, 1*:19–24.

Hsiung, R. C. (2000). The best of both worlds: An online self-help group hosted by a mental health professional. *CyberPsychology & Behavior, 3*:935–950.

International Society for Mental Health Online (2000). ISMHO/PSI suggested principles for the online provision of mental health services. Retrieved October 19, 2002, from http://ismho.org/suggestions.html.

Kanz, J. E. (2001). Clinical-supervision.com: Issues in the provision of online supervision. *Professional Psychology: Research and Practice, 32*:415–420.

King, S. A., & Moreggi, D. (1998). Internet therapy and self-help groups—The pros and cons. In J. Gackenbach (Ed.), *Psychology and the Internet: Intrapersonal, interpersonal, and transpersonal implications* (pp. 77–109). San Diego: Academic Press.

Klein, B., & Richards, J. C. (2001). A brief Internet-based treatment for panic disorder. *Behavioural and Cognitive Psychotherapy, 29*:113–117.

Maheu, M. M., & Gordon, B. L. (2000). Counseling and therapy on the Internet. *Professional Psychology: Research and Practice, 31*:484–489.

Murphy, L. J., & Mitchell, D. L. (1998). When writing helps to heal: e-mail as therapy. *British Journal of Guidance and Counseling, 26*:21–32.

National Board for Certified Counselors (2001). The practice of online counseling. Retrieved May 19, 2002, from http://www.nbcc.org/ethics/webethics.htm.

Ookita, S. Y., & Tokuda, H. (2001). A virtual therapeutic environment with user projective agents. *CyberPsychology & Behavior, 4*:155–167.

Oravec, J. A. (2000). Online counselling and the Internet: Perspectives for mental health care supervision and education. *Journal of Mental Health, 9*:121–135.

Rheingold, H. (2002). The virtual community. Retrieved October 19, 2002, from http://www.rheingold.com/vc/book/intro.html.

Robinson, P. H., & Serfaty, M. A. (2001). The use of e-mail in the identification of bulimia nervosa and its treatment. *European Eating Disorders Review, 9*:182–193.

Stofle, G. S. (2001). Choosing an online therapist: A step-by-step guide to finding professional help on the Web. Harrisburg, PA: White Hat Communications.

Suler, J. (2001). The online clinical case study group: An e-mail model. *CyberPsychology & Behavior, 4*:711–722.

Suler, J. (2002). The psychology of cyberspace. Retrieved October 19, 2002, from http://www.rider.edu/users/suler/psycyber/psycyber.html.

Suler, J., & Fenichel, M. (2000). The online clinical case study group of the International Society for Mental Health Online: A report from the Millennium Group. Retrieved May 19, 2002, from http:/ismho.org/casestudy/ccsgmg.htm.

Wiederhold, B. K., Wiederhold, M. D. (1998). A review of virtual reality as a psychotherapeutic tool. *CyberPsychology & Behavior, 1*:45–52.

REFERENCES

Barak, A. (2001, November). SAHAR: An Internet-based emotional support service for suicidal people. Paper presented at a conference of the British Psychological Society, "Psychology and the Internet: A European Perspective," Farnborough, England.

Barak, A., & Wander-Schwartz, M. (2000). Empirical evaluation of brief group therapy conducted in an Internet chat room. *Journal of Virtual Environments, 5*(1). Retrieved October 19, 2002 from http://www.brandeis.edu/pubs/jove/HTML/v5/cherapy3.htm.

Bellak, L., & Small, L. (1978). *Emergency psychotherapy and brief psychotherapy.* Larchmont, NY: Grune & Stratton.

Fenichel, M. (1997). "Internet Addiction": Addictive behavior, transference or more? Retrieved October 19, 2002 from http://www.fenichel.com/addiction.shtml.

Fenichel, M. (2000). Online psychotherapy: Technical difficulties, formulations and processes. Retrieved October 19, 2002 from http://www.fenichel.com/technical.shtml.

Fenichel, M. (2002). The here and now of cyberspace. Retrieved October 19, 2002 from http://www.fenichel.com/herenow.shtml.

Fenichel, M., Suler, J., Barak, A., et al. (2002). Myths and realities of online clinical work. *CyberPsychology and Behavior, 5*:481–497.

LaRose, R., Eastin, M. S., Gregg, J. (2001). Reformulating the Internet paradox: Social cognitive explanations of Internet use and depression. *Journal of Online Behavior, 1*(2). Retrieved June 20, 2003 from http://www.behavior.net/JOB/v1n2/paradox.html.

Malan, D. (1976). *The frontier of brief psychotherapy: An example of the convergence of research and clinical practice.* New York: Plenum Publishing.

Pew Internet and American Life Project (March 3, 2002). Getting serious online: As Americans gain experience, they use the web more at work, write emails with more significant content, perform more online transactions, and pursue more serious activities. Retrieved October 19, 2002 from http://www.pewinternet.org/reports/toc.asp?Report=55.

Suler, J. (1997). Psychological dynamics of online synchronous conversations in text-driven chat environments. Retrieved October 19, 2002 from http://www.rider.edu/~suler/psycyber/texttalk.html.

Suler, J. (2000). Psychotherapy in cyberspace: A 5-dimensional model of online and computer-mediated psychotherapy. *CyberPsychology & Behavior, 3*:151–159.

Suler, J. (2002). The online disinhibition effect. Retrieved June 20, 2003 from http://www.rider.edu/~suler/psycyber/disinhibit.html.

Suler, J., Barak, A., Chechele, P., et al. (2001). Assessing a person's suitability for online therapy. *CyberPsychology & Behavior, 4*:675–679. (See Correction, 2002, *CyberPsychology & Behavior, 5*, p. 93.)

2

THE PSYCHOLOGY OF
TEXT RELATIONSHIPS

JOHN SULER, PH.D.

Editors' Note: Most online interactions take place via the exchange of text messages, either in realtime chat or asynchronous emails. In text-based communication, perhaps more than in any other setting, there is a crucial relationship between what is said and how it is said. In this chapter, the author explains the nature of text-based communication.

I'll begin this chapter by pointing out the obvious: text communication is as old as recorded history, hence the psychology of text communication dates just as far back. Letter writing and the creation of postal systems enabled more people to interact more personally via text. However, the advent of computer networks made the exchange of text more accessible, efficient, and faster than ever before in history. Online text communication offers unprecedented opportunities to create numerous psychology spaces in which human interactions can unfold. We truly have entered a new age, the age of *text relationships*.

In this chapter I will explore the psychology of these relationships while pointing out the implications for online clinical work. Many of the psychological dimensions of text communication in general apply across the board to the various types of text communication tools in particular—chat, email, message boards, instant messaging, blogs, and others more esoteric or yet to be invented. These different modalities differ in sometimes obvious, sometimes subtle ways that make each a unique psychological environment—a fact the online clinician might keep in mind when choosing a communication tool for working with a particular client. Because email is the most widely used, much of my discussion will pertain to that modality, although I also will address important issues concerning the other modalities. I believe that a true understanding of the therapeutic value of any particular online communication tool rests on a wider appreciation of how it compares and contrasts to the others. Online clinicians might strive to specialize in a particular type of text medium, while recognizing its pros and cons vis-à-vis the others.

Before I proceed into my discussion of the unique aspects of text relationships, I'd like to point out that text is but one dimension of online communication. To encourage a wider view of the whole horizon of possibilities for online clinical work, I'll refer the reader to my conceptual model for understanding the larger set of dimensions that shape the various psychological environments of cyberspace: asynchronous versus synchronous communication, imaginary versus realistic environments, automated versus interpersonal interactions, being invisible versus present, and the extent to which communication is text-driven or sensory-rich with sight, sound, even smells (Suler, 2000). All these dimensions interact with text to create a fascinating variety of therapeutic interventions. Clinicians can combine and sequence these different modalities to address the needs of a particular client.

LET'S TEXT: WRITING SKILLS, STYLES, ATTITUDES

Text talk is a skill and an art, not unlike speaking, yet in important ways different than speaking. Proficiency in one does not guarantee success in the other. Some truly great authors and poets might sound bumbling or shallow during in-person conversation. A person's ability to communicate effectively in text talk obviously depends highly on writing abilities. People who hate to write, or are poor typists, probably will not be drawn to text-based therapy. Self-selection is at work. Others report that they prefer writing as a way to express themselves. They take delight in words, sentence structure, and the creative opportunity to subtly craft exactly how they wish to articulate their thoughts and moods. In asynchronous communication, such as email and message boards, they may enjoy the *zone of reflection* where they can ponder on how to express themselves. In those cases, asynchronous text may be a less spontaneous form of communicating than speech and online synchronous communication, such as chat. Unlike verbal conversation, in which words issue forth and immediately evaporate, writing also places one's thoughts in a more visible, permanent, concrete, objective format. An email message is a tiny packet of self-representation that is launched off into cyberspace. Some people experience it as a piece of themselves, a creative work, a gift sent to their online companion. They hope or expect it to be treated with understanding and respect. Clinicians might look for how these skills and preferences for writing versus speaking might be associated with important differences in personality and cognitive style.

The quality of the text relationship rests on these writing skills. The better people can express themselves through writing, the more the relationship can develop and deepen. Poor writing can result in misunderstandings and possibly conflicts. In the absence of an accurate perception of what the other is trying to say, people tend to project their own expectations, anxieties, and fantasies onto the other. A disparity in writing ability between people can be problematic. The equivalent in face-to-face (f2f) encounters would be one person who is very eloquent and forthcoming talking to another who speaks awkwardly and minimally. The loquacious one eventually may resent putting so much effort into the relationship and taking all the risks of self-disclosure. The quiet one may feel controlled, ignored, and misunderstood. As in f2f clinical work, therapists might modify their writing techniques—even basic elements of grammar and composition—to interact more effectively and empathically with the client.

We might tend to think of writing abilities as a fixed skill—a tool for expressing oneself that is either sophisticated, unsophisticated, or something in between. It's also possible that the quality of one's writing interacts with the quality of the relationship with the other. As a text relationship deepens and trust develops, people may open up to more expressive writing. They become more willing to experiment, take risks—not just in what specific thoughts or emotions they express but also in the words and composition used. Composition can advance when people feel safe to explore; it regresses when they feel threatened, hurt, or angry. Those changes reflect the developmental changes in the relationship. Writing isn't just a tool for developing the text relationship. Writing affects the relationship and the relationship affects the quality of the writing.

This same reciprocal influence exists between the text relationship and *writing style*. Concrete, emotional, and abstract expression; complexity of vocabulary and sentence structure; the organization and flow of thought—all reflect one's cognitive/personality style and influence how the other reacts. People who are compulsive may strive for well-organized, logically constructed, intellectualized messages with sparse emotion and few, if any, spelling or grammatical errors. Those with a histrionic flair may offer a more dramatic presentation, where neatness plays a back seat to the expressive use of spacing, caps, unique keyboard characters, and colorful language. Narcissistic people may write extremely long, rambling blocks of paragraphs. People with schizoid tendencies may be pithy, whereas those who are more impulsive may dash off a disorganized, spelling-challenged message with emotional phrases highlighted in shouted caps. Different writing/ personality styles may be compatible, incompatible, or complementary to other styles.

One's attitude about writing also plays an important role. Composition conjures up memories from the school years of one's past. Self-concept and self-esteem may ride on those memories. In the course of an email relationship, those issues from the past may be stirred up.

The International Society for Mental Health Online (ISMHO) Clinical Case Study Group (2001) suggests that the clinician, as part of the initial phase of counseling, assess the client's skills, attitudes, and past experiences regarding both reading and writing. A person's reading, writing, as well as typing skills may not be equivalent, but all are necessary for a text relationship. Some may prefer reading over writing, or vice versa. What does reading and writing mean to the person? What needs do these activities fulfill? Are there any known physical or cognitive problems that will limit the ability to read and write? The clinician might find it helpful to discuss how the person's attitudes and skills regarding in-person communication compare to those regarding text communication. When assessing the person's suitability for text communication, the clinician should remember that developing and enhancing the person's reading and writing skills may be intrinsic to the therapeutic process. Because synchronous text talk (chat, instant messaging) is quite different than asynchronous text talk (email, discussion boards), the clinician might also determine the client's skills and preferences regarding each. How does the person feel about the spontaneous, in-the-moment communication of chat as opposed to the opportunity to compose, edit, and reflect, as in email?

Our skills in text-based clinical work will deepen as we continue to explore the benefits of simply *writing*. Encouraging clients to express themselves in prose may help them tap and strengthen a variety of therapeutic processes. It may encourage an observing ego, insight, working through, a reinforcing of positive mental resources, and, especially in asynchronous text, the therapeutic construction of a personal narrative, as in journal writing and bibliotherapy.

THE ABSENCE OF FACE-TO-FACE CUES

As we'll see throughout this chapter and book, the absence of f2f cues has a major impact on the experience of a text relationship. You can't see other people's faces or hear them speak. All those subtle voice and body language cues are lost, which makes the nuances of communicating more difficult. But humans are creative beings. Avid text communicators develop all sorts of innovative strategies for expressing themselves through typed text—in addition to the obvious fact that a skilled writer can communicate considerable depth and subtlety in the written word. Despite the lack of f2f cues, conversing via text has evolved into a sophisticated, expressive art form. The effective text clinician understands and attempts to master this art.

The lack of f2f cues may create ambiguity. Without hearing a person's voice or seeing body language and facial expressions, you may not be sure what the person means. This ambiguity activates the imagination, stirs up fantasies, enhances the tendency to project your own expectations, wishes, and anxieties onto the somewhat shadowy figure sitting at the other end of the online connection. When in doubt, we fall back on our old expectations about how people relate to us, expectations that formed in our early relationships with our parents and siblings—what psychoanalytic clinicians would call a *transference reaction*. As a text relationship develops over time, these reactions toward the other person may ebb and flow. When you first communicate via text, transference might be minimal because you do not know the other person well and have yet to develop a strong psychological investment in the relationship. Transference reactions more readily surface when emotional attachments begin to form but you still do not have a good "feel" for the person because of that lack of f2f cues. Other peak moments occur when emotional topics come up but you are unable to pinpoint exactly where the other person stands on the issue.

Under ideal conditions, as we spend more and more time conversing with a person via text, we begin to understand and work through those transference reactions so that we can see the other person as he/she really is. However, even under the best of circumstances, some aspect of our mental image of the other person rests more on our own expectations and needs than on the reality of the other person. With online communication, our mental image of the other person may be affected by what we think he might look like or how her voice might sound. We may not even be consciously aware that we've formed that impression until we meet the person f2f or talk to her on the phone, only to discover, much to our surprise, that she is in some important way very different than what we expected. In general, transference reactions are unconscious. We don't see them coming and don't fully realize how they are steering our behavior. That's why they can get lead us astray and sometimes into trouble.

In online therapy the client is not alone in this susceptibility to misperceptions, projections, and transference. Faced with those silent words scrolling down the screen, the clinician may develop countertransference. The ability to catch oneself possibly misinterpreting and projecting, to always entertain the possibility that one might be in the midst of a text transference, to suspend final judgments about the client until more data comes in, are the keys to effective online therapy. Helping clients also develop this self-correcting awareness, helping them explore and understand their text-based transference as it interacts with the therapist's countertransference, may be a crucial component of their therapy, especially in the psychodynamic varieties.

Some incoming email or discussion board posts may be prepackaged with transference even though the person is a complete stranger to us. If you have a professional or personal website or other information about you is available on the Internet, people can form inaccurate impressions that they launch your way via an "out of the blue" message. They may idealize you, detest you, or anything in-between. These kinds of transference reactions often are deeply ingrained, prepared responses in the person that are ready to leap out at any opportune moment. On a fairly regular basis, I receive email from people whom I call "spoon-feeders." There is no greeting, no sign-off line or name—just a terse request, or should I say *demand*, for something. Another common transference reaction is the "chip on my shoulder" email. People who have antagonistic conflicts with authority figures may feel free to send a flaming email to someone they perceive as a parental figure. The bottom line with these kinds of unrequested emails is this: You may not have a relationship with them, but they think they have a relationship with you. When beginning work with new clients, an online therapist might encourage them to discuss their impressions of the therapist as a result of seeing the website or other online information about the therapist.

The absence of f2f cues will have different effects on different people. For some, the lack of physical presence may reduce the sense of intimacy, trust, and commitment in the therapeutic relationship. Typed text may feel formal, distant, unemotional, lacking a supportive and empathic tone. They want and need those in-person cues. Others will be attracted to the silent, less visually stimulating, nontactile quality of text relationships—which may be true for some people struggling to contain the overstimulation of past trauma. A person's ambivalence about intimacy may be expressed in text communication because the format is a paradoxical blend of allowing people to be honest and feel close, while also maintaining their distance. People suffering with social anxiety or issues regarding shame and guilt may be drawn to text relationships because they cannot be seen. Some people even prefer text because it enables them to avoid the issue of physical appearance, which they find distracting or irrelevant to the relationship. Without the distraction of in-person cues, they feel they can connect more directly to the mind and soul of the other person. Text becomes a transitional space, an extension of their mind that blends with the extension of the other person's mind. Consider this woman's experience with her online lover:

> Through our closeness, we are easily able to gauge each other's moods, and often type the same things at the same time. We are able to almost read each other's thoughts in a way I have rarely found even in ftf [face-to-face] relationships (only my sister and I have a similar relationship in this respect). . . . It is in the cybersexual relationship where the most interesting aspects have developed. We are now able to actually 'feel' each other, and I am often able to tell what he is wearing, even though we live more than 6000 miles away. I can 'feel' his skin and smell and taste senses have also developed during sexual episodes. I have only seen one very small and blurred picture of this person so I have no idea what he really looks like, but

I'm able to accurately describe him. He is able to 'feel' me too. I'm sure that in the main it is just fantasizing, but to actually and accurately describe the clothing and color and texture of skin is really something I have never experienced before.

Although we may be skeptical about the validity of such reports—or not fully agree with the idea that physical presence is irrelevant—we clinicians should take seriously this subjective experience some people have of connecting more directly to the online companion's psyche. If a client experiences the clinician in this way, how might that determine a diagnosis and the therapeutic plan for that person?

Even though in this section I've been underplaying the sensory component of text relationships, I should emphasize that important visual components are present. As I'll discuss later, creative keyboarding techniques (emoticons, spacing, caps, font color and size, etc.) offer a wide visual range of possibilities for presenting ideas and optimizing self-expression, often in ways that mimic f2f cues. As human factor engineers will tell us, the visual interface of our communication software also affects how we think, perceive, and express ourselves. Clinicians might be wise to compare software before choosing one for their work.

TEMPORAL FLUIDITY: SYNCHRONICITY AND ASYNCHRONICITY

Unlike in-person encounters, cyberspace offers the choice of meeting in or out of realtime. In *asynchronous* communication, such as email and message boards, people do not have to be sitting at their computers at the same time. Usually this means there is a stretching of the time frame in which the interaction occurs, or no sense of a time boundary at all. You have hours, days, or even weeks to respond. Cyberspace creates a flexible temporal space where the ongoing, interactive time together can be stretched out or shortened, as needed. The perception of a temporally locked "meeting" disappears, although sitting down to read a message may subjectively feel as if one has entered a fluid temporal space with the other person, a more subjective sense of here and now. The opportunity to send a message to the therapist at any time can create a comforting feeling that the therapist is always there, always present, which eases feelings of separation and allows clients to articulate their thoughts and feelings in the ongoing stream of their lives, immediately during or after some important event, rather than having to wait for the next appointment.

This asynchronous communication does not require you to respond on-the-spot to what the other has said. You have time to think, evaluate, and compose your reply. This *zone of reflection* comes in very handy for those awkward or emotional situations in a relationship. Some people take advantage of this zone. Others, perhaps acting more spontaneously or at times impulsively, do not. When people receive a message that stirs them up emotionally, they might apply what I call the 24-Hour Rule. They may compose a reply without sending it (or write nothing), wait 24 hours, then go back to reread the other person's message and their unsent reply. "Sleeping on it" may help process the situation on a deeper, more insightful level. The next day, from that new temporal perspective, they may interpret the other person's message differently, sometimes less emotionally. The reply they do send off may be very different—hopefully much more rational and mature—than the one they would have sent the day before. The "Stop and Think" rule of thumb can save people from unnecessary misunderstandings and arguments. A wait-and-revise strategy helps avert impulsiveness, embarrassment, and regret. In online therapy, clinicians can experiment with creative ways of encouraging clients to use this zone of reflection, to take advantage of the opportunity to self-reflect before responding to the clinician's message, perhaps as a way to stimulate an observing ego or enhance the process of working through an issue. In other cases the clinician may suggest that clients *not* delay their response to encourage a more spontaneous, uncensored reply. For the therapist, the zone of reflection allows interventions to be more carefully planned and countertransference reactions to be managed more effectively.

Because email and other asynchronous forms of communication have this adjustable conversing speed, the pacing of message exchanges will vary over the course of a text relationship. There will be a changing rhythm of freely spontaneous and carefully planned messages that parallels the ebb and flow of the relationship itself. Significant changes in cadence may indicate a significant change in feelings, attitudes, or commitment. The initial excitement of making contact may lead to frequent messages. Some people may even unconsciously experience the interaction as if it is an f2f encounter and therefore expect an almost immediate reply. Later in the relationship, the pacing may level off to a rate of exchange that feels comfortable to both partners. As a general rule, the more frequently people email each other, the more important and intimate the relationship feels to them. Some people email each other every day, or several times a day. Bursts in the intensity of the pace occur when hot topics are being discussed or when recent events in one's life need to be explained. These bursts may reflect a sudden deepening of the intimacy in the relationship. Declines in the pace may indicate a temporary or long-term weakening of the bonds between the couple—either due to a lagging interest in the relationship or distractions from other sectors of one's life. Drastic drops in the pace, or an apparent failure of the partner to respond at all, throws you into the *black hole experience*. The partner's silence may be a sign of anger, indifference, stubborn withdrawal, punishment, laziness, or preoccupation with other things. But you don't know for sure. The ambiguity inherent in the no-reply easily can become a blank screen onto which we project our own expectations, emotions, and anxieties.

Some clients will be avid text communicators. The computer is a major feature of their interpersonal and professional life. They do email all day long. Other clients will be novices in the online world. They log on only once or twice a week. To effectively adjust the pacing of their work, the clinician needs to take such differences into consideration.

Asynchronicity presents potential problems. Spontaneity and a sense of commitment to the relationship may decline without that in-the-moment contact. Without being together in realtime, some clients may experience the therapist as less "present." Although time zones seem irrelevant, clinicians need to sensitize themselves to the fact that the client's temporal experience of the therapeutic encounter may not match that of the clinician. I "see" the client in the morning, but the client "sees" me at night. Pauses in the conversation, coming late to a session, and no-shows are lost as psychologically significant cues. Although we eliminate the scheduling difficulties associated with an "appointment," we also lose the professional boundaries of that specific, time-limited appointment. In our culture we are not used to interacting with a professional in an asynchronous time frame. Because online therapists run the risk of being overwhelmed with messages from the client, or having the client drift away, they must be careful to create guidelines for an effective, reliable, manageable pacing of messages.

In *synchronous* communication, such as chat and instant messaging, the client and therapist are sitting at their computer at the same time, interacting with each other in that moment. Text chat includes the more common message-by-message exchanges in which a button is clicked to transmit the composed and perhaps edited message, as well as chat conversations where everything that both parties type can be seen as it is being typed, including typos, backspacing, and deletions, which enhances the synchronicity, spontaneity, and meaning of the experience. In all types of chat the act of typing does slow down the pace, thus making the conversation a bit asynchronous compared to f2f meetings. Technical factors, especially transmission speeds, also determine just how closely a chat meeting approaches the tempo of an in-person encounter. In text-only chat, for example, "lag" due to busy networks may slow down the conversation between the client and therapist, resulting in temporal hiccups of several or even dozens of seconds between exchanges. This creates a small zone of reflection, which can be useful. However, it's not easy knowing when to wait to see if someone will continue to type, when to reply, when to change the topic of discussion. A conversation may accidentally become crisscrossed until both partners get "in sync." Users skilled in online chat create incomplete sentences or use dot trailers at the end of a sentence fragment. . . . that lead the companion into the next message. To allow the other user to express a complex idea, you may need to sit back into a listener mode. Some users will even type "listening" to indicate this posture to others. Some people have a greater intuitive sense of how to pace the conversation: when to talk, when to wait and listen. They possess an empathic understanding of the synchronous text relationship and of the particular person with whom they are conversing.

The temporal pros and cons of synchronous communication are the mirror image of those for synchronous communication. Synchronous communication provides the opportunity to schedule sessions defined by a specific, limited period of time—the culturally familiar "appointment." It can create a point-by-point connectedness that enhances feelings of intimacy, presence, interpersonal impact, and "arriving together" at ideas. People may be more spontaneous, revealing, uncensored in their self-disclosures. Pauses in the conversation, coming late to a session, and no-shows are not lost as temporal cues that reveal important psychological meanings.

On the down side, the zone of reflection diminishes. Clients may lose the opportunity to compose their message, to say exactly what they want to say. In fact, some people feel they can create a stronger presence in asynchronous communication because they have more opportunity to express complexity and subtlety in what they write about themselves. They present themselves more fully. In synchronous communication clients also may associate "therapy" specifically with the appointment rather than experiencing it as a process that generalizes to their outside life.

DISINHIBITION

It's well known that people say and do things in cyberspace that they ordinarily wouldn't in the f2f world. They loosen up, feel more uninhibited, and express themselves more openly. Researchers call this the *disinhibition effect*. It's a double-edged sword. Sometimes people share very personal things about themselves. They reveal secret emotions, fears, wishes, show unusual acts of kindness and generosity, and as a result intimacy develops. Clinicians dare to make important interventions that they would have withheld f2f. On the other hand, the disinhibition effect may not be so benign. Out spills rude language, harsh criticisms, anger, hatred, even threats. People act out in all ways imaginable. Intimacy develops too rapidly resulting in regret, anxiety, and a hasty termination of the relationship. Clinicians say something better left unsaid. On the positive side, disinhibition indicates an attempt to understand and explore oneself, to work through problems and find better ways of relating to others. And sometimes it is simply a blind catharsis, an acting out of unsavory needs and wishes without any personal growth at all. Earlier in this article I cited an email in which a woman, a complete stranger to me, intimately described her relationship with her online lover. Consider also this email from another stranger:

> i am so suicidal every day that i have to tell somebody i would die and it would be all my parents fault for beating me every day and my classmates faults for making my life miserable every day and my dealers fault for going out of town and my fault for being manic depressive and suicidal and it would all be yalls fault cause your

fuckin site is to god damn confusing and i couldnt talk to anybody. *thank you for your time* please feel just fucking free to email me back

What causes this online disinhibition? What is it about cyberspace that loosens the psychological barriers that normally block the release of these inner feelings and needs? Several factors are operating, many of them driven by the qualities of text communication that I've described previously. For some people, one or two of these factors produces the lion's share of the disinhibition effect. In most cases these factors interact with each other and supplement each other, resulting in a more complex, amplified effect.

Anonymity (You Don't Know Me).   As you move around the Internet, most of the people you encounter can't easily tell who you are. People only know what you tell them about yourself. If you wish, you can keep your identity hidden. As the word *anonymous* indicates, you can have no name— at least not your real name. That anonymity works wonders for the disinhibition effect. When people have the opportunity to separate their actions from their real world and identity, they feel less vulnerable about opening up. Whatever they say or do can't be directly linked to the rest of their lives. They don't have to own their behavior by acknowledging it within the full context of who they "really" are. When acting out hostile feelings, the person doesn't have to take responsibility for those actions. In fact, people might even convince themselves that those behaviors "aren't me at all." This is what many clinicians would call *dissociation*.

Invisibility (You Can't See Me).   In many online environments other people cannot see you. They may not even know that you're present. Invisibility gives people the courage to do things that they otherwise wouldn't. This power to be concealed overlaps with anonymity because anonymity is the concealment of identity. But there are some important differences. In text communication others may know a great deal about who you are. However, they still can't see or hear you—and you can't see or hear them. Even with everyone's identity visible, the opportunity to be "physically" invisible amplifies the disinhibition effect. You don't have to worry about how you look or sound when you type something. You don't have to worry about how others look or sound. Seeing a frown, a shaking head, a sigh, a bored expression, and many other subtle and not-so-subtle signs of disapproval or indifference can slam the breaks on what people are willing to express. The psychoanalyst sits behind the patient to remain a physically ambiguous figure, without revealing any body language or facial expression, so that the patient has free range to discuss whatever he or she wants without feeling inhibited by how the analyst physically reacts. In everyday relationships people sometimes avert their eyes when discussing something personal and emotional. It's easier not to look into the other's face. Text communication offers a built-in opportunity to keep one's eyes averted.

Delayed Reactions (See You Later). In asynchronous relationships people may take minutes, hours, days, or even months to reply to something you say. Not having to deal with someone's immediate reaction can be disinhibiting. The equivalent in real life might be saying something to someone, magically suspending time before that person can reply, and then returning to the conversation when you're willing and able to hear the response. Immediate, realtime feedback from others tends to have a powerful effect on the ongoing flow of how much people express. In email and message boards, where there are delays in that feedback, people's train of thought may progress more steadily and quickly toward deeper expressions of what they are thinking and feeling. Some people may even experience asynchronous communication as running away after posting a message that is personal, emotional, or hostile. It feels safe putting it out there where it can be left behind. Kali Munro, an online clinician, aptly calls this an "emotional hit and run."

Solipsistic Introjection (It's All in My Head). As I described earlier, people sometimes feel online that their mind has merged with the mind of the other person. Reading another person's message might be experienced as a voice within one's head, as if that person magically has been inserted or introjected into one's psyche. Of course, we may not know what the other person's voice actually sounds like, so in our head we assign a voice to that person. In fact, consciously or unconsciously, we may even assign a visual image to what we think that person looks like and how that person behaves. The online companion now becomes a character within our intrapsychic world, a character who is shaped partly by how the person actually presents himself or herself via text communication, but also by our expectations, wishes, and needs. Because the person may remind us of other people we know, we fill in the image of that character with memories of those other acquaintances. As the character now becomes more elaborate and "real" within our minds, we may start to think, perhaps without being fully aware of it, that the typed-text conversation is all taking place within our heads, as if it's a dialogue between us and this character in our imagination—as if we are authors typing out a play or a novel. Even when it doesn't involve online relationships, many people carry on these kinds of conversations in their imagination throughout the day. People fantasize about flirting, arguing with a boss, or very honestly confronting a friend about what they feel. In their imagination, where it's safe, people feel free to say and do all sorts of things that they wouldn't in reality. At that moment, reality *is* one's imagination. Online text communication can serve as the psychological tapestry in which a person's mind weaves these fantasy role-plays, usually unconsciously and with considerable disinhibition.

When reading another's message, it's also possible that you "hear" that person's words using your own voice. We may be subvocalizing as we read, thereby projecting the sound of our voice into the other person's message. Perhaps unconsciously, it feels as if I am talking to/with myself. When we talk to ourselves, we say all sorts of things that we wouldn't say to others.

Neutralizing of Status (We're Equals).   In text communication we don't see the trappings of status and power—the fancy office, expensive clothes, diplomas on the walls and books on the shelves. In addition, a long-standing attitude on the Internet is that everyone should be equal, everyone should share, everyone should have equivalent access and influence. Respect comes from your skill in communicating (including writing skills), your persistence, the quality of your ideas, your technical know-how. Everyone, regardless of status, wealth, race, and gender, starts off on a level playing field. These factors combined tend to reduce the perception of authority. Usually people are reluctant to say what they really think as they stand before an authority figure. A fear of disapproval and punishment from on high dampens the spirit. But online, in what feels more like a peer relationship, people are much more willing to speak out or misbehave.

Of course, the online disinhibition effect is not the only factor that determines how much people open up or act out in cyberspace. The strength of underlying feelings, needs, and drive level has a big influence on how people behave. Personalities also vary greatly in the strength of defense mechanisms and tendencies toward inhibition or expression. People with histrionic styles tend to be very open and emotional. Compulsive people are more restrained. The online disinhibition effect will interact with these personality variables, in some cases resulting in a small deviation from the person's offline behavior, and in other cases causing dramatic changes.

FLUID AND TRANSCENDED SPACE

In text relationships geographical distance poses as no barrier to accessing other people online. Despite hundreds or thousands of miles of distance, the connection is always seconds away, always available, always on. The therapist can reach into the client's environment, intervening *in vivo*, in ways not possible during f2f counseling. In return, clients may experience the therapist as "here" (e.g., immediately present in their life space). Issues of separation and individuation take on a new meaning, which may be an advantage or disadvantage, depending on the client and the therapeutic circumstances.

A much more subjective, psychological sense of space replaces the physical or geographical sense of space. As I mentioned earlier, people may experience text relationships as an intermediate zone between self and other, an interpersonal space that is part self, part other. Sitting down at one's computer and opening up the communication software activates the feeling that one is entering that space. However, the very nature of text relationships—reading, writing, thinking, and feeling, all inside our head as we sit quietly at the keyboard—encourages us to continue carrying that internalized interpersonal space with us throughout the day. How often do we compose email messages in our head as we wash dishes and drive the car?

Although text relationships transcend geographical distance, they don't transcend the cultural differences associated with geography. People around the world have different customs for conversing and developing relationships, including text relationships. Some of the ideas discussed in this chapter will be culture-bound. A good rule of thumb in conversing with people from other lands is to be appropriately polite, friendly, and as clear as possible in what you write. Stretch your email empathy muscles. Unless you're very sure of your relationship with the person, avoid colloquialisms, slang, humor, innuendoes, and especially subtle attempts at cynicism and sarcasm, which are difficult to convey in text even under the best of circumstances. Starting off polite and later loosening up as the relationship develops is safer than inadvertently committing a faux pas and then trying to patch up the damage.

SOCIAL MULTIPLICITY

Spatial fluidity contributes to another important feature of cyberspace—social multiplicity. With relative ease a person can contact hundreds or thousands of people from all walks of life, from all over the world. By posting a message on bulletin boards read by countless numbers of users, people can draw to themselves others who match even their most esoteric interests. Using a Web search engine, they can scan through millions of pages in order to zoom their attention onto particular people and groups. The Internet will get more powerful as tools for searching, filtering, and contacting specific people and groups become more effective.

But why do we choose only some people to connect with and not others? A person will act on unconscious motivations—as well as conscious preferences and choices—in selecting friends, lovers, and enemies with whom to establish a text relationship. Transference guides them toward specific types of people who address their underlying emotions and needs. Pressed by hidden expectations, wishes, and fears, this unconscious filtering mechanism has at its disposal an almost infinite candy store of online alternatives from which to choose. As one experienced online user once said to me, "Everywhere I go in cyberspace, I keep running into the same kinds of people!" Carrying that insight one step further, another said, "Everywhere I go, I find . . . ME!"

As I mentioned earlier, online clinicians might keep in mind that a person who contacts them for counseling may already have seen their website or learned a substantial amount about them. The client-to-be may have been shopping around the Internet for a therapist who seemed right for him or her. Knowing how and why the client came to you, what pre-contact impressions the client formed, and why the client decided against other online therapists, all may be important issues to discuss. The therapist might also keep in mind that the client knows those other online clinicians are still waiting off in the wings. Ending one relationship and beginning another involves just a few clicks. Online social multiplicity may magnify the factors contributing to early termination, such as counterde-pendence, flights into health, a fear of intimacy and vulnerability, and other forms of resistance. Clinicians with a prominent online presence may also receive many unsolicited contacts from strangers with varying degrees of transference reactions and a wide variety of requests for help, advice, and information. They will need to develop strategies for deciding when and how to respond to such contacts from strangers whose motivations and needs may not be obvious.

Social multiplicity creates opportunities for a fascinating variety of group work. People experiencing similar problems, even unusual problems, easily can join together with a clinician in an email or message board group, regardless of their geographical location. In addition to this ability to form unique, topic-focused groups, online social multiplicity also creates opportunities for group format and process not always possible in f2f meetings. Using layered interactions a group could function at two different levels using two different channels of communication, with one channel perhaps functioning as a metadiscussion of the other, a computer-mediated enhancement of the "self-reflective loop." The group process becomes layered, with perhaps a core, spontaneous, synchronous experience and a superimposed asynchronous metadiscussion. In a nested group, people could communicate with each other while also being able to invisibly communicate with one or more people within that group. Although such private messaging could create subgrouping and conflict, it also could be useful in enabling group members and the therapist to offer hidden coaching and support that ultimately enhances the whole group. In overlapping groups, individuals or subgroups within one group can communicate with individuals or subgroups from a sister group, which enables a comparing of experiences across groups. Some online clinicians also use a metagroup that silently observes a meeting and then offers its feedback to the whole group, or privately to individuals during or after the online meeting. In a wheel group, the clinician might multiconverse with several clients at the same time, as in chat or instant messaging, essentially serving as the hub of the group with all lines of communication directed at the clinician. The clients may not even know that other clients are present or that a "group" even exists.

RECORDABILITY: ARCHIVES AND QUOTED TEXT

Most text communication, including email and chat sessions, can be recorded and saved. Unlike real-world interactions, we have the opportunity to keep a permanent record of what was said, to whom, and when. Most email programs enable users to create filters and a special folder to direct and store messages from a particular person or group, thereby creating a distinct space or "room" for those relationships. If we've only known certain people via text, we may even go so far as to say that our relationships with them *are* the messages we exchanged, that these relationships can be permanently recorded in their entirety as perfectly preserved in bits and bytes. Stored email communication is not unlike a novel that isn't a record of characters and plot, but rather *is* the characters and plot.

At your leisure, you can review what you and your partner said, cherish important moments in the relationship, reexamine misunderstandings and conflicts, or refresh a faulty memory. The archive offers clinicians an excellent opportunity to examine nuances of the therapeutic relationship and the progress of their work with the client. Clinicians also might encourage clients to create their own archives, as well as invent a variety of therapeutic exercises that have specific objectives in guiding the client's reviewing of that stored text.

Left to their own design, people differ in how much of a text relationship they save. The person who saves less—or maybe none at all—may have a lower investment in the relationship. Or they may not be as self-reflective about relationships as people who wish to reread and think about what was said. On the other hand, that person may simply have less of a need to capture, preserve, or control the relationship. Some people like to "live in the moment." They may not feel a need to store away what was said, which doesn't necessarily indicate less of an emotional attachment.

When people save only some of the text, they usually choose those chunks of the relationship that are especially meaningful to them—emotional high points, moments of intimacy, important personal information, or other milestones in the relationship. Comparing the text saved by one person to that saved by the partner could reveal similarities and discrepancies in what each finds most important about the relationship. One person might savor humor, practical information, personal self-disclosures, emotional recollections, or intellectual debate, whereas the other may not. Saving mostly one's own messages, or mostly the other person's messages, may reflect a difference in focus on either self or other. The area of significant overlap in saved messages reflects the common ground of interest and attitude that holds the relationship together.

Unless you're simply searching for practical information (e.g., phone number, address), what prompts you to go back and read old text may indicate something significant happening in the relationship or your reaction to it. Doubt, worry, confusion, anger, nostalgia? What motivates you to search your archive? The curious thing about rereading old text (even if it is just a few days old) is that it sounds different than it did the first time you read it. You see the previous communication in a new light or from a new perspective, or you notice nuances that you did not see before. You might discover that the emotions and meanings you previously detected were really your own projections and really nothing that the sender put there (i.e., your transference reaction). You might realize that your own feelings have distorted your recall of the history of the relationship.

We are tempted to think that a text archive is a factual record of what was said. In some ways it is. But saved text also is a container into which we pour our own psyche. We invest it with all sorts of meanings and emotions depending on our state of mind at the moment. Herein lies the therapeutic potential of encouraging clients to reread previous conversations, as well as the opportunity for the therapist to understand countertransference reactions.

An advantage of email conversations over those f2f is the ability to quote parts or all of what the other person said in the previous message. Hitting "reply" and then tacking your response to the top or bottom of the quoted email is a quick and easy rejoinder. In some cases it's a very appropriate strategy—especially when the other person's message was short, which makes it obvious what you are replying to. However, inserting a reply at the top or bottom of a long quoted message may be perceived by the other person as laziness or indifference on your part—as if you simply hit the reply button, typed your response, and clicked on "send." The person may not be sure exactly what part of the message you are responding to and also may feel annoyed at having to download an unnecessarily long file. Sticking a reply at the end of the lengthy quoted message can be particularly annoying because it forces the person to scroll and scroll and scroll, looking for the reply. All in all, quoting the entirety of a hefty message may not come across as a considerate and personal response. The impersonal tone may be exacerbated by those email programs that automatically preface a block of quoted text with a standardized notice such as, "On Saturday, May 28, Joe Smith said:". Whereas this automated notation may work fine for formal, businesslike relationships, or on email lists where multiple conversations are taking place, it may leave a bad taste in the mouth during more personal relationships.

The alternative to quoting the whole message is to select out and respond individually to segments of it. It takes more time and effort to quote segments rather than the whole message, but there are several advantages. People may appreciate the fact that you put that time and effort into your response. It makes your message clearer, more to the point, and easier to read. It may convey to your partner a kind of empathic attentiveness because you are responding to specific things that he or she said. Applying Rogerian reflection, you are letting the person know exactly what from their communication seemed most important. Replying to several segments can create an intriguingly rich email in which several threads of conversation occur at the same time, each with a different content and emotional tone. In one multilevel email, you may be joking, explaining, questioning, recalling a past event, and anticipating a future one. To establish continuity over several back-and-forth exchanges, you can create embedded layers of quoted segments, with each layer containing text from an earlier message. However, too many layers result in a confusing message in which it is unclear who said what and when. Messages with multiple quoted segments need to be formatted clearly.

Usually, one quotes lines from the most recent message received from the email partner. If you have an email archive, you also can quote lines from earlier messages, including messages from long ago. This may have a dramatic impact on your partner. On the positive side, people may be pleased to realize that you are saving their messages—in a sense, holding them in your memory, even cherishing their words. On the negative side, they may feel uncomfortable seeing their words revived from the distant past—especially when they don't quite remember when or in what context they said it. It's a reminder that you have a record of them. The situation can be even more unnerving when they don't have a record of the message themselves, so they can't verify the accuracy of the quote. A slightly paranoid feeling seeps in. "Am I being deceived, held hostage? Why didn't *I* save that message?" Of course, all of these negative reactions are amplified when people use old quoted text in an accusatory or hostile manner.

Quoting segments can create other problems too. Divvying up the other person's message into numerous quotes, with your comments interspersed, may be experienced by other people as impatient, interruptive, or unempathically disrespectful of the integrity of their message. In flame wars you often see people citing more and more of what the opponent said, using it as ammunition to launch counterattacks. A series of point-by-point retorts becomes a verbal slicing up of the foe, almost as if it reflects an unconscious wish to tear up the person by dissecting his or her message. Often attackers want to legitimize their arguments by citing the opponent's exact words, as if the citation stands as concrete, unquestionable evidence. "This is precisely what you said." However, it's very easy to take sentences out of context, completely misread their emotional tone, or juxtapose several segments extracted from different parts of the other person's emails in order to draw a false conclusion from that forced composite of ideas. It's an attempt to create a contrived reality that Michael Fenichel has aptly called a "cut and paste reality."

MEDIA DISRUPTION

With the exception of such things as laryngitis and noisy heating systems, we take for granted the accuracy and stability of the communication channel during f2f conversations. Online, we need to be more cognizant of possible communication disruptions. There will be moments when software and hardware do not work properly, when noise intrudes into the communication, when connections break. Busy servers result in lag that drastically slows down a chat conversation. A server crashes, preventing everyone from getting to the message board. Our email that we carefully constructed with special indentations and different fonts of different colors may lose all that formatting as it passes through mail servers that don't notice our creative keyboarding—essentially, a problem in translation. There will even be moments in a text relationship when we receive no reply and no error message at all, leaving us wondering if the problem is technical or interpersonal. That lack of response opens the door for us to project all sorts of worries, anxieties, and fantasies into this black hole experience.

Some computer-mediated environments are more robust than others, a fact online clinicians need to take into consideration when choosing their tools. Even in stable channels, therapists might take measures to confirm that the mechanical translation of the message is accurate ("Can you see this font?") and to create backup communication procedures if the primary channel fails.

THE MESSAGE BODY

In email and message boards, the body of the message contains the meat of the communication. I like the metaphor of "the body" because it captures the connotation of the physical self—how people appear, move, their sound and tone, their body language, even the elusive and rather mysterious dimensions of "presence." The message body is the most complex component of the communication. Messages can vary widely in length, organization, the flow of ideas, spelling errors, grammar sophistication, the spacing of paragraphs, the use of quoted text, caps, tabs, emoticons and other unique keyboard characters, as well as in the overall visual "feel" of the message. As I mentioned earlier in this chapter, the structure of the email body reflects the cognitive and personality style of the individual who creates it.

One interesting feature of the message body—not unlike the physical body—is the extent to which it is planned and controlled versus spontaneous and free. Carefully constructed text, even when intended to be empathic, may lack spontaneity. It is possible to overthink and micromanage the message to the point where it sounds contrived. Nevertheless, despite conscious attempts to present oneself exactly as one wishes, hidden elements of one's personality unconsciously may surface. On the other hand, completely freeform, loosely constructed text may confuse or annoy people. The most effective message is one that strikes a balance between spontaneity and carefully planned organization. Short messages with a few obvious spelling errors, glitches, or a slightly chaotic visual appearance can be a sincere expression of affection and friendship—as if the person is willing to let you see how they look hanging around the house, wearing an old T-shirt and jeans. Or such a message can be a genuine expression of the person's state of mind at that moment. "I'm in a hurry, but I wanted to dash this off to you!" In the course of an ongoing text relationship, there will be an engaging rhythm of spontaneous and carefully thought out messages that parallels the ebb and flow of the relationship itself. Composition can become more casual, detailed, and expressive as the relationship develops and people feel safe to explore; it regresses when they feel threatened, hurt, or angry. In some cases chaotic, regressed text may indicate decompensation and psychosis.

Text construction reflects an important personality trait—text empathy. Is there just the right measure of organization so the reader understands, along with the right measure of spontaneity so the reader appreciates the writer's genuineness? Does the sender pay attention to and anticipate the needs of the recipient? Empathic people specifically respond to what their text partners have said. They ask their partners questions about themselves and their lives. They also construct their messages anticipating what it will be like for the recipient to read it. They write in a style that is both engaging and readily understood. With appropriate use of spacing, paragraph breaks, and various keyboard characters (. . . .///**) to serve as highlights and dividers, they visually construct the message so that it is easy and pleasing to read. They estimate just how long is too long. Essentially, they are good writers who pay attention to the needs of their reader. This is quite unlike people with narcissistic tendencies who have difficulty putting themselves into the shoes of the recipient. They may produce lengthy blocks of unbroken text, expecting that their partner will sustain an interest in scrolling and reading for seemingly endless screens of long-winded descriptions of what the sender thinks and feels. Paradoxically, the narcissistic person's need to be heard and admired may result in the recipient hitting the delete key out of frustration or boredom.

Text empathy includes an intuitive feeling for what the others might be feeling and thinking. Curiously, people report that even in the stripped-down sensory world of text relationships—even in the bare bones of chat communication—others sometimes sense what's on your mind, even when you didn't say anything to that effect. Did they detect your state of mind from subtle clues in what or how you typed? Are they picking up on some seemingly minor change in how you typically express yourself? Or does their empathy reach beyond your words appearing on the screen? Obviously, this intuitive insight into the message body is a skill crucial to the success of an online clinician. It's a skill that may be different than intuition in f2f communication.

Humans are curious creatures. When faced with barriers, they find all sorts of creative ways to work around those barriers, especially when those barriers involve communication. Despite the auditory and visual limitations of text relating, experienced onliners have developed a variety of keyboard techniques to overcome some of the limitations of typed text—techniques that lend a vocal, kinesthetic quality to the message, that indeed create a metaphorical message "body." They attempt to make text conversations less like postal letters and more like an f2f encounter. In addition to the expressive use of fonts, colors, spacing, and indentations, some of these creative keyboarding strategies include the following:

Emoticons like the smiley, winky, and frown, which are seemingly simple character sets that nevertheless capture very subtle nuances of meaning and emotion. The smiley often is used to clarify a friendly feeling when otherwise the tone of your sentence might be ambiguous. It also can reflect benign assertiveness, an attempt to undo hostility, subtle denial or sarcasm, self-consciousness, and apologetic anxiety. The winky is like elbowing your email partner, implying that you both know something that doesn't need to be said out loud. It often is used to express sarcasm. The frown is used to express personal displeasure or sadness, or to show sympathy for an email partner who is unhappy.

Parenthetical expressions that convey body language or "subvocal" thoughts and feelings (sigh, feeling unsure here). It's an intentional effort to convey some underlying mood or state of mind, almost implicitly saying, "Hey, if there is something hidden or unconscious going on inside me, this is probably it!"

Voice accentuation via the use of caps, asterisks, and other keyboard characters in order to place vocal *EMPHASIS* on a particular word or phrase.

Trailers to indicate a pause in thinking. . . . or a transition in one's stream of thought. Combined with such vocal expressions as. . . . uh. . . . um. . . . trailers can mimic the cadence of in-person speech, perhaps simulating hesitation or confusion.

LOL, the acronym for "laughing out loud," which serves as a handy tool for responding to something funny without having to actually say "Oh, that's funny!" It feels more natural and spontaneous—more like the way you would respond in an f2f situation.

Exclamation points that tend to lighten up the mood of otherwise bland or serious sounding text. Text peppered lightly with exclamations, at just the right spots, provides a varying texture of energy that highlights mood and enthusiasm. Too many exclamation points may result in text that seems contrived, shallow, or even uncomfortably manic.

Expressive acronyms, such as imo (in my opinion) and jk (just kidding), used as shorthand expressions.

As with all things, practice makes perfect, so people tend to fine-tune and enhance their text expressiveness over time. As a relationship develops, the partners also become more sensitive to the nuances of each other's typed expression. Together they develop their own emoticons, acronyms, and unique communication techniques not immediately obvious to an outsider. They develop a private language that solidifies their relationship and the distinctness of their identity together. Usually that language crystallizes around issues that are discussed frequently and therefore are personally important to them. To understand and enhance the therapeutic relationship, clinicians might pay attention to—even encourage—the development of this private language with the client.

MESSAGE PERIPHERALS

Important features of interpersonal communication surround the message body in discussion board posts and especially email. Sometimes we overlook these peripheral features and head directly for the meat of the message. Nevertheless, as experienced online clinicians well know, these message peripherals can yield sometimes obvious, sometimes subtle, but always useful insights into the psychology of the other person and our relationship with that person. As seemingly insignificant aspects of the communication, they often become small gems of communication, deceptively packed with meaning. When they change over time they serve as signposts indicating changes in the relationship.

The Username

The username people choose reflects the identity that they wish to present online. The name chosen may be one's real name, a pseudonym, or a combination thereof. Using one's real name indicates a wish to simply be oneself. It is a straightforward presentation. Pseudonyms can be more mysterious, playful, revealing approaches. They may express some hidden aspect of the person's self-concept. They may reveal unconscious motivating fantasies and wishes (or fears) about one's identity. A change in username may reflect an important change in how a person wishes to relate to others and be perceived by others. Moving from a pseudonym to one's real name may express the wish to drop the "mask" (albeit a meaningful mask).

The Subject Line

The subject line is a tiny microcosm unto itself. Often people use it to simply summarize or introduce the major idea(s) contained in the text body. Experienced onliners understand the more subtle techniques for communicating meaning and emotion in the titles they bestow to their text. The subject line can lead into, highlight, or elaborate a particular idea in the text body. It can ask a definitive question, shoot back a terse answer, joke, tease, prod, berate, shout, whisper, or emote. Sometimes its meaning may blatantly or discreetly contradict the sentiment expressed in the text body. A creative application of caps, commas, slashes, parentheses, and other keyboard characters adds emphasis and complexity to the thoughts and emotions expressed in the subject line. Here are some examples illustrating these ideas:

> the solution is . . .
> loved it!
> Jim! help, Help, HELP!!
> I'm so impressed (yawn)
> Have To Do This
> Things afoot . . .
> Even more/sorry
> ????
> OK folks, settle down
> &**%$#))(*@#%%$
> Bob/battles/techniques/bullshit
> sigh. . . .

In an email archive, examining the list of subject lines across he development of the relationship is like perusing the headlines of a newspaper over the course of months or years. That list of titles reflects the flow of important themes in the history of the email encounter. These patterns or trends over time might reveal subtle or unconscious elements in the relationship. Even if online clinicians are reluctant to devote much time to rereading old messages, they can gain considerable insight into the progress of therapy by creating pithy subject titles, paying attention to the titles created by the client, and periodically scrolling through their archives to peruse those titles.

The use of "re:" versus creating a new subject title reflects an interesting dynamic interchange between text partners. Creating a new title means taking the lead in the relationship by introducing a new caption for the interaction. It is an attempt to conceptualize, summarize, and highlight what the person perceives as the most important feature of the conversation. Creating a new title calls into play the "observing ego"—that ability to step back and reflect on what is happening. It also reveals a sense of responsibility and ownership for the dialogue—in some cases maybe even an attempt to control the dialogue. In this fashion, some text partners "duel" with each other via the subject line. Simply clicking on reply without creating a new title may indicate less of an observing ego and more of a spontaneous reaction. It suggests a "I want to reply to what you said" mode of operation. Some people chronically fail to create a new title and persistently use "re:". They may be a bit passive in the relationship, indifferent, lazy. They may not feel that sense of responsibility, ownership, or control. Even if none of this is true, their partner may still perceive them as being that way. Online clinicians might pay special attention to when and how they create new titles versus using "re:" to maintain the captioned continuity of the discussion.

The Greeting

Similar to writing letters or meeting someone on the street, the text conversation usually begins with the greeting. Different greetings convey slightly different emotional tones and levels of intimacy. It sets the mood for the rest of the message—and sometimes may contradict the tone of the message. Starting with "Dear Jane" is somewhat formal, reminiscent of writing letters, and rarely used among experienced text communicators. "Hello Jane" is more casual, but still polite as compared to the looser "Hi Jane." The more enthusiastic "Hi Jane!" or "Hi there!" may have quite a significant impact on the reader when it appears for the first time, as well as when later it defaults to a plain "Hi Jane," perhaps indicating indifference, anger, or depression. "Jane!!" conveys an even higher level of enthusiasm, surprise, or delight. On the contrary, a simple "Jane" as a greeting tends to be a very matter-of-fact, "let's get to the point" opening, sometimes suggesting an almost ominous tone, as if the sender is trying to get your attention in preparation for some unpleasant discussion. Of course, adding the person's name to the greeting as in "Hi Jane" rather than simply "Hi" always indicates a deeper level of intimacy—or, at the very least, the fact that the person made the small extra effort to personalize the message. Over the course of a batch of messages, the back-and-forth changes in the greeting become a revealing little dance—sometimes playful, sometimes competitive. Who is being polite, friendly, intimate, enthusiastic, emotional?

No greeting at all is an interesting phenomenon that cuts two ways. In some cases, it may reveal that the sender is lazy or passive, or that he/she lacks any personal connection to you or any desire for a personal connection. In some messages I've received of this type, I felt almost as if the sender perceived me as a computer program ready to respond to his or her needs—with no identity or needs of my own. On the other hand, no greeting may indicate the exact opposite motive. The sender indeed feels connected to you—so much so that a greeting isn't required. She assumes you know that it's you who's on her mind. Or he never felt like he left the conversation and the psychological "space" he inhabits with you, so why inject a greeting into the message? In an ongoing, back-and-forth dialogue, there may be no greetings at all throughout a string of exchanged text. In the f2f world, you don't say "hello" in the midst of an energetic discussion. In cyberspace, the same principle holds. Although each email message looks like a letter that, according to tradition, should start off with a greeting, it isn't. It's a segment of an ongoing conversation.

The Sign-off Line

Whereas the greeting is the way people say hello and "sign in," the sign-off line is the way they exit from their message. As with the greeting, the sign-off is a fingerprint revealing the status of the person's mood and state of mind—sometimes obvious, sometimes subtle. "Here's where I'm at as I say good-bye." A contrast between the greeting and the sign-off may be significant, as if writing the message altered the person's attitudes and feelings. Across a series of messages the sign-off lines may be a string of repartees between the partners that amplifies, highlights, or adds nuance to their dialogue in the message bodies. The progression of exchanged sign-off lines may itself become an encapsulated, Morse-code dialogue between the partners. "Sincerely," "Regards," or other similar sign-offs are rather safe, all-purpose tools borrowed from the world of postal mail. They are formal, polite ways to exit. Some avid email users use them sparingly because they suggest a snail-mail mentality and a lack of appreciation for the creatively conversational quality of email. Here are some examples of sign-off lines that are a bit more revealing of the person's state of mind and his or her relationship to the email partner:

HUGZZ,
an unusually annoyed,
just my 2 cents,
stay cool,
still confused,
sheesh . . .

Almost invariably, the person's name follows the sign-off line, which demonstrates how intrinsically connected the sign-off line is to his or her identity. Simply typing one's real name is the easiest, most straightforward tactic. Some people creatively play with the sign-off name as a way to express their state of mind, some aspect of their identity, or their relationship to the text partner. Usually this type of play only feels appropriate with friends, or it indicates that one wishes to be friendly, loose, and imaginative.

Leaving out the sign-off line and/or name may be an omission with meaning. It might suggest a curt, efficient, formal, impersonal, or even angry attitude about the conversation. The ending could appear especially bureaucratic or impersonal if the person inserts his signature block and nothing else. On the other hand, friends may leave out a sign-off line and name as a gesture of informality and familiarity. "You know it's me." They may assume that the conversation is ongoing as in an f2f talk, so there's no need to type anything that suggests a good-bye.

Many email programs offer the option of creating a signature block that automatically will be placed at the bottom of the message, unless that feature is turned off. People usually place factual or identifying information into that file—such as their full name, title, email address, institutional affiliation, phone number, etc. It's a prepackaged stamp indicating "who, what, and where I am." What a person puts into that file reflects what they hold dear to their public identity. Some programs offer the feature of writing alternative signature files, which gives the person the opportunity to create several different fingerprints, each one tailored for a specific purpose. For example, one block may be formal and factual, another more casual and playful. Each one is a slightly different slice of the person's identity. Because all signature blocks have a nonspontaneous, prepackaged feeling to them, friends often make a conscious effort to turn this feature off when writing to someone who knows them well. In a sense they are dropping their formal status and title. The message in which the signature block first disappears may reflect the sender's move toward feeling more friendly and casual in the relationship. As with the sign-off line and name, a change in a person's signature block reflects a shift in his or her identity or in how he or she wishes to present his or her identity.

Some email users place an ASCII drawing or a quote into their signature block. Sometimes the quotes are serious, humorous, intellectual, tongue-in-cheek, famous, or homespun. Whatever people use can reveal an important slice of their personality, lifestyle, or philosophy of life. In online counseling the clinician might consider talking with the client about the meaning of the drawing or quote and any changes the client makes in them.

TEXT TALK IN REALTIME

The synchronous forms of text communication—as in instant messaging and chat—have evolved into a style of relating quite different than the asynchronous methods. The exchange of text usually involves only short sentences and phrases, what I like to call staccato speak. Some people find that experience too sparse. They feel disoriented in that screen of silently scrolling dialogue. Other people enjoy that minimalist style. They love to see how people creatively express themselves despite the limitations. They love to immerse themselves in the quiet flow of words that feels like a more direct, in the moment, intimate connection between one's mind and the minds of others. Some clinicians also prefer this point-by-point exchange of ideas. They feel it creates a greater sense of presence and a more full interpersonal influence "in the here and now."

Staccato speak influences communication in a variety of ways. The terse style works well for witty social banter and sometimes elicits that type of relating. Conversations may involve very short, superficial exchanges, or very honest and to-the-point discussions of personal issues. One doesn't have the verbose luxury of gradually leading the conversation to a serious topic, so self-disclosures sometimes are sudden and very revealing. To make conversations more efficient experienced synchronous communicators develop a complex collection of acronyms, which accelerates the development of a private language. In public chat settings, when people are meeting for the first time, they often quickly test the waters to determine the characteristics of the users around them and whom they want to engage. Questions that would be considered less than tactful in f2f encounters are a bit more socially acceptable here. Terse inquiries tossed out to a fellow user, or the entire room, might include "Age?", "M/F?", "Married?"

Synchronous communication in groups is considerably more challenging than one-on-one discussions—a fact the clinician interested in group work might consider. Chat room banter can seem quite chaotic, especially when many people are talking, or you have just entered a room and attempt to dive into the ongoing flow of overlapping conversations. There are no visual cues indicating what pairs or groups of people are huddled together in conversation, so the lines of scrolling dialogue seem disconnected. If people don't preface their message with the other user's name, it's not easy to tell who is reacting to whom or if someone is speaking to the whole group. Messages appear on your screen in an intermixed, slightly nonsequential order. The net result is a group free association where temporality is suspended, ideas bounce off each other, and the owner and recipient of the ideas become secondary.

You have to sit back and follow the flow of the text to decipher the themes of conversation and who is talking with whom. Consciously and unconsciously, you set up mental filters and points of focus that help you screen out noise and zoom in your concentration on particular people or topics of discussion. Often, you become immersed in one or two strings of dialogue and filter out the others. With experience, you develop an eye for efficiently reading the scrolling text. Some people may be better at this specific cognitive-perceptual task than others.

Saved transcripts of chat sessions often are more difficult to read after the fact than reading the text when you are there at the time the chat occurs. In part, this is because during a post hoc reading of a log you read at the pace you usually read any written material—which is quickly, but much too quickly to absorb the chat conversation. While online, the lag created by people typing and by thousands of miles of busy Internet wires forces the conversation into a slower pace. And so you sit back, read, wait, scan backward and forward in the dialogue (something you can't do in f2f conversation), and think about what to say next. There's more time for those perceptual/cognitive filters to operate. There's also more time for a psychological/emotional context to evolve in your mind—a context that helps you follow and shape the nuances of meaning that develop in the conversation.

Quite unlike f2f encounters, people can send private messages to others in a chat room—a message that no one else in the room can see. There may be very few or no messages appearing on your screen but people may be very busy conversing. In f2f encounters the equivalent would be a silent room filled with telepaths! If you are engaged in one of those private discussions, as well as conversing with people out loud, you are placed in the peculiar situation of carrying on dual social roles—an intimate you and a public you, simultaneously. Even more complex is when you attempt to conduct two or more private conversations, perhaps in addition to public ones. You may be joking privately with Harold, conducting a serious personal discussion with Elizabeth, while engaging in simple chitchat out loud with the rest of the room. This complex social maneuver requires the psychological mechanism of dissociation—the ability to separate and direct the components of your mind in more than one direction at the same time. It takes a great deal of online experience, mental concentration, and keyboarding skill (eye–hand coordination) to pull it off. A clinician needs to be aware of how these complex communication patterns might be affecting the group's dynamics, as well as hone the skills of conducting public and private conversations simultaneously. Most important is the ability to coordinate efforts with a co-therapist via private messaging while also speaking to the group.

INTEGRATION: CROSSING THE TEXT BOUNDARY

If there are any universally valid principles in psychology, one of them is the importance of integration: the fitting together and balancing of the various elements of the psyche to make a complete, harmonious whole. A faulty or pathological psychic system often is described with terms connoting division and fragmentation, such as *repression*, *dissociation*, and *splitting*. Health, on the other hand, is usually specified with terms that imply integration and union, such as *insight*, *assimilation*, and *self-actualization*. Integration—like commerce—creates synergy. It leads to development and prosperity. The exchange enriches both sides of the trade.

Even though I've devoted this chapter to a discussion of text relationships, I cannot emphasize enough the importance of the clinician considering the therapeutic possibilities of moving beyond the text relationship, of crossing the text boundary into other modes of communication. People learn by reading and writing, but they learn more by combining reading and writing with seeing, hearing, speaking, and doing. The integration of different modes of communication accelerates the process of understanding, working through, and assimilating psychological change. The clinician might consider the therapeutic possibilities of embedding graphics, audio, and video files into the text relationship. The clinician might also consider if, when, and how speaking with the client on the phone or in-person might enhance the progress of therapy.

The developmental path in most online relationships leads toward becoming more and more real to the other person—a process accelerated by bringing the relationship into new channels of communication. At first the companions may converse only via email or chat. If they try chat in addition to email, or vice versa, they often experience that move as a deepening of the relationship. Crossing any communication boundary often is perceived as reaching out to the other in a new way, as a gesture of intimacy. The big move of crossing the text boundary into phone and later in-person contact often becomes an important turning point in the relationship.

Hearing the other's voice on the phone and especially meeting f2f, you have the opportunity to test out the image of the other person that you had created in your mind. While conversing via text, how did you accurately perceive this person and where did your perceptions go astray? By answering those questions, you may come to understand how your own mind-set shaped your online impressions. You may have wanted or needed the person to be a certain way. Steered by your past intimate relationships, you may have expected them to be a certain way. You may have completely overlooked something in the text relationship that couldn't be ignored in the real world encounter. Afterward you may together discuss, assimilate, reminisce, and build on the encounter. You can share the ways in which the meeting confirmed and altered your perceptions of each other. But the in-person meeting doesn't always enhance the relationship for some people. They may be disappointed after the meeting. The other person was not what they had hoped. This unfortunate outcome may indicate that their online wishes were strong but unrealistic.

Some people choose not to phone or meet in-person their email companion, even though such meetings could be arranged. They prefer to limit the relationship to cyberspace. Perhaps they fear that their expectations and hopes will be dashed, or they feel more safe and comfortable with the relative anonymity of email contact. They may be relishing the online fantasy they have created for themselves. Or they simply enjoy the text relationship as it is and have no desire to develop the relationship any further. In all cases, choosing not to increase f2f contact with the text companion is a choice not to make the relationship more intimate, well-rounded, or reality-based.

The implications of these ideas for online counseling and psychotherapy can be profound. Although therapists sometimes may choose to communicate with a client only via text—given the needs of that client or perhaps of the therapist—they might keep in mind the therapeutic possibilities of using different modes of communication and, especially, of crossing the text boundary. Combining different modes, or progressing from one mode to another, offers opportunities for a more robust understanding of the other person, for deepening intimacy and trust, and for exploring transference and countertransference reactions.

An important dimension of what I call the integration principle is the process of bringing together one's online lifestyle with one's in-person lifestyle. Encourage clients to discuss and translate their f2f behaviors within the text relationship. Encourage them to take whatever new, productive behaviors they are learning via text and apply them to their in-person lifestyle. Encourage them to talk to trusted friends and family members about their online text relationships, including their therapy. If you are working with someone via text and in-person, help them discuss the text relationship when meeting in-person and the in-person relationship when online. This will prevent a dual relationship in which certain issues are isolated to one channel of communication (probably text) and never fully worked through. Encourage clients to communicate via online text with their in-person family members and friends, while also encouraging (but not forcing) them to meet in-person or via phone the people they know online.

If a goal of life is to "know thyself," as Socrates suggested, then it must entail knowing how the various elements of thyself fit together to make that Big Self that is you. Reaching that goal means understanding and taming the barriers between the sectors of self. Barriers are erected out of the need to protect or out of fear. Those barriers and anxieties too are a component of one's identity. Sequencing, combining, and integrating different modalities of communication help us explore the different dimensions of self that are expressed in those modalities and also helps us understand our resistances to communicating in new and perhaps growth-promoting ways.

SUMMARY

The Internet makes text relationships more accessible than ever before in history. The unique aspects of text relationships open up new possibilities for online clinical work: reading and writing skills shape the communication; there are minimal visual and auditory cues; communication is temporally fluid; a subjective sense of interpersonal space replaces the importance of geographical space; people can converse with almost anyone online and with multiple partners simultaneously; conversations can be saved and later reexamined; and, the environment is more susceptible to disruption. Several of these factors cause social disinhibition. Although we tend to focus on the body of the message, the peripheral components of a text communication—such as the username and message title—also enhance meaning. As effective as text work can be, we should not overlook the therapeutic possibilities of moving outside text and integrating other communication modalities into our work.

KEY TERMS

24-hour rule: The principle indicating the value of waiting one day before sending off a message related to an emotional situation.

Anonymity: A partial or complete invisibility of one's identity.

Black hole experience: A situation in cyberspace when one receives no response from either a computer or a person.

Creative keyboarding: The use of keyboard characters to convey emotion, body language, and subvocal thinking.

Cut and paste reality: A term coined by Michael Fenichel that refers to the distortion of the meaning of a person's text message by quoting excerpts of it out of context, or by inappropriately juxtaposing excerpts.

Delayed reactions: In asynchronous communication, the postponing of a reply to someone's text message.

Disinhibition effect: The tendency for people to do or say things in cyberspace that they normally would not say or do in their f2f life.

Dissociation: The process of isolating components of one's self or identity from each other.

Dual relationship: Somehow relating to someone differently online as compared to the in-person relationship with that person.

Emoticons: Keyboard characters that mimic facial expressions, such as the smiley, winky, and frown.

Integration principle: A principle stating the salutary effects of bringing together one's online and offline lifestyles.

Invisibility: Also known as "lurking," the condition of being unnoticed or unseen in an online environment.

Media disruption: A situation in which technical problems interfere with effective communication in an online environment.

Message body: The actual message written by a person in an email.

Message peripherals: The additional features of an email surrounding the message. body, such as the subject, username, greeting, and signature block.

Parenthetical expressions: In text messages, expressions in parentheses that indicate body language and underlying thoughts and feelings.

Presence: The sensation of actually being present in an online environment, or of another person being present in an online environment.

Private language: The idiosyncratic patterns of conversing that develop over time between people in text communication.

Recordability: The ability to save text messages.

Social multiplicity: The ability in cyberspace to establish relationships with numerous and different types of people.

Solipsistic introjection: In text relationships, the tendency to perceive the other person. as a character or voice within one's own internal psychological world.

Staccato speak: The terse style of communicating in chat and instant messaging.

Subject line: The title of an email message or discussion board post.

Synchronicity/asynchronicity: Online communication that occurs in realtime as in chat and instant messaging, or outside of realtime as in email and discussion boards.

Temporal fluidity: The flexible quality of when to respond to other people in asynchronous communication.

Text empathy: The intuitive ability to sense another person's thoughts and feelings in text communication.

Trailers: A string of periods to indicate a pause in speech or a transition of thought in text communication.

Transference reactions: The distorted perception of a person based on one's wishes, needs, and emotions stemming from past relationships with other people.

Voice accentuation: The use of capital letters and asterisks to emphasize words in a text message.

Zone of reflection: The period of time one can reflect on a message before replying to it.

STUDY QUESTIONS

1. What makes text relationships unique compared to in-person relationships?

2. How do writing skills and styles interact with the text relationship?

3. What are the pros and cons of absent f2f cues?

4. What are the factors that contribute to the disinhibition effect?

5. How can clinicians therapeutically use temporal fluidity, spatial fluidity, and recordability?

6. What are the basic creative keyboarding techniques?

7. How do message peripherals add to the meaning of text communication?

8. How can crossing the text boundary and integrating communication modalities be therapeutic?

REFERENCES

ISMHO Clinical Case Study Group (2001). Assessing a person's suitability for online therapy, *CyberPsychology & Behavior*, 4:675–680.

Suler, J. R. (2000). Psychotherapy in cyberspace: A 5-dimension model of online and computer-mediated psychotherapy. *CyberPsychology & Behavior*, 3:151–160. Also available in *The Psychology of Cyberspace*, www.rider.edu/users/suler/psycyber/psycyber.html. Retrieved August 25, 2003.

3

ONLINE COUNSELING: A HISTORICAL PERSPECTIVE

JOHN M. GROHOL, PSY.D.

Editors' Note: In this chapter, the author reviews the development of the field of online counseling. We are introduced to the earliest forms of therapeutic communication with a computer and taken on a tour of the major developments and key events in the unfolding of this new modality.

To understand the history of online counseling, or e-therapy (Grohol, 1997), it helps to understand three diverse fields and their convergence: computer-mediated communication, the Internet, and psychotherapy. Some people believe that online therapy began in the 1990s, but that is a simplistic understanding of the rich history that brought together people through the use of globally networked computers. What the history of e-therapy does not include is a discussion of the history of telemedicine and telehealth, distinct clinical applications that use other types of technology and that share little in common with the basic nature of e-therapy.

THE EARLY ROOTS OF ONLINE COUNSELING

One can trace e-therapy's roots all the way back to a time when researchers first envisioned uses of computers that went beyond simple number-crunching. One area that researchers looked at is computer-mediated communication, that is, communication between an individual and another individual done via computer.

Online Counseling: A Handbook for Mental Health Professionals

51

ELIZA

While the Internet was being developed in the 1960s, other researchers were using computers to let individuals communicate, or "talk," to a software program. This software, dubbed *ELIZA* by its Massachusetts Institute of Technology creator Joseph Weizenbaum, was first described in a 1966 journal article (Weizenbaum, 1966).

Using simple keyword associations, the *ELIZA* software (Carnegie Mellon University, 1995a) examined user-entered sentences and phrases and returned preprogrammed return phrases and sentences. Based on its own scripting language, the software could be programmed to respond to different topical areas of conversation. The default script, and the one for which the software is best known, is for *ELIZA* to, "play (or rather, parody) the role of a Rogerian psychotherapist engaged in an initial interview with a patient" (Weizenbaum, 1976). This is the first well-documented example of humans interacting with computers for a therapeutic purpose. Although Weizenbaum didn't intend the program to seriously be used as a substitute for a psychotherapist, many studies over the next three decades illustrated such usage (see, for example, O'Dell & Dickson, 1984).

ELIZA is not a traditional example of computer-mediated communication because an individual interacting with *ELIZA* is actually communicating with a computer program, not another person. But what makes this computer program different, however, is that most of the initial *ELIZA* users *thought* they were chatting with another person via the computer screen.

PARRY

Kenneth Mark Colby, a psychiatrist at Stanford University, worked with Weizenbaum on *ELIZA* and believed it had greater potential for psychotherapy and counseling applications. But this belief that *ELIZA* could one day substitute for a real-world therapist led to a split between the two scientists. Weizenbaum vehemently disagreed with Colby on the nature of computer-based psychotherapy, with Weizenbaum believing that psychotherapy could only be conducted face-to-face (f2f) between the therapist and his or her client (K. M. Colby, personal communication, April 1999). Colby went off on his own, eventually creating a program called *PARRY,* based on Weizenbaum's *ELIZA* (Colby, 1975; Carnegie Mellon University, 1995b). *PARRY* simulated a client in therapy who exhibited paranoid behavior. Where *ELIZA* lacked an internal model of communication that could track the flow of the conversation, *PARRY* could rudimentarily follow its own conversation. Based on different dimensions, *PARRY* simulated its paranoid behavior by keeping track of its "emotional state." Unlike *ELIZA, PARRY* was subjected to formal Turing testing. A

Turing test is a technical term for a procedure, designed by A. M. Turing, to determine whether a respondent is a person or a computer, and the test was originally used to determine whether a computer is intelligent. The Turing test results for *PARRY* showed that both scientists and psychiatrists did no better than chance in distinguishing *PARRY* from real patients (Colby, 1975; Colby, Weber & Hilf, 1971).

One of the first demonstrations of the Internet was a simulated psychotherapy session between two computer programs at UCLA, which was then repeated during the International Conference on Computer Communication held in Washington, D.C., in October 1972 (Zakon, 2002). The conversation took place between *PARRY* (at Stanford University in California) and the *DOCTOR,* another name for *ELIZA.* (*ELIZA* was also known as the *DOCTOR* at the time because of the common role it took on of playing a psychiatrist, yet it was also capable of playing other roles.) The transcript of the conversation is available and illustrates the limitations of both programs, while providing some amusing conversation (Cerf, 1973).

ELIZA was eventually ported (i.e., converted) to a more modern programming language, Perl, and was made available on the Internet by John Nolan in 1997 (Nolan, 1997). There are now hundreds of implementations of *ELIZA* online, allowing individuals to interact with the first and most well-known examples of rudimentary artificial intelligence. These types of programs are known as "chatterbots," owing to their ability to sustain some type of conversation with a human. Researchers continue to explore future applications for these programs as they become more complex and able to hold more meaningful conversations.

TALKING TO A COMPUTER

The importance of *ELIZA* and *PARRY* to online counseling lies in their text-based, interactive nature of communication between human and computer. Researchers discovered not only that individuals could communicate with a computer program and feel as though they were engaging in a conversation, but also that they did so easily and without reinforcement. These programs illustrated some of the very first social uses for computers and demonstrated that people would willingly engage in text-based communication for therapeutic purposes. Both programs simulated the traditional roles of individuals in a psychotherapy relationship. Users who tested and interacted with the programs more often than not could not tell they were not communicating with a human. More important, individuals readily accepted the novel idea of expressing their feelings and thoughts to a computer screen, which reportedly infuriated Weizenbaum (K. M. Colby, personal communication, April 1999). This easy acceptance would later lay the groundwork for online support groups and, eventually, online counseling itself.

THE RISE OF SUPPORT GROUPS ONLINE

Online support groups allow individuals to talk to others that are suffering from a similar disorder or grappling with similar issues as their own. An online support group serves much the same purpose and is used in much the same way as a real-world, f2f support group. A self-help support group is beneficial because it allows individuals to share common experiences about a specific issue, disorder, or event. The only real difference between the online and real-world groups is that people don't see one another while sharing their experiences and offering advice to one another in the online version.

Support groups initially began forming on the Internet around two types of problems: rare diseases and disorders that carry a stigma. Online support groups for rare diseases make sense because often there are not enough similarly afflicted individuals living in the same geographical locale to form a local support group. Bulletin board services (BBSs), and eventually the Internet, made distances inconsequential in socializing and connecting with others. For many people with a disorder that carries a stigma, visiting a doctor's or therapist's office often is an insurmountable hurdle. Online support groups offer individuals a safe, easy-to-access social group that reduces the problems associated with stigmatized disorders.

Support groups also offer an important benefit often overlooked or dismissed by many professionals—they provide the individual a first step toward change. Since people often turn to other methods of help before seeking out professional care, healthy online support groups can help people realize the extent of their problem and direct them to professional assistance if need be. Before online support groups were available, most individuals were limited in their ability to gather information on their malady or share their experiences with others. In addition to having a long, well-accepted history in the f2f world, support groups also have demonstrated positive, therapeutic effects for their participants (Humphreys, 1997; Kyrouz & Humphreys, 1997). Being available online, support groups offer a greater variety of topics from which to choose, as well as the convenience of participating in them at will. Of course, the online world's other greatest benefit—anonymity—serves these support groups' participants as well.

BULLETIN BOARD SYSTEMS

In the 1970s the personal computer came into existence, which was quickly followed by the introduction of the world's first BBSs. The Internet at the time was limited to universities, the government and military, and certain companies that helped build it. Ordinary individuals who owned computers could not yet access it. BBSs were the average home user's answer to the Internet and computer networking, because all that was required was a computer and a modem. The system worked by an individual dialing a phone number that connected his or her computer to somebody else's computer running BBS software. That software operated much like America Online (AOL) and CompuServe do today, providing email and messaging functionality. The significant difference between BBSs and larger commercial systems was that in most cases only one BBS user could be logged on at any given time. Given this limitation, most messaging was asynchronous or time-delayed.

BBSs hosted their own message boards, similar to Internet message boards today. Some BBSs were started to host an online community (such as the San Francisco Whole Earth 'Lectronic Link' [WELL] and the East Coast's Echo); others were devoted to specific themes or hobbies. And some BBSs hosted message boards that acted as online support groups. BBSs that did host online support groups for a mental health issue or medical disease tended to be the larger ones that had enough members to support such groups. These groups were very similar in style of interaction to the Web-based bulletin boards of today. They also shared one other component more difficult to find online today—a close-knit, closed community of people in a mostly similar geographical area. Because of this component, these communities tended to be more intimate and, therefore, more appealing.

NEWSGROUPS AND SPECIAL INTEREST FORUMS

As the Internet grew in the 1980s, connecting most of the world's universities, another form of message boards began to emerge. These message boards were called newsgroups, and the universe of newsgroups on the Internet was referred to as Usenet. Usenet newsgroups were organized by topical hierarchies (as is the popular website directory Yahoo!). In each newsgroup, an individual could start a new "thread," or topic, of conversation. Because each topic was kept to its own thread, discussions were easier to follow than in the other major format available at the time (mailing lists, discussed in the next section). If a person wasn't interested in a particular topic in a newsgroup, he or she could simply choose not to read that entire thread. It made browsing the discussion quick and easy, and allowed individuals to participate in groups even if the groups had a great many members and discussions occurring at the same time.

One of the first Internet-based online support groups, alt.support.depression, started on Usenet. Soon, dozens more support groups popped up in the alt.support hierarchy, and by 1995 there were hundreds of such support groups, covering not only mental health topics but medical diseases as well. Today, thousands of people participate in these groups—some are regulars, some are first-time participants, some post to the newsgroup often, and some have never posted a single message to the group, instead preferring to sit back and simply follow conversations of interest.

The downside to newsgroups became apparent as their numbers grew in the early 1990s and the Internet was opened to commercial use. Inappropriate and off-topic postings became more frequent and many groups suffered from an exodus to other online forms of communication and community.

MAILING LISTS

Some individuals who abandoned newsgroups turned to electronic mailing lists (also sometimes referred to as *listservs,* a term that came from the brand of software running many of the earliest mailing lists). Mailing lists have been around since shortly after the advent of email, because users wanted a way of emailing a group of individuals without having to remember to carbon copy each of them. Mailing list software provides for this functionality and list management, allowing a group of individuals to email the group back and forth without worrying about each person's email address. But an important difference with email as opposed to other online modalities is that a person doesn't have to do anything to participate in a list once subscribed. Emails are sent, or *pushed,* automatically to each user on the list, a behavior that's referred to as *push* technology. This is very different than all other online modalities for communication (except instant messaging), which require the active participation of the user to, for example, visit the newsgroup or Web-based message board.

Mailing lists still host thousands of support groups online around the world. In addition to being less susceptible to off-topic postings or advertisements, they are also more private. Subscribing to a mailing list to read others' comments or to contribute those of your own requires a specific set of actions on the user's part. With the advent of modern email software, such as Outlook and Eudora, mailing list messages can be easily filtered into separate folders and can be viewed as threads, much like newsgroups. This makes them nearly as easy to participate in.

OPENING THE DOOR TO ONLINE COUNSELING

In addition to online communities provided by BBSs, Internet newsgroups, and mailing lists, proprietary commercial services begun in the 1980s, such as CompuServe, Prodigy, and, later, AOL, also hosted their own online communities, sometimes referred to as Special Interest Groups (or SIGs, a term popularized by CompuServe's forums). Each one of these services had numerous support groups online for everything ranging from depression and anxiety to relationships and careers. At the time, these services were not connected to each other or the Internet, so each was an online island community, just as the BBSs continued to operate on their own. What these larger commercial service providers could offer that BBSs could not were larger online communities. So whereas a typical BBS might have up to 500 or 1000 members, Prodigy and services like it had hundreds of thousands of users. With the greater numbers came greater diversity and needs. One of those needs, helping people organize self-help groups, was readily filled by the commercial services. Not only did it serve the community's needs, it also made the service more profitable because they typically charged per-minute connection fees.

Support groups even formed in realtime, interactive text games, such as multiuser Dungeons (MUDs, named after the popular multiplayer fantasy game of the 1980s, Dungeons and Dragons) and object-oriented multiuser dungeons (MOOs). Such environments allowed people to role-play, a behavior that can often have therapeutic benefits. After people tired of playing the game, they would simply log in to the gaming environment to chat with fellow characters and socialize. In some instances, the chatting turned into real social support about serious emotional issues. In the 1990s another service called The Palace provided a more graphical environment for users to interact in real-time and role-play within. Because all of these areas offered users a somewhat closed system with a limited number of users—all of whom were taking on roles very different from their real-world personas—these technologies provided what felt like a closer-knit, more intimate social environment.

What all of these online forums shared was the ability to bring together individuals from around the world into a virtual community. Although the technologies of these communities differed significantly, their basic social underpinnings were similar, bringing together people from around the world to communicate through computers. People found it simple, rewarding, and nearly limitless in its potential to change many social conventions.

THE EARLY DAYS OF ONLINE COUNSELING

The early days of online counseling were characterized by professionals looking to use the advances of online technology to reach out to more people than was ever before possible. Never in history had it been so easy and inexpensive for one person to communicate with an audience of hundreds or thousands of others. Before the Internet, one-to-many communication was traditionally done by publishers, through books, magazines, newspapers, and broadcast media, such as television and radio. The Internet drastically changed this, making it possible to publish psychoeducational material easily and inexpensively online. Online technology also made it extremely simple to participate in communities and support groups. This allowed professionals to disperse information that was traditionally reserved to books and graduate or medical school classes. Few of the pioneers saw any significant commercial potential in the work they did. They did it for numerous reasons, but mainly because the Internet made it possible to help others in a way no one had thought possible a few years earlier and because the need was there.

THE FREE PIONEERS

The advent of advice-giving online by professionals, and eventually online counseling itself, can be traced back to universities. At university campuses, students often enjoyed unlimited access to the Internet and related computing resources, despite their archaic interface and mainframe technology. This lent itself to a problem constantly faced at universities—handling the overflow of students seeking counseling and health advice from the free university health clinics and counseling centers.

In 1986, then Assistant Dean of Students and former Director of the Cornell Counseling Center Jerry Feist and Cornell Computer Service's Steve Worona developed a revolutionary solution to this perennial problem: use the vast computing resources at the university to help answer some of the students' questions. The system they devised was named *Dear Uncle Ezra,* taking on the namesake of the university's founder, Ezra Cornell (Feist & Worona, 1986). Two dozen public computer sites around campus provided free access to students to ask and read *Uncle Ezra* inquiries (as a part of the campus-wide Cornell University Information System, CUinfo). The queries were answered by university workers and posted on the university's proprietary computer system for all to read. The service (still in use, having been transferred to the Web in the 1990s) is free but only provides simple, advice-driven answers; in-depth consultations aren't available through the system. Real names aren't used, so the submitter's privacy is protected. Other universities have followed Cornell's lead and offer similar online health systems of their own.

In 1991 John Grohol was a graduate student in psychology in Florida and began fielding psychology and mental health questions asked of him from his participation in numerous Usenet newsgroups. Creating the first online index of mental health support groups online, he used his growing knowledge in the field to answer basic questions about mental disorders, corrected misperceptions about mental health treatments, and responded to inquiries both in private and on newsgroups to help guide people to appropriate care. In 1995 Grohol continued this work on his website, Psych Central, which has operated continuously since then (Grohol, 1995). Also in 1995, Grohol began offering an online mental health chat on the Webchat Broadcasting System (WBS). This chat, conducted weekly, has continued uninterrupted to this day, but is now hosted on a different chat system. Grohol has never charged for any of the services he provides to the public.

A handful of other mental health professionals were also joining and becoming more active in different online forums. Ivan Goldberg was a psychiatrist and clinical psychopharmacologist in New York City who specialized in treatment-resistant cases. He often could help individuals who were having troubles with typical medications prescribed for depression or bipolar disorder, by changing the dose or type of medication. Beginning around 1993, he started fielding questions by email as a result of his participation on depression support mailing lists and Internet newsgroups. Like Grohol, Goldberg never charged for the educational answers he gave nor the advice he doled out. In 1996 he created a website, called Depression Central, to house his answers (Goldberg, 1996).

Professionals and individuals interested in support groups weren't the only ones who saw the great potential the Internet brought. A United Kingdom charity organization begun in 1953 called the Samaritans originally began by fielding phone calls from suicidal people throughout the UK and Ireland. It expanded in the 1970s beyond the UK's borders and is also known internationally as Befrienders International. With more than 18,000 trained volunteers throughout the world currently, these same people sometimes staff the volunteer suicide hotlines that are available locally in most U.S. communities. Such telephone hotlines are answered 24 hours a day and have saved hundreds of thousands of lives in the past four decades. In 1994 the Samaritans set up the first email address specifically to answer the emails of despair and lost hope from suicidal individuals around the world. As with the hotlines, the email service is available without charge and individuals accessing it can be anonymous if they choose. This email service now answers more than 60,000 queries per year and is distributed among 68 international Befrienders branches (Samaritans, 2002).

FEE-FOR-SERVICE COMES OF AGE

The Internet was finally opened to commercial use in the 1990s, and the realities of commerce soon made themselves felt in this new medium. As early as 1994, the popular media saw the emerging potential for therapy online, as characterized by the start of this article in the *San Francisco Examiner:*

> Driven by a medical system that begs for cost containment, many mental health professionals are looking for ways to offer their patients more for less, and technotherapy fits the bill. Using computers as an adjunct to, or even in place of, traditional therapy for all but the most severely mentally ill, they find, not only speeds up the therapeutic process, but in some cases makes it more effective (Kelley, 1994).

There was no single "first" psychotherapist who began offering his or her services online for a fee; many professionals began around the same time in different parts of the world. A few therapists, however, are repeatedly mentioned and recognized as being among the first online counselors. David Sommers was one of those people, a psychologist who offered a fee-for-service arrangement on the Internet, beginning in 1995. Sommers's sessions were not single advice-giving sessions; they usually consisted of ongoing therapeutic relationships with his clients. While he mainly used email as the therapy modality, he also occasionally used chat and video-conferencing. He eventually provided services to more than 300 clients while offering e-therapy services until 1998, when he quit because he found his online practice too time-consuming (Beckett, 1998).

Leonard Holmes, another psychologist, also began in 1995 offering what he called "Shareware Psychological Consultations." *Shareware* is a term for software that a person may download and try out for free, but if the person finds the software useful, he or she is expected to pay a fee to continue its use. Applying the term to psychological consultations, Holmes expected that if clients found his one-time consultations of use, they would pay a suggested fee. According to Holmes's accounts of his experience, most individuals did not pay and he stopped the practice in the later 1990s. Unlike Sommers, most of Holmes's online counseling sessions were one-time only consultations, not ongoing psychotherapy.

Ed Needham, a master's-level counselor in Indiana, opened his Cyberpsych counseling service on the Internet in August 1995 (Needham, 2000). He used real-time chat to conduct his counseling. Using a modality called Internet Relay Chat (IRC), he charged $15 for a 1-hour session. Needham worked with more than 40 clients until he closed his service in 1998. Richard Sansbury was among other early adopters of e-therapy. Sansbury is a licensed psychologist and began his online practice in 1997. Since that time, he has seen hundreds of patients through his website, which continues to this day (Sansbury, 2002).

Other entrepreneurs were beginning to realize the potential of computers to help people, much in the same vein as the early *ELIZA* program. *Overcoming Depression* was a software program developed in 1991 by Malibu Artificial Intelligence Works, a company started by psychiatrist Kenneth Colby (who also developed *PARRY*) and his son Peter (Colby, 1991). In the 1980s a psychiatrist named Roger Gould developed a program called the *Therapeutic Learning Program (TLP)*. Based on decades of research in adult development, the program provided users an interactive tool that systematically assessed a person's problem, learned about the person's way of coping with his or her problem, and provided the appropriate tools to help the person overcome the problem. In 1997 Gould translated one of the modules onto a website called MasteringStress.com. Backed by seven separate published research studies concerning its effects on 20,000 subjects, the *Therapeutic Learning Program* was a significant milestone in providing text-based, interactive self-help.

These programs provide a research base that illustrates how specific, personalized text-based techniques can help people with specific issues. They also show that individuals have little difficulty in expressing complex, personal thoughts and feelings to a computer by typing. Such research has positive implications for goal-based, solution-oriented online counseling.

HEADING INTO THE MAINSTREAM

The world of online counseling was beginning to pick up as the Internet experienced significant growth in the mid-1990s. With the large commercial online service providers merging into one (AOL), and with AOL's connection to the Internet cemented at about the same time, hundreds of thousands of new users were going online every month. It is not surprising that some of these individuals would be interested in obtaining e-therapy services. Driven by the promise of offering direct therapy services in their spare time without having to worry about insurance claims, more therapists turned to the potential that online therapy offered.

Martha Ainsworth (2002) has helpfully tracked the rise and growth of the field within her directory of online counselors. She first started compiling the directory as early as 1995, when she discovered a dozen counselors offering services online. This number slowly grew in the late 1990s, to approximately 200 by 1998. Because some counselors began joining the emerging online clinics, often the same professional might be listed more than once (and in more than one online clinic). This makes reliable statistics about the number of actively practicing professionals online somewhat difficult to obtain.

GROWTH OF COMMERCIAL SERVICES

As the 1990s drew to a close, users saw the rise (and sometimes fall) of commercial enterprises aimed at filling the needs of online counselors and their respective clients. These businesses, sometimes referred to as online clinics or e-clinics, typically brought together dozens and sometimes hundreds of professionals offering mental health services. In this section, I will highlight some of the business failures and success stories of these online clinics.

Many Business Models, Some That Failed ...

It is said that the road to hell is littered with good intentions. If that is true, then the road of the Internet is littered with failed dot-coms with mostly good intentions. The term *dot-com* refers to a company whose central business is online. And in the late 1990s, starting a dot-com was all the rage. With astronomical valuations being placed on businesses that had little more than a fantasy business plan, it wasn't surprising when some businesspeople started thinking about the online therapy field. Here was an area that seemingly had a large potential market (anybody who was online and had an issue they would like to discuss with a professional), low cost (e-therapy allowed lower costs than other professional services), and simple technology requirements (just provide a secure email and chat system). Businesspeople thought it sounded like a good idea and found willing investors to put up initial funding to get a number of companies started.

A number of companies entered the field but never made a significant impact. Two of those were LifeHelper.com. and etherapy.com. Life-Helper.com was started, as were many of the online clinics, in 1999 by a businessman, Roy Lee, who thought that such services could help people who were afraid of the stigma associated with seeking mental health services in person. With initial funding by individual investors and a small board of directors, Lee gathered a team of technologists and psychology professionals to help him build it. After putting together a large advisory group of mental health professionals, some of whom were experts in the field and some of whom were offering e-therapy on their own, they set about developing the actual software that would host the online clinic.

Virtually all of the online clinic companies had similar business plans. Their plans tended to include the building and development of an extensive online clinical record-keeping system to allow mental health professionals to schedule, see, and bill for online patient sessions. The details of the plans varied somewhat, but they all relied on building a platform on which therapists could conduct their sessions; the system typically used a regular Web browser and the browser's built-in security technology. Some systems offered more bells and whistles, such as videoconferencing capabilities, than other systems. The companies planned to earn revenue by charging the professionals a small monthly fee or a small transaction fee for each client session. With small numbers of professionals, the companies would lose a significant amount of money each month. With larger numbers of professionals (usually the numbers would require more than 200 paid professionals to sustain the company's business needs), the company could sustain itself and grow.

Like many dot-coms of the era, however, LifeHelper.com underestimated the costs of building a custom system from scratch to offer secure therapy online. Consumer marketing costs to tell people about the service would be significant, and reaching enough professionals to subscribe to the network would cost more money than at first estimated. In the meantime, the drain of having so many professionals on the management team caused monthly costs to balloon. The company experienced short-term cash flow problems and closed in 2000, even before publicly launching its website.

About this same time, another set of businessmen in South Florida had a similar idea with etherapy.com. This company's site got further along than LifeHelper.com's: etherapy.com did launch a public beta site and eventually did open for business. But with most of its money poured into development costs and salaries, there was little money to hold the company over for the time it takes to build the professional network of therapists needed to make the business model work. Etherapy.com operated under the same assumption as most similarly structured dot-coms: that mass consumer marketing was needed to attract the customers that would give the professionals business. Without that marketing, the professionals would often be associated with a site not providing them any business, never mind income. Without income, there was little reason to pay a monthly fee, or any fee, to remain with the company's network. As it did for so many other start-ups, the formula failed for etherapy.com and the company shuttered its doors shortly after its launch.

These dot-com companies that came and went did so with little debt and with little impact on practitioners or potential clients, because they were not operational or were just beginning operation. While the closing of a company is usually traumatic on some level, these companies left behind little in terms of a legacy. In a field in its infancy, that is a good behavior. Others to follow were not so kind.

Some That Worked . . . Sort Of

For e-therapy dot-coms to be successful, they need to sustain a delicate balance between professionals in their network and consumers seeking mental health services. Too many professionals and not enough clients, and the professionals will leave the company or simply refuse to renew their membership. Too many consumers seeking services and professionals will be overwhelmed with clients, turning away paying customers. Few achieved that balance, but two that nearly did were here2listen.com and HelpHorizons.com.

Here2listen.com is a perfect example of a dot-com gone wrong. It began in a blaze of glory, subscribed hundreds of practitioners to its network, then abruptly shut its doors and closed down its website when the money ran out, abandoning hundreds of its customers. Cofounded by Gunny Cho, a former international corporate lawyer, and Don Sheu in June 1999, the company boasted an advisory board of renowned psychology experts. Its advisory board included well-respected university professors, such as Larry Beutler from the University of California, Peter Kramer, well-known author of *Listening to Prozac,* and Philip G. Zimbardo, the president of the American Psychological Association in 2002. This board gave the company instant legitimacy, which businesspeople understand but academics seemingly rarely do. The company subscribed to the Health on the Net Foundation's (HON) code of ethics and proclaimed the endorsement of the Pacific Graduate School of Psychology. According to a 2000 article in *Wired News,* here2listen.com was also backed by Stanford University (Burke, 2000). The company's revenue was garnered by charging 10 percent of the therapist's fees.

The specific causes of here2listen.com's failure are still mired in mystery, because few involved in the company will speak about its closure. But symptoms of the problems in the company appeared as writers started lining up for payment in early 2001 and took their complaints public (see, for example, http://www.writersweekly.com/warnings/here2listen.html). Although many at the time complained publicly about the lack of defined ethical standards for e-therapy encounters, few questioned the ethics or business acumen of the businesspeople and investors providing the clinical workspace for the therapists; it was assumed that they would be responsible to their customers. But without warning or prenotification to its clients or therapists, here2listen.com shuttered its doors in late 2001 and its remaining assets were sold to help pay off some of its debts.

Here2listen.com's failure might be related to its infrastructure and development costs, salaries, and policy of paying freelance writers for articles. Begun on disparate technology platforms, the company underwent a development effort to simplify the site's architecture. Salary costs for management, customer service representatives, media relations, technologists, and others needed to be paid despite the platform's failure to generate significant revenues early in its development. It was also thought that a website needed a wealth of original content to be unique and original enough to attract large numbers of consumers. The simplest way to obtain such content quickly and regularly was to pay freelance writers for it. For historical purposes, here2listen.com is still archived at the Internet archive (http://www.archive.org).

Another dot-com of the time was HelpHorizons.com. It was founded in 1999 by Michael Tagatac, a former Wall Street financial analyst who believed in the potential for the Internet to reach people who otherwise would not seek mental health services. He assembled a small team of professionals and energetic people he knew, raised some initial funding from individual investors, and proceeded to build not only a platform on which to conduct e-therapy, but a full-fledged practice management system for professionals.

Unlike many other dot-com founders, Tagatac understood the need for strict financial management of the limited funds he had to work with. Still in business as of this writing, HelpHorizons.com tightened the company's purse strings in 2001 when it was clear additional financing would be difficult to obtain. The technology platform HelpHorizons.com built was designed to be largely self-sustaining, requiring little maintenance or technical oversight once in production. This helped the company trim its costs, cut unneeded staff, and continue to offer a reliable, stable "virtual office" for professionals to provide online mental health services.

THE NEED FOR GUIDANCE

As more and more therapists were coming online, they were looking for guidance on how to practice online in an ethical and professional manner. The American Counseling Association understood the need to provide such guidance to counselors. In October 1999 the association published the Ethical Standards for Internet Online Counseling. These were the first standards adopted by a national professional organization and paved the way for later efforts.

In 1997 at the American Psychological Association's annual convention in Chicago, Illinois, a group of online mental health professionals and consumers gathered for a historic luncheon. More than a dozen individuals attended the lunch and discussed their passion and energy for mental health online. The group was more diverse than a traditional professional organization and had interests encompassing more than just e-therapy. They agreed in principle to start an organization to promote the varied projects and interests of mental health online. That organization was the International Society for Mental Health Online, a nonprofit society created to serve that purpose.

In 1999 the Society collaborated with the Psychiatric Society for Informatics to create the Suggested Principles for the Online Provision of Mental Health Services (ISMHO, 2000). These were adopted and approved by both organizations, providing an additional framework for professionals.

Editors' Note: Among the early clinics that began emerging online was OnlineClinics.com, which was founded in 1999 by Ron Kraus, a New York clinical and child psychologist. Dr. Kraus and his colleagues believe that online counseling requires service standards that are equal to those practiced in the clinician's office. As a result, OnlineClinics' team developed EthicsCode.com to set professional and ethical standards for the forming modality. After a promising start with the registration of hundreds of clinicians nation-wide and some positive media attention, the company suffered greatly from the dot-com crash, especially when its web development group went belly up, and with it, a large portion of the company's initial investment. Still, OnlineClinics managed to somehow stay in the market, as well as online, without interruption to service but not fully interactive for a time. A new technological development team was found in 2003, and now OnlineClinics continues to grow.

ONLINE COUNSELING TODAY

Today, e-therapy has found a niche. It is not a large niche, nor one that will attract millions of dollars in investment capital. Some small online networks of mental health practitioners continue to thrive and will likely gradually grow as more and more people learn of the benefits of online mental health services. Without large marketing budgets, consumers will continue to trickle in to online therapist's offices through search engines and the handful of online clinics still in existence.

Some of e-therapy's rise can be attributed to mainstream press coverage of the online clinics' efforts in 1999 and 2000, before the dot-com crash. Television networks such as CNN and ABC gave online therapy ample coverage, and publications such as *Time, Newsweek* and *USA Today* quoted one expert after another proclaiming its benefits. Although there appears to be some interest among consumers in this new modality, there is little critical mass as of this writing.

Some professional associations, such as the American Counseling Association and the National Board for Certified Counselors, immediately understood the benefits online therapy might offer certain clients and provided their professional members guidelines on how to offer it. Other associations, such as the American Psychiatric Association and the American Psychological Association, were much more conservative in their initial assessment of e-therapy and offered their members little guidance. More recently, however, even these associations have altered their stance and now offer some guidance and direction to their members on how best to integrate the Internet into their service and research offerings.

Online counseling is still largely based on fee-for-service, requiring consumers to pay for online services out of their own pocket. As of this writing, most insurance companies still do not reimburse for e-therapy or similar services. As the research base grows, it's likely that insurance companies will change their stance and offer payment to professionals for their online practice. As a more cost-effective means of providing some level of service, it seems that such a change is not a matter of whether or not it will occur, but when.

Some individual online therapists are thriving, having learned the skills of marketing themselves successfully online through search engines, word-of-mouth, and other methods. Others are still learning how to market their practice and make a successful splash on the Internet. Turning toward professional organizations such as the International Society for Mental Health Online for guidance is a simple way for professionals interested in this field to keep updated on the latest developments.

KEY TERMS

Bulletin Board System (BBS): A computer setup to exchange messages among a group of users, including email and public messages. BBSs were more popular before the Internet became accessible to the general public in the early 1990s.

Dot-com: A business that conducts most of its activities and business transactions on the Internet.

ELIZA: A software program written by Joseph Weizenbaum in the 1960s to mimic a therapist's communications. It is the first example of a computer-mediated interaction using a very simple form of psychotherapy.

E-therapy: A new modality of psychotherapy that provides clients a way of accessing a mental health professional online. Emphasizing anonymity, introspection, immediacy, convenience, and lower costs, e-therapy is most often conducted via email communication with a therapist. It can also include chat and videoconferencing, although these are less often used. Also referred to as online therapy or online counseling.

Message board: A discussion forum on the Internet. Message boards are usually organized by topics.

MUDs/MOOs: Multiuser Dungeons, named after Dungeons and Dragons (the popular multiplayer fantasy game of the 1980s), and object-oriented multiuser dungeons. Some people refer to "dungeons" as the more generic "domains."

Newsgroup: A specific type of message board characterized by its communications protocol.

Samaritans: A United Kingdom charity organization begun in 1953. Referred to internationally as Befrienders International.

Telemedicine/telehealth: The practice of medicine or health services over distance via technology (such as the Internet, videoconferencing, etc.).

Thread: A series of contributions made by individuals in an online discussion that constitute a single topic.

Usenet: The universe of newsgroups on the Internet.

STUDY QUESTIONS

1. What are e-therapy's origins?
2. What is *ELIZA*'s association with e-therapy?
3. What organization offered the first ethical guidelines for e-therapy professionals online?
4. What two types of problems did online support groups originally form around?
5. Who were two of the original therapists to offer online counseling in exchange for payment?
6. What do the Samaritans offer online?
7. Name two companies that pioneered e-therapy in an online clinic setting?
8. What is the name of the international organization that offers professionals a place to network with others interested in online therapy?

REFERENCES

Ainsworth, M. (2002). E-therapy: History and survey. Retrieved September 20, 2002, from http://www.metanoia.org/imhs/history.htm.

68

THE NEW MEDIUM

American Counseling Association (1999). Ethical standards for Internet online counseling. Retrieved September 20, 2002, from http://www.counseling.org/resources/internet.htm.

Beckett, J. (1998). Sorting out cybershrinks: Online psychotherapy can provide short-term relief. *San Francisco Chronicle,* August 11, 1998. Retrieved September 20, 2002, from http://sfgate.com/cgi-bin/article.cgi?file=/chronicle/archive/1998/08/11/BU79806.DTL.

Burke, L. (2000). Online therapy isn't shrinking. *Wired News.* Retrieved September 20, 2002, from http://www.wired.com/news/medtech/0,1286,36584,00.html.

Carnegie Mellon University's (CMU) Artificial Intelligence Repository (1995a). *PARRY: Paranoia mental hospital patient.* Retrieved September 20, 2002, from http://www-2.cs.cmu.edu/afs/cs/project/ai-repository/ai/areas/classics/*parry*/0.html.

Carnegie Mellon University's (CMU) Artificial Intelligence Repository (1995b). Implementations of *Eliza.* Retrieved September 20, 2002, from http://www-2.cs.cmu.edu/afs/cs/project/ai-repository/ai/areas/classics/eliza/0.html.

Cerf, V. (1973). *PARRY* encounters the *DOCTOR.* Retrieved September 20, 2002, from http://www.faqs.org/rfcs/rfc439.html.

Colby, K. M. (1975). *Artificial paranoia: A computer simulation of paranoid process.* New York: Pergamon Press.

Colby, K. M., Weber, S., & Hilf, F. D. (1971). Artificial paranoia. *Artificial Intelligence, 2*(1):1–25.

Colby, K. M. (1991). Overcoming depression. Retrieved September 20, 2002, from http://www.maiw.com.

Feist, J., & Worona, S. (1986). Dear Uncle Ezra. Retrieved September 20, 2002, from http://cuinfo.cornell.edu/Dialogs/EZRA.

Goldberg, I. (1996). Ivan Goldberg's depression central. Retrieved September 20, 2002, from http://www.psycom.net/depression.central.html.

Grohol, J. M. (1995). Dr. John Grohol's psych central. Retrieved September 20, 2002, from http://psychcentral.com.

Grohol, J. M. (1997). Personal communication to *Research in Psychology* mailing list, April 1997.

Humphreys, K. (1997). Individual and social benefits of mutual aid/self-help groups. *Social Policy, 27*(3):12–20.

International Society for Mental Health Online (2000). Suggested principles for the online provision of mental health services. Retrieved September 20, 2002, from http://www.ismho.org/suggestions.html.

Kelley, B. B. (1994). New therapy: Cybershrink. *San Francisco Examiner,* May 1, 1994, A-10.

Kyrouz, E. M., & Humphreys, K. (1997). Research on self-help/mutual aid support groups. Retrieved September 20, 2002, from http://psychcentral.com/library/support_groups.htm.

Needham, E. (2000). Cyberpsych. Retrieved September 20, 2002, from http://www.win.net/cyberpsych.

Nolan, J. (1997). ELIZA chatbot. Retrieved September 20, 2002, from http://www.cpan.org/modules/by-module/Chatbot/Chatbot-Eliza-0.40.readme.

O'Dell, J. W., & Dickson, J. (1984). ELIZA as a "therapeutic" tool. *Clinical Psychologist, 40*(4):942–945.

Samaritans, The (2002). Statistics. Retrieved September 20, 2002, from http://www.samaritans.org.uk/know/statistics.html.

Sansbury, R. (2002). Headworks. Retrieved September 20, 2002, from http://www.headworks.com.

Weizenbaum, J. (1966). ELIZA—A computer program for the study of natural language communication between man and machine. *Communications of the ACM, 9*(1):36–35.

Weizenbaum, J. (1976). *Computer power and human reason.* New York: Freeman.

Zakon, R. (2002). Hobbes' Internet timeline v5.6. Retrieved September 20, 2002, from http://www.zakon.org/robert/internet/timeline.

4

ONLINE COUNSELING RESEARCH

MICHAEL J. MALLEN

Editor's Note: In this chapter, the author reviews the current research related to online counseling. Although research in this field has just begun, much has been learned that can inform the online counselor's clinical practice. Readers are also presented with ideas that will inspire future research in this exciting new area.

> *"There's no emoticon for what I'm feeling!"*
> —*Comic Book Guy from* The Simpsons
> *"Since it was possible, it was necessary."*
> —*Jacques Soustelle*

The ability to communicate across vast distances 24 hours a day using a keyboard and computer monitor has existed for a long time. However, in the past 10 years, the ease of access to the Internet has reached a critical mass (Oliver, Marwell, & Teixeira, 1985) and the use of computer-mediated communication has skyrocketed. By critical mass, it is meant that enough people in our society have begun to use online communication in their lives—the technology has become absorbed into all facets of life, including work, education, and leisure. It comes as no surprise that people have used the new technologies to reach out and communicate with other individuals around the world and the implications of this process have already been explored (Arnett, 2002). The field of psychology is only beginning to explore the potential of computer-mediated communication. However, a panel of 67 psychotherapy experts predicted in 2002 that Internet therapy services would be the second fastest increasing service area in the next 10 years (Norcross, Hedges, & Prochaska, 2002). As this prediction from well-respected members of the psychological community indicates, the time for research in the realm of online therapeutic services is right now.

The purpose of this chapter is to integrate the research in the domain of online counseling up to this point in time. Also, research from other fields, such as computer-mediated communication, will be used to bolster existing psychological research. The chapter will cover:

A brief introduction to face-to-face (f2f) process and outcome research to provide a background for computer-mediated counseling research

Early approaches to online counseling research, including a special look at work done in the treatment of eating disorders with the assistance of computer-mediated communication

The current acceptance of online counseling from clients and counselors

Studies that have directly compared online counseling to f2f counseling

Guidelines for developing and implementing a study on online counseling, and ways to manage possible resistance to future research endeavors

The chapter will conclude with a brief discussion of the available literature and future directions of online counseling research.

INTRODUCTION TO PROCESS AND OUTCOME RESEARCH

For years researchers have been examining the counseling relationship in traditional f2f therapy. A glance through the process and outcome literature (e.g., Hill & Corbett, 1993; Hill, Nutt, & Jackson, 1994) demonstrates the trials and tribulations of such investigation. A professor once advised me, half-jokingly, "Whatever you do, stay away from process and outcome research!" The dynamics of the relationship between a counselor and a client are multitudinous and complex. The questions for those interested in researching the counseling relationship have always been, "Why does it work, for whom does it work, and how does it work?"

Researchers have devoted countless hours investigating counselors' behaviors within the session, client satisfaction, the therapeutic alliance, and a litany of client outcome measures, just to name a few dynamics of the counseling relationship that have been examined up to this point.

Greenberg and Pinsof (1986) assert that since the 1970s psychotherapy research has taken an unprecedented interest in the process of change. The accessible technology to record sessions by audio and video and the open atmosphere in which therapists were trained led to opportunities to review and discuss what went on in the therapy room. As outcome measurement became more sophisticated and its findings more stable, researchers realized that "to say that something worked (or failed) without being able to specify what it was that worked undermines the replicability criterion of scientific research" (p. 5). A review of individual psychotherapy process and outcome research (Goldfried, Greenberg, & Marmar, 1990) summarized the burgeoning repertoire of process descriptions and measures, which was added to two years later by Hill, Corbett, Kanitz, Rios, Lightsey, and Gomez (1992). Process variables ranging from aspects of language and vocal quality of the counselor to the working alliance between the client and the therapist have been investigated. The advent of computer analysis of discourse brought about content analytic approaches to transcribed therapy sessions (Holzer et al., 1996).

This cornucopia of research includes a variety of points of view, representing ratings from clients, therapists, and outside observers and at levels of analysis ranging from single utterances to episodes to relationships. Making the choice of which variables to use in a process and outcome research study is a difficult, complicated, multidetermined act and, whether admittedly or not, idiosyncratic. Keep in mind, the studies discussed so far investigated the traditional mode of therapy, which is in an f2f environment. To measure the therapeutic alliance, which is one of the critical factors related to process and outcome in therapy (Bachelor, 1991; Eckert, 1993; Henry et al., 1994; Horvath & Symonds, 1991), in an online environment will require researchers to determine the best way to measure these variables in the absence of traditional cues. As should be obvious by this short introduction to the literature, research in process and outcome is time-consuming, complicated, often frustrating, but fascinating and rewarding.

MOVING TOWARD ONLINE COUNSELING RESEARCH

The process and outcome of therapy is difficult enough to measure in the traditional f2f modality of treatment. The task becomes more burdensome when you factor in the unknowns related to computer-mediated communication. Also, the field of online counseling is only beginning to take shape. Several online counseling websites launched during the Internet boom are no longer functional; they were casualties of the boom's collapse. However, thousands of counselors are offering their services online to meet the demand from consumers (Grover et al., 2002), with the majority of the work being conducted through email (Maheu & Gordon, 2000; VandenBos & Williams, 2000), and materials are now being published to guide counselors through online interactions with clients (e.g., Boer, 2001; Fink, 1999).

Psychologists have entered the Internet fray with personal homepages advertising their services and companies such as HelpHorizons (www.helphorizons.com) have solicited the services of psychologists and made them available in one location on the Internet. All this being said, no one is entirely certain if the process of online counseling is effective. Nevertheless, a growing number of consumers are seeking mental health care via these online modes of treatment. The slow-moving wheels of research have not been able to keep up with the ever-spawning technology. For the above reasons, the research in the area of online counseling is, sadly, currently minimal.

EARLY APPROACHES TO ONLINE COUNSELING RESEARCH

The earliest attempts to understand the new modes of computer-mediated counseling were usually in the form of a snapshot of the process or a case study. Sander (1996) examined his couples' group therapy, which moved from an f2f to a computer-mediated synchronous chat environment when several of the members could no longer attend f2f sessions. The researcher was clear that the "experiment in using computer-mediated communication to run a couples' group was largely characterized by a certain clumsiness and disjointedness" (p. 309). Overall, the participants in the study did not enjoy the computer-mediated sessions as well as their previous f2f encounters. It is interesting to note that the study may have reported the first documented "Freudian slip" in an online counseling session. The study does not offer a great amount of insight into the process of online counseling but it does indicate that taking clients from an established f2f routine and placing them into an online environment does not necessarily yield positive results.

Shernoff (2000) detailed his use of the Internet to reach out to gay and lesbian clients. It was demonstrated that the Internet could be a boon to a practitioner's business and make it possible to continue relationships with clients who tended to travel frequently. For gay and lesbian individuals, who may be socially isolated in their f2f environments, the role of the Internet is that of a potential lifeline for those who feel too stigmatized to seek out counseling or are isolated in remote areas. Many other groups of individuals that feel isolated or alone have used the Internet to reach out to one another and provide social support. Countless support groups exist on the Internet and those groups have been shown to be beneficial through numerous studies (Braithwaite, Waldron, & Finn, 1999; Bresnahan & Murray-Johnson, 2002; Finn, 1999; Sharf, 1997; Shaw et al., 2000).

For example, one study investigated an email group of parents of children with autism (Huws, Jones, & Ingledew, 2001). In an analysis of more than 6000 messages, it was clear that individuals were able to convey and gain a sense of interpersonal warmth through the computer-mediated communication. Special characters or emoticons (Walther & D'Addario, 2001; Wolf, 2000) were often used to convey physical contact or to demonstrate facial expressions, such as smiles or frowns. Meier (2000) offers a review of the online support group literature and describes potential risks and benefits of the process.

In a more unique study, Hsiung (2000) studied an online self-help group that was hosted by a mental health professional. In an analysis of more than 20,000 messages, the asynchronous online bulletin board demonstrated that the dialogues on the message board were effective as measured by the participants' self-reports. It is recognized that online support groups can have negative consequences, such as the proliferation of misinformation, but the fact that a mental health professional monitored and administered the group eliminated some of these potential drawbacks. A trained professional can identify negative group dynamics and intervene when necessary to keep those posting on the message board from becoming disruptive and maintain a sense of support between members.

Another aspect of psychological services that has been investigated in an online environment is consultation. In a study involving four school psychologist–teacher dyads, which used email to facilitate client-centered consultation, both teachers and school psychologists perceived that email in consultation reduced teachers' feelings of isolation and enhanced their knowledge of working with students (Kruger et al., 2001). These feelings about the computer-mediated consultation were strong even though the participants had relatively little experience with email prior to the study.

The early research devoted to online counseling offers several insights:

It appears that suddenly shifting an existing f2f therapeutic relationship to a computer-mediated environment is not ideal for therapeutic outcomes. If the mode of therapy is to be changed, the client should be made aware of the possible shortcomings ahead of time.

It does appear that individuals are capable of establishing a warm and caring environment even without the assistance of f2f cues, indicating that it may be possible to establish a working alliance through computer-mediated communication.

The studies highlighted above only offer us a glimpse of how therapeutic relationships could form online, but it is becoming clearer that the possibility does exist for therapy to work through computer-mediated communication. With this in mind, the chapter will now turn to research conducted in the area of eating disorders, which has been remarkably active in exploiting the potential benefits of computer-mediated treatment options.

COMPUTER-MEDIATED TREATMENT FOR
EATING DISORDERS

One area of interest that has been focused on in the literature is the treatment of eating disorders with the aid of computer-mediated communication. At first glance, it would seem that a problem as complex and difficult as eating disorders, difficult to treat even in an f2f setting, would not benefit from online interventions. However, several lines of research have demonstrated that the treatment of eating disorders is perhaps possible with the use of computer-mediated communication.

A study conducted by Winzelberg (1997) focused on an electronic support group for individuals with eating disorders. Over a three-month period, the researchers analyzed the content of 306 messages posted on an eating disorders electronic support group. "Members of this ESG [electronic support group] used similar helping strategies to those that are found in f2f support groups. Members provided emotional support, information, feedback, and acknowledged that they were experts on their problems" (p. 404). It is interesting to note that two-thirds of the messages were posted between 6 PM and 7 AM, a period during which members would least be able to obtain support from f2f professionals. The research team later demonstrated the effectiveness of Internet-based programs in the treatment of eating disorders (Celio, Winzelberg, & Taylor, 2002; Winzelberg, 2000). Walstrom (2000) also investigated the content of an online support group for eating disorders and concluded that an online support group could be "a viable alternative to f2f eating disorder support groups for coping with eating disorder–related problems" (p. 779).

Yager (2001) investigated the use of emails as an adjunct to f2f therapy for anorexia nervosa and found that the patients readily accepted and adhered to the new mode of treatment. Similar results were found in the use of email in the identification and treatment of bulimia nervosa. Nineteen participants that met the *Diagnostic and Statistical Manual of Mental Disorders (DSM)* criteria for bulimia nervosa showed significant reduction in scores of depression, symptoms and severity after 3 months of meeting with a clinician through only email (Robinson & Serfaty, 2001). Results from a related study indicate that synchronous chat is an acceptable and feasible format for treatment of eating disorders. Descriptive and qualitative data suggested that this method of treatment delivery is potentially effective as well (Zabinski et al., 2001). The findings above provide preliminary evidence of the efficacy and effectiveness of online interventions in the treatment of eating disorders.

Initially, it would not seem that individuals with a presenting problem such as an eating disorder would be suitable for online counseling services. However, these studies suggest the following:

Various forms of online counseling are a potential option for the treatment of clients with eating disorders.

If clients with eating disorders can benefit from online counseling services, there is no reason to believe that other presenting issues could not be handled by the new modes of treatment.

Of course, we are still far from determining which individuals are most suited for online therapy services or which problems are beyond the scope of an online counseling format. It is vital that these questions begin to be addressed through systematic and well-designed research.

THE ACCEPTANCE OF ONLINE COUNSELING

The application of computer-mediated communication to the field of psychology is currently only limited by the imagination. The Internet has already been used by researchers to investigate the usefulness of a computerized screening tool for *DSM* classifications (Krol et al., 2001) and the validation of an online personality scale (Buchanan & Smith, 1999). Peyrot (2000) reported the use of a telehealth system by correctional psychologists to consult with prison inmates. The telehealth system used an audiovisual feed with a 1-second transmission delay. Inmates reported that they were satisfied with various aspects of the online consultation process and were willing to return for a follow-up to the consultation. Inmates with more severe pathology still reported they were satisfied with the process, although some problems did arise when inmates became angry or frustrated. At times, the early signs of frustration and anger were not readily apparent to the psychiatrist because of the slow transmission speed and low resolution of the technology. First, the potential for online services to expand access to care is demonstrated by the study. Second, even prisoners who are typically thought to be a difficult population to work with were accepting of the new mode of treatment, highlighting the possibility of psychological services reaching a population that might otherwise be without the resources of a therapist. The possible applications of online counseling and consultation seem promising in this environment.

Another difficult population that has been examined is emotionally disturbed adolescents (Zimmerman, 1987b). Eighteen severely disturbed adolescents were instructed in the use of a computer-mediated communication system. The online communication was then compared to their communication in their f2f groups. The results suggest, "computer-mediated communication may represent a new resource for eliciting emotionally rich, relationship-oriented verbal interaction among emotionally disturbed adolescents" (Zimmerman, 1987a, p. 228). This is one of the first studies to empirically demonstrate the potential benefits of computer-mediated interventions over the traditional f2f mode of treatment. The adolescents were much more likely to focus on emotional issues and resolve problems in an adaptive way in their online group than in the f2f group. The differences in the mode of writing were also analyzed and it was found that emotionally disturbed adolescents that use a word processor, as opposed to handwriting, were more likely to be relationally oriented and expressive of psychological states (Zimmerman, 1989).

It has been demonstrated that difficult populations readily accept computer-mediated treatments, and this finding has been stretched to include less severe groups as well (Wright & Wright, 1997). A multimedia technology was designed and used in conjunction with traditional f2f treatment for almost 100 subjects to help them learn cognitive therapy skills. Once again, the participants readily accepted the computer-assisted therapy and there were significant improvements on a measure of cognitive therapy knowledge (Wright et al., 2002). A strong point to be made from the lines of research mentioned above is the following:

> It is becoming clear that individuals are open to receiving services through computer-mediated communication, even clients who may be thought of as difficult to treat in f2f environments.

Another aspect to consider is the generational gap in computer experience and expertise. Emotionally disturbed adolescents readily accepted the technology and seemed to function better in their groups than in an f2f situation. Although communicating through a keyboard and computer monitor may be difficult to comprehend or enjoy for some people, the next generations of clients will have grown up with the technology. For them, it is just another way of communicating, like using a telephone (a device that is often overlooked in discussions of distance counseling).

ONLINE COUNSELING COMPARED TO FACE-TO-FACE COUNSELING

The focus will now be placed on empirical work that has actually compared f2f treatments to computer-mediated treatments. Currently, this type of research is scant but preliminary results are promising for the validation of online counseling as a new mode for treatment. Initial investigations into the use of online counseling compared to control groups that did not receive treatment have been positive (Ghosh & Marks, 1987; Ghosh, Marks, & Carr, 1988; Selmi et al., 1990). For example, students experiencing grief and posttraumatic stress were enrolled in an online therapy experiment. A significant difference was found between the groups: more than 80% of the participants in the online condition showed clinically reliable improvement in various categories (Lange et al., 2001).

Cohen and Kerr (1998) made an early attempt to examine online counseling. Clients were assigned to either one session of f2f or computer-mediated counseling. Clients showed significant decreases in anxiety in both modes of treatment but there was no difference in the level of change in the two modes. Clients also reported similar ratings of counselor's expertness, attractiveness, and trustworthiness. These findings are interesting because clients in the computer-mediated counseling condition could not see the counselor, yet they still rated the counselor as attractive and trustworthy. It may be that the online clients idealized their counselors, and future research should closely investigate this phenomenon to determine the positives and negatives of such a process.

In another line of research the effectiveness of videoconferencing-based family counseling has been compared to f2f family counseling for families with epileptic children (Hufford, Glueckauf, & Webb, 1999). In examining a host of outcome variables, including problem severity and frequency and overall treatment adherence, it was found that both treatments were effective but the mode of treatment did not influence the results (Glueckauf et al., 2002). The research demonstrates the usefulness of computer-mediated communication in connecting families with unique problems and challenges from distant rural areas to a therapeutic environment. There are surely other isolated populations that could benefit from being connected to other individuals who are experiencing similar issues. Once again, the possible applications of online counseling are limitless, but we need solid research such as the work of Glueckauf and his colleagues to justify the broadening of online counseling to include new types of clients and populations.

Day and Schneider (2002) analyzed process and outcome variables across three modes of psychotherapy: f2f, video teleconference, and two-way audio. Results from 80 randomly assigned clients indicated that the differences between the three modes of treatment were minimal. Even though the researchers set significance levels at 0.15, no significant differences were found between the three modes of therapy on any of the outcome measures, $F(12,144) = 0.67$, $p > 0.15$, including closing symptom checklists, assessments of functioning, levels of target complaints, and a satisfaction measure. A significant difference of note in the process variables was found for a measure of client participation, $F(6,150) = 2.51$, $p < 0.05$. However, it was shown that clients participated less in the f2f mode than in either of the technologically mediated conditions. The researchers discussed the implications of the research by stating, "The similarities among the three treatment groups—f2f, video teleconference, and audio conference—came through more strongly than any differences" (p. 501).

Whereas these studies focused on the client, a few studies have examined the counselor's responses to the differences between online and f2f modes of treatment. Stevens and colleagues (1999) found that patients involved in a pilot study for televideo psychiatric assessments gave high ratings for satisfaction with the experience but also reported that they were able to achieve sufficient rapport with the psychiatrist. However, the psychiatrists in the study expressed significantly lower levels of satisfaction with the televideo interviews compared to the f2f interviews, although their ratings for the televideo communication were still positive. Another study focused on the reactions of the counselor in an online environment (Mallen & Vogel, 2002). Counselors were informed that they would be meeting with a client in a synchronous chat environment for one session only. Counselors were able to accurately assess the client's presenting problems and were generally satisfied with the process, even though their experience with the computer-mediated communication technology was extremely low overall. Future research should continue to analyze the responses of therapists in the new modes of treatment. A word of caution should be heeded:

> If therapists are not comfortable with the technology or not convinced that the new modes of treatment are useful, then they should not be conducting sessions with clients in a computer-mediated environment.

Another process-related variable that is noteworthy from the Mallen and Vogel study is the analysis of the transcripts. Transcripts from the online sessions were compared to similar f2f transcripts from a study conducted by Day and Schnieder (2000). The most dramatic finding was the difference in the amount of discourse that could flow between the counselor and the client in an f2f session. F2f transcripts had a mean of close to 6000 words, while the synchronous chat transcripts only had a mean of 2000 words. Of course, it should not be determined that quantity of words equals quality of service or care, but it can not be denied that the amount of information in an f2f session far exceeds synchronous chat sessions of the same length. Counselors' responses were coded using Hill and O'Brien's (1999) coding system; it was found that counselors in the f2f condition offered more approval, reassurance, and interpretations, challenged the client more often, asked more questions, and focused more often on immediacy issues. These are preliminary data, but it certainly appears that the counselor is more comfortable taking risks in an f2f session than in an online counseling session.

Future research should closely examine process-related differences related to the mode of treatment and how they may affect the therapeutic relationship. A great place for psychological research to start is exemplified by the above studies, which used traditional f2f therapy as a comparison group for new modes of treatment. In the meantime, the following conclusions can be drawn from the current literature:

> New modes of treatment may allow isolated groups of individuals to connect for services that are simply not feasible in an f2f setting.

Studies that have compared online modes of treatment to traditional f2f therapy have demonstrated significant effectiveness for clients.
Early research from Day & Schnieder indicates that online modes of counseling could compare favorably to f2f treatments, even when the level of significance is raised to catch potential differences.
The amount of information that can be transmitted during an online counseling session is significantly less than a traditional f2f counseling session.

COMPUTER-MEDIATED COMMUNICATION LITERATURE

The field of psychology, especially for those interested in online applications, could benefit from the study of existing literature in the domain of computer-mediated communication. There is already a long line of research investigating differences between f2f and online environments on a wide variety of variables. Research comparing computer-mediated communication and f2f communication has examined:

Team decision making and group process (Adrianson & Hjelmquist, 1991; Barkhi, Jacob, & Pirkul, 1999; Olaniran, 1996; Thompson & Coovert, 2002)
Electronic negotiation (Croson, 1999)
Student learning (Ocker & Yaverbaum, 1999)
Work meetings (Lantz, 2001)
Focus groups (Schneider et al., 2002)

The literature provides a mixed bag of findings with computer-mediated communication prevailing over f2f in some instances, not performing as well in other studies, and no differences found between the modes of communication at times.

For example, it has already been demonstrated that computer-mediated communication is often more uninhibited and contains more disclosures of personal information than f2f communication (Sproull & Kiesler, 1986; Kiesler, Siegel, & McGuire, 1984). However, in a study of f2f and synchronous chat conversations, it was found that participants in the f2f groups felt they disclosed more personal information and that their partner disclosed more information (Mallen, Day, & Green, 2003). The debate continues about the nature of self-disclosure and its relation to the available anonymity in computer-mediated communication. Future researchers should investigate the possible differences as they relate to a client's willingness to disclose information about his or her background or presenting problems. If computer-mediated communication does indeed foster greater self-disclosure on the part of the client, an interesting study could determine if it would be helpful to hold sessions in an online environment from time to time, even if the main mode of treatment remains in the f2f realm. Research has already shown that f2f discussions preceded by synchronous chat or asynchronous email are perceived as more enjoyable and include a greater diversity of perspectives than f2f discussions not preceded by a form of computer-mediated communication (Dietz-Uhler, & Bishop-Clark, 2001). The possible implications for online counseling are striking. The most likely future of online counseling resides in a mixture of treatments for clients. For example, counselors may meet with a client in a traditional f2f session twice a month and meet through a synchronous chat room twice a month. A client that seeks therapy for the first time in an online environment may be opening the door to further counseling in the more traditional f2f setting.

The initial reaction to the possible applications of online communication by many of those established in the field of psychology was that the nature of the technology could not possibly allow enough social cues to be exchanged in order to establish meaningful relationships. Social information processing theory states, "The critical difference between FtF [face-to-face] and CMC [computer-mediated communication] . . . is a question of rate, not capability" (Walther, 1995; p. 190). In a long line of research, Walther (1993) points out a critical flaw in existing literature comparing f2f and computer-mediated communication, stating that many studies do not allow a significant amount of time for online communication to develop. The key difference may be that the *rate* of relationship building and impression formation is affected by the differences in computer-mediated communication and f2f communication. Relationships in computer-mediated communication groups have been shown to gradually strengthen over time to similar levels of f2f groups. It has also been demonstrated that there are times when computer-mediated communication actually surpasses normal f2f communication in relational strength, a phenomenon that has been labeled *hyperpersonal* communication. "When users even so much as expect to have a long-term association, CMC is no less personal than FtF" (Walther, 1996; p. 33).

Although the literature in computer-mediated communication is still developing, the field of psychology should build upon this research and use existing data to drive research on computer-mediated counseling.

GUIDE FOR RESEARCHERS

As we have seen, computer-mediated counseling has tackled a wide variety of presenting issues. The strengths and limitations of online counseling are still unclear. Research on the therapeutic use of the Internet is needed to establish a reasonable standard of care for the delivery of mental health services. Without such research, it is possible that a standard of care may develop without sufficient empirical validation regarding its appropriateness and efficacy (Childress & Asamen, 1998). One group that is attempting to clear the muddled waters is the International Society for Mental Health Online (ISMHO; ismho.org). Through a clinical case study group, a proposed set of guidelines has been developed to assess a client's suitability for online therapy (Suler, 2001). The current guidelines are by no means complete but the ISMHO offers an example of clinicians being proactive in attempting to develop and examine the field of online counseling.

The nuances of computer-mediated communication must be factored into any study involving online process and outcome research. Factors such as previous online experience and the potential of technological glitches must be accounted for in the study. For instance, during a study of graduate counselors in training (Mallen & Vogel, 2002), the Internet connection was lost, interrupting a session between a counselor and the client. The research team was quickly able to reconnect the session but backup plans for instances such as this should always be a part of any study investigating computer-mediated communication. One should always plan for a worst-case scenario, especially when dealing with potentially intense psychological issues and the connection between the client and therapist is broken. A client in a very emotional state in an online session could feel abandoned and disoriented if he or she is in the middle of disclosing personal information or feelings to a counselor when suddenly the proverbial plug is pulled. Your research should include f2f crisis management even if you have screened for possible severe pathologies ahead of time. It can never be predicted if work in session will arouse latent intense emotions for the client. Again, your study should be prepared for emergency situations as well as any possible worst-case scenarios.

One of the more glaring shortcomings up to this point in the online counseling literature that your research could address is the lack of heterogeneous samples. Most of the participants in the research literature have been college-aged Caucasians and there has been little research including individuals with multicultural backgrounds. It will be interesting for future researchers to examine if there are differences in these domains. For instance, there is a growing interest in the dynamics of multicultural individuals and the counseling relationships that develop with a counselor. In the absence of verbal and nonverbal cues, such as speech and appearance, it will be interesting to see if multicultural clients and their counselors feel safer and more at ease during online sessions because the surface level differences would not be as present in the sessions.

The potential for investigations into transference and countertransference issues are extraordinary, with an online counselor providing a literal "blank screen" for the client. New inventories and assessment techniques are needed to investigate online relationships between a counselor and a client but it is important for future researchers to adequately operationalize their variables, and they should build off the existing process and outcome literature.

The procedure for designing and conducting research related to online counseling should not be entirely different from any other study you might construct. This being said, extra precautions should be taken with the unique factors involved in computer-mediated communication. Some things to consider are:

Ethical issues—Distance counseling presents several ethical hurdles, including state-to-state licensure problems, confidentiality issues, and possible duty-to-warn problems. (Refer to Chapter 6 for a discussion of the various ethical dilemmas that are presented in online counseling.)

Technological failure—Even the best computer or program can crash or fail at times. It is important to account for possible breakdowns with contingency planning ahead of time. Also, one should properly inform participants that disconnection of an online session is possible, and present them with a plan of action if the connection is lost.

Logistical issues—You will have to manage at least two schedules for each online session that you are studying. Scheduling sessions can become confusing when connecting individuals who are separated by several time zones. For instance, residing in Iowa and collecting data from an online session between a counselor in Maryland and a client in California can be daunting. Questions can be sent and received by fax or email but this process can become cumbersome. Let your participants know ahead of time about possible delays in order to reduce confusion and irritation.

Lack of nonverbal cues—A common challenge to online counseling is that the mode of treatment does not allow the counselor and client to react to nonverbal cues. As a researcher, be prepared to compensate for the lack of cues because this could also present problems as you attempt to schedule, manage, and monitor online sessions.

Previous online experience—It is my feeling that any study analyzing the dynamics and process of online relationships use some measure of online acumen. Communicating effectively through asynchronous email or synchronous chat takes time, patience, and most of all, sheer practice. The more accustomed you are to online communication, the more likely you are to feel comfortable with the technology and understand subtle nuances in the rate, presentation, style, and idiosyncrasies of the text involved. Including this variable in your study may help to explain differences in your results, which otherwise might go unnoticed.

In summary, one should abide by existing research design standards and should not ignore established norms in order to study these new modes of treatment. Research on online counseling may be difficult to effectively design and implement, but you may reap the rewards of carrying out innovative and groundbreaking work.

One final note regarding research in this field concerns the new trend toward online data collection. Paper-and-pencil inventories are quickly being posted on websites for easy data collection and entry. Software such as Perseus Software Solutions (www.perseus.com) allows researchers to post their questionnaire online. Participants are then given access to the website hosting the questionnaire where they can complete the measure in the comfort of their own home. Another benefit of online surveys are that they can be linked to databases for quick data analysis; researchers no longer have to suffer through the process of entering, checking, and rechecking data, which can be tedious and time-consuming. Other options for online data collection are email and instant message programs. Participants could be emailed the questionnaire as a file attachment, which would then be downloaded, completed, and emailed back to the researcher as a file attachment. Another interesting option is online interviews, which could take place through an instant message program.

DEALING WITH RESISTANCE

It is entirely possible that you may encounter resistance in attempting to study this topic but it will be difficult to deny a study that is well constructed and built on a solid foundation of research (this foundation is continuously growing as more and more psychologists are becoming aware of online counseling). Hopefully, as the literature on computer-mediated counseling evolves, the subject of online counseling will no longer be considered taboo by institutions or individual psychologists. It is vital that more psychologists get involved in online counseling and claim the field from possible impostors, who will only give the field of psychology a bad name. The old saying "the more, the merrier" certainly applies when it comes to research in the area of online counseling.

Ethical issues are present in any attempt at online counseling research and must be added into the mix when proposing a study to an ethical review board. For many institutions, your study may be the first to address computer-mediated communication and the unique experimental design issues that are involved. Because of this, it will be important to clearly explain how participants will be recruited and how you will ensure that no harm will come to them. There may be initial resistance to such a study but if you have all your bases covered and include fail-safe procedures into your research agenda, it should not be a problem to get approved from an ethical review board if your research is well-designed and thoughtfully planned.

CONCLUSION

An understanding of the dynamics involved in online counseling is still outside of our grasp at this point. However, from this brief review, it seems logical to conclude that online counseling will continue to grow. Surely, there will be roadblocks in the development of online services and more research is needed to accurately judge the limits of the treatments that could be offered. The existing literature in the field is generally positive, which may surprise some individuals. There does not appear to be lines of research that are declaring significant impairments of online counseling. The ventures into this field so far have demonstrated that clients accept online services, and that those services tend to produce positive outcomes. Certainly, we are a long way from confirming or disconfirming the efficacy and effectiveness of computer-mediated modes of treatment, but the current literature points in the direction of justifying the practice of online counseling.

It is an exciting time to be exploring online counseling. There is so much we do not yet know and currently so few investigating the strengths and limitations of this potential mode of treatment. Professional journals are becoming increasingly interested in this line of research, as noticed by several special issues that have been published in recent years and the number of presentations devoted to the topic during recent professional conventions. Every researcher who studies online counseling has the opportunity to make a significant contribution to the field. In so doing, he or she will help establish the foundation for a new era of mental health service delivery.

KEY TERMS

Between-subjects design: Research design in which each subject experiences only one of the conditions in an experiment.

Case study: Exploratory study of an existing situation as a means of creating and testing a hypothesis.

Clinical significance: The practical importance of a result from a study.

Control: Providing a standard against which to compare the effect of a particular variable.

Control group: Subjects in an experiment who are like the experimental group in every respect except that they do not receive treatment.

Debriefing: The process of informing subjects after participation of the experiment's true purpose in order to increase their understanding and to remove possible harmful effects of deception.

Experiment: Research procedure in which the scientist has complete control over all aspects, including the manipulation of variables and assignment of subjects.

Experimental group: Subjects in an experiment who receive treatment.

F statistic: Result from an analysis of variance (ANOVA) test; the ratio of the mean square between subjects to the mean square within subjects.

Informed consent: A document that clarifies the nature of an experiment, and provides an agreement on the responsibilities of both the participant and researcher; this is to ensure that the participant is taking part voluntarily and is aware of what is about to happen in the experiment.

Likert scale: A question that asks for a rating of the extent of agreement or disagreement with a statement; a rating scale.

Observational research: Study method in which the researcher observes and records ongoing behavior but does not attempt to change it.

Operational definition: A statement of precise meaning of a procedure or concept within an experiment.

Participant-observer research: Observational research in which the observer participates in the group to record behavior.

Pilot study: Tentative, small-scale study done to pretest and modify study design and procedures.

Statistical significance: The probability that an experimental result happened by chance.

Therapeutic alliance: The bond formed between a client and therapist; includes the therapist and client respecting each other, and agreeing on goals and tasks for each session.

Validity: An indication of accuracy in terms of the extent to which a research conclusion corresponds with reality.

Within-subject design: Research design in which each subject experiences every condition of the experiment.

STUDY QUESTIONS

1. What do you feel are the potential roadblocks to online counseling effectiveness? How might they be overcome in the future?

2. Are you surprised by the current findings regarding online counseling? What were your expectations, given your existent knowledge of f2f therapy?

3. Given that preliminary results indicate that online counseling may be a viable alternative or supplement for mental health services, why do you think the topic is rarely addressed in the mainstream of psychology?

4. If you were meeting with a client in an online environment, how would you navigate around the lack of nonverbal cues? What questions might you ask to gather this type of information?

5. Would the effectiveness of online counseling challenge fundamental tenets of what therapy is? Why or why not?

6. Do you believe that younger generations will readily accept online forms of psychology treatment? Why or why not?

7. Briefly outline a study investigating online counseling. Decide on independent and dependent variables, and state your hypothesis. How would you complete your study?

REFERENCES

Adrianson, L., & Hjelmquist, E. (1991). Group processes in face-to-face and computer-mediated communication. *Behaviour & Information Technology, 10*:281–296.

Arnett, J. J. (2002). The psychology of globalization. *American Psychologist, 57*:774–783.

Bachelor, A. (1991). Comparison and relationship to outcome of diverse dimensions of the helping alliance as seen by client and therapist. *Psychotherapy, 28*:534–549.

Barkhi, R., Jacob, V. S., & Pirkul, H. (1999). An experimental analysis of face to face versus computer mediated communication channels. *Group Decision and Negotiation, 8*:325–347.

Boer, P. M. (2001). *Career counseling over the Internet: An emerging model for trusting and responding to online clients.* Mahwah, NJ: Lawrence Erlbaum Associates, Inc.

Braithwaite, D. O., Waldron, V. R., & Finn, J. (1999). Communication of social support in computer-mediated groups for people with disabilities. *Health Communication, 11*:123–151.

Bresnahan, M. J., & Murray-Johnson, L. (2002). The healing web. *Health Care for Women International, 23*:398–407.

Buchanan, T., & Smith, J. L. (1999). Research on the Internet: Validation of a world-wide web mediated personality scale. *Behavior Research Methods, Instruments, & Computers, 31*: 565–571.

Celio, A. A., Winzelberg, A., Dev, P., et al. (2002). Improving compliance in on-line, structured self-help programs: Evaluation of an eating disorder prevention program. *Journal of Psychiatric Practice, 8*:14–20.

Childress, C. A., & Asamen, J. K. (1998). The emerging relationship of psychology and the Internet: Proposed guidelines for conducting Internet intervention research. *Ethics & Behavior, 8*:19–35.

Cohen, G. E., & Kerr, B. A. (1998). Computer-mediated counseling: An empirical study of a new mental health treatment. *Computers in Human Services, 15*:13–26.

Croson, R. T. A. (1999). Look at me when you say that: An electronic negotiation simulation. *Simulation & Gaming, 30*:23–37.

Day, S. X., & Schneider, P. (2000). The subjective experiences of therapists in face-to-face, video, and audio sessions. In J. W. Bloom & G. R. Walz (Eds.), *Cybercounseling and cyber-learning: strategies and resources for the new millennium* (pp. 203–218). Alexandria, VA: American Counseling Association.

Day, S. X., & Schneider, P. L. (2002). Psychotherapy using distance technology: A comparison of face-to-face, video, and audio treatment. *Journal of Counseling Psychology, 49*:499–503.

Dietz-Uhler, B., & Bishop-Clark, C. (2001). The use of computer-mediated communication to enhance subsequent face-to-face discussions. *Computers in Human Behavior, 17*:269–283.

Eckert, P. A. (1993). Acceleration of change: Catalysts in brief therapy. *Clinical Psychology Review, 13*:241–253.

Fink, J. (1999). *How to use computers and cyberspace in the clinical practice of psychotherapy.* Northvale, NJ: Jason Aronson Inc.

Finn, J. (1999). An exploration of helping processes in an online self-help group focusing on issues of disability. *Health and Social Work, 24*:220–231.

Ghosh, A., & Marks, I. M. (1987). Self-treatment of agoraphobia by exposure. *Behavior Therapy, 18*:3–16.

Ghosh, A., Marks, I. M., & Carr, A. C. (1988). Therapist contact and outcome of self-exposure treatment for phobias: A controlled study. *British Journal of Psychiatry, 152*:234–238.

Glueckauf, R. L., Fritz, S. P., Ecklund-Johnson, E. P., et al. (2002). Videoconferencing-based family counseling for rural teenagers with epilepsy: Phase 1 findings. *Rehabilitation Psychology, 47*:49–72.

Goldfried, M. R., Greenberg, L. S., & Marmar, C. (1990). Individual psychotherapy: Process and outcome. *Annual Review of Psychology, 41*:659–688.

Greenberg, L. S., & Pinsof, W. M. (1986). Process research: Current trends and future perspectives. In L. S. Greenberg & W. M. Pinsof (Eds.), *The psychotherapeutic process: A research handbook* (pp. 3–19). New York: Guilford.

Grover, F., Wu, H. D., Blanford, C., Holcomb, S., et al. (2002). Computer-using patients want Internet services from family physicians. *Journal of Family Practice, 51*:570–572.

Henry, W. P., Strupp, H. H., Schacht, T. E., et al. (1994). Psychodynamic approaches. In A. E. Bergin & S. L. Garfield (Eds.), *Handbook of psychotherapy and behavior change* (4th ed., pp. 467–508). New York: Wiley.

Hill, C. E., Corbett, M. M., Kanitz, B., et al. (1992). Client behavior in counseling and therapy sessions: Development of a pantheoretical measure. *Journal of Counseling Psychology, 39*:539–549.

Hill, C. E., & Corbett, M. M. (1993). A perspective on the history of process and outcome research in counseling psychology. *Journal of Counseling Psychology, 40*:3–24.

Hill, C. E., Nutt, E. A., & Jackson, S. (1994). Trends in psychotherapy process research: Samples, measures, researchers, and classic publications. *Journal of Counseling Psychology, 41*:364–377.

Hill, C. E., O'Brien, K. M. (1999). *Helping skills: Facilitating exploration, insight, and action.* Washington, DC: American Psychological Association.

Holzer, M., Mergenthaler, E., Pokorny, D., et al. (1996). Vocabulary measures for the evaluation of therapy outcome: Re-studying transcripts from the Penn Psychotherapy Project. *Psychotherapy Research, 6*:95–108.

Horvath, A. O., & Symonds, B. D. (1991). Relations between working alliance and outcome in psychotherapy: A meta-analysis. *Journal of Counseling Psychology, 38*:139–149.

Hsiung, R. C. (2000). The best of both worlds: An online self-help group hosted by a mental health professional. *CyberPsychology & Behavior, 3*:935–950.

Hufford, B. J., Glueckauf, R. L., Webb, P. M. (1999). Home-based interactive videoconferencing for adolescents with epilepsy and their families. *Rehabilitation Psychology, 44*:176–193.

Huws, J. C., Jones, R. S. P., & Ingledew, D. K. (2001). Parents of children with autism using an email group: A grounded theory study. *Journal of Health Psychology, 6*:569–584.

Kiesler, S., Siegel, J., & McGuire, T. W. (1984). Social psychological aspects of computer-mediated communication. *American Psychologist, 39*:1123–1134.

Krol, N. P. C. M., De Bruyn, E. E. J., van Aarle, E. J. M., et al. (2001). Computerized screening for DSM classifications using CBCL/YSR extended checklists: A clinical try-out. *Computers in Human Behavior, 17*:315–337.

Kruger, L. J., Struzziero, J., Kaplan, S. K., et al. (2001). The use of email in consultation: An exploratory study of consultee outcomes. *Journal of Educational and Psychological Consultation, 12*:133–149.

Lange, A., van den Ven, J., Schrieken, B., et al. (2001). Treatment of posttraumatic stress through the Internet: A controlled trial. *Journal of Behavior Therapy and Experimental Psychiatry, 32*:73–90.

Lantz, A. (2001). Meetings in a distributed group of experts: Comparing face-to-face, chat and collaborative virtual environment. *Behaviour & Information Technology, 20*:111–117.

Maheu, M. M., & Gordon, B. L. (2000). Counseling and therapy on the Internet. *Professional Psychology: Research and Practice, 31*:484–489.

Mallen, M. J., Day, S. X., & Green, M. A. (2003). Online versus face-to-face conversations: An examination of relational and discourse variables. *Psychotherapy: Theory, Research and Practice, 40*:(1/2)155–163.

Mallen, M. J., & Vogel, D. L. (2002, August). Working toward online counselor training: Dynamics of process and assessment. In A. B. Rochlen (Chair), *Appeal and relative efficacy of online counseling: Preliminary findings.* Symposium conducted at the annual convention of the American Psychological Association, Chicago, Illinois.

Meier, A. (2000). Offering social support via the Internet: A case study of an online support group for social workers. *Journal of Technology in Human Services, 17*:237–266.

Norcross, J. C., Hedges, M., & Prochaska, J. O. (2002). The face of 2010: A delphi poll on the future of psychotherapy. *Professional Psychology: Research and Practice, 33*:316–322.

Ocker, R. J., & Yaverbaum, A. J. (1999). Asynchronous computer-mediated communication versus face-to-face collaboration: Results on student learning, quality and satisfaction. *Group Decision and Negotiation, 8*:427–440.

Olaniran, B. A. (1996). A model of group satisfaction in computer-mediated communication and face-to-face meetings. *Behaviour & Information Technology, 15*:24–36.

Oliver, P., Marwell, G., & Teixeira, R. (1985). A theory of the critical mass: Interdependence, group heterogeneity, and the production of collective action. *American Journal of Sociology, 91*:522–556.

Peyrot, M. F. (2000). Telehealth in the federal bureau of prisons: Inmates' perceptions. *Professional Psychology: Research and Practice, 31*:497–502.

Robinson, P. H., & Serfaty, M. A. (2001). The use of e-mail in the identification of bulimia nervosa and its treatment. *European Eating Disorders Review, 9*:182–193.

Sander, F. M. (1996). Couple group therapy conducted via computer-mediated communication: A preliminary case study. *Computers in Human Behavior, 12*:301–312.

Schneider, S. J., Kerwin, J., Frechtling, J., et al. (2002). Characteristics of the discussion in online and face-to-face focus groups. *Social Science Computer Review, 20*:31–42.

Selmi, P. M., Klein, M. H., Greist, J. H., et al. (1990). Computer-administered cognitive-behavioural therapy for depression. *American Journal of Psychiatry, 141*:51–56.

Sharf, B. (1997). Communication breast cancer online: Support and empowerment on the Internet. *Women and Health, 26*:65–4.

Shaw, B. R., McTavish, F., Hawkins, R., et al. (2000). Experiences of women with breast cancer: Exchanging social support over the CHESS computer network. *Journal of Health Communication, 5*:135–159.

Shernoff, M. (2000). Cyber counseling for queer clients and clinicians. *Journal of Gay & Lesbian Social Services, 11*:105–979.

Sproull, L., & Kiesler, S. (1986). Reducing social context cues: Electronic mail in organizational communication. *Management Science, 32*:1492–1512.

Stevens, A., Doidge, N., Goldbloom, D., et al. (1999). Pilot study of televideo psychiatric assessments in an underserved community. *American Journal of Psychiatry, 156*:783–785.

Suler, J. (2001). Assessing a person's suitability for online therapy: The ISMSO clinical case study group. *CyberPsychology & Behavior, 4*:675–679.

Thompson, L. F., & Coovert, M. D. (2002). Stepping up to the challenge: A critical examination of face-to-face and computer-mediated team decision making. *Group Dynamics: Theory, Research, and Practice, 6*:52–64.

VandenBos, G. R., & Williams, S. (2000). The Internet versus the telephone: What is telehealth, anyway? *Professional Psychology: Research and Practice, 31*:490–492.

Wadland, W. C., Soffelmayr, B., & Ives, K. (2001). Enhancing smoking cessation of low-income smokers in managed care. *Journal of Family Practice, 50*:138–144.

Walstrom, M. K. (2000). "You know, who's the thinnest?": Combating surveillance and creating safety in coping with eating disorders online. *CyberPsychology & Behavior, 3*:761–783.

Walther, J. B. (1993). Impression development in computer-mediated interaction. *Western Journal of Communication, 57*:381–398.

Walther, J. B. (1995). Relational aspects of computer-mediated communication: Experimental observations over time. *Organization Science, 6*:186–203.

Walther, J. B. (1996). Computer-mediated communication: Impersonal, interpersonal, and hyperpersonal interaction. *Communication Research, 23*:3–43.

Walther, J. B., & D'Addario, K. P. (2001). The impacts of emoticons on message interpretation in computer-mediated communication. *Social Science Computer Review, 19*:324–347.

Wolf, A. (2000). Emotional expression online: Gender differences in emoticon use. *Cyber Psychology & Behavior, 3*:827–833.

Winzelberg, A. (1997). The analysis of an electronic support group for individuals with eating disorders. *Computers in Human Behavior, 13*:393–407.

Winzelberg, A. J., Eppstein, D., Eldredge, K. L., et al. (2000). Effectiveness of an Internet-based program for reducing risk factors for eating disorders. *Journal of Consulting and Clinical Psychology, 68*:346–350.

Wright, J. H., & Wright, A. S. (1997). Computer-assisted psychotherapy. *Journal of Psychotherapy Practice and Research, 6*:315–329.

Wright, J. H., Wright, A. S., Salmon, P., et al. (2002). Development and initial testing of a multimedia program for computer-assisted cognitive therapy. *American Journal of Psychotherapy, 56*:76–86.

Yager, J. (2001). E-mail as a therapeutic adjunct in the outpatient treatment of anorexia nervosa: Illustrative case material and discussion of the issues. *International Journal of Eating Disorders, 29*:125–138.

Zabinski, M., Wilfley, D. E., Pung, M. A., et al. (2001). An interactive Internet-based intervention for women at risk of eating disorders: A pilot study. *International Journal of Eating Disorders, 30*:129–137.

Zimmerman, D. P. (1987a). A psychological comparison of computer-mediated and face-to-face language use among severely disturbed adolescents. *Adolescence, 22*:827–840.

Zimmerman, D. P. (1987b). Effects of computer conferencing on the language use of emotionally disturbed adolescents. *Behavior Research Methods, Instruments, & Computers, 19*:224–230.

Zimmerman, D. P. (1989). Electronic language: A study of word processing by emotionally disturbed children and adolescents in residential treatment. *Behavior Research Methods, Instruments, & Computers, 21*:181–186.

PART

II

THE PRACTICAL
ASPECTS OF ONLINE
COUNSELING

5

TECHNOLOGY OF
ONLINE COUNSELING

JASON S. ZACK

In this chapter, we will discuss the technological underpinnings of online counseling. That is, the hardware, software, and networking infrastructure that allow counselors and clients to communicate and conduct business with clients via the Internet.

Much as every introductory psychology course requires students to complete a unit on brain physiology (often the most challenging and dreaded section of the course), a study of online counseling should include a review of Internet fundamentals; we think it is important for online counselors to understand what goes on behind the curtain, so to speak. Such an understanding will help the online counselor best take advantage of technology's many possibilities and also address and cope with its limits.

Our goal for this chapter is not to turn you into a computer scientist, nor will we guide you to the fabled and mysterious land of computer geekdom. Rather, we will try to provide a clear and sufficient discussion of each of the technologies you are likely to encounter during your work as an online counselor. We are well aware that readers of this text will have varying degrees of computer literacy—from the complete novice (or "newbie," in Net lingo) to the accomplished "power user." Where you belong on this continuum is probably related to how you became interested in online counseling to begin with. Novice users are likely to be clinicians or clinicians-in-training wanting to expand their practice into a new medium. Power users may be computer enthusiasts eager to incorporate their passion for computers into their professional work. Thus, we take a middle-of-the-road approach to presenting this material. We will make some assumptions (e.g., that you know what a computer is and have used one before, that you are aware of the existence of the Internet, etc.), but we will not tell you more than what we believe you *need* to know to be a competent online mental health professional. You will not find a detailed discussion of computer programming, transmission protocols, advanced cryptography, server maintenance, etc. We will, however, provide references and referrals to other sources of advanced information, should you wish to learn more.

So what do you *need* to know? We'll divide this chapter into the following sections:

1. General Considerations
2. Getting Started—The Basics
3. Understanding the Internet
4. Understanding the Web
5. Understanding Email
6. Understanding Text-Chat
7. Understanding Videoconferencing
8. Understanding Forms
9. Understanding Document Sharing
10. Understanding Security
11. Common Problems
12. Technology Trends in Online Counseling

GENERAL CONSIDERATIONS

In this chapter we want to stick close to the technology issues and avoid discussing theory (other chapters address them sufficiently). That being said, we want to mention a few theoretical issues. First and foremost, it must be acknowledged that with online counseling, the technology cannot be divorced from the practice. As much as new users might wish, technology has simply not advanced to the stage where you can push a button, talk, and you're done with it. For now, technology will inevitably affect the process of online counseling interactions. Glitches are inevitable, and must be expected. Some clients may personify the computer as an interloper in your relationship, or they may attach the technical problems to their conception of the therapist ("my therapist just crashed my computer").

For some people, especially at the beginning before a routine is established, online counseling interactions are fraught with a constant sense of fragility. Imagine doing sessions in a conventional office with the constant fear that the roof will cave in unexpectedly, possibly just after you or the client says something *really important*. Online counseling can be like that, at least the first few times. Hence, any online counseling training must be done within the framework of the technical platform that will be used to deliver services. At the very least you need to know what modality you'll be using: email, text-chat, videoconferencing, etc.

Although there are theoretical constructs, discussed elsewhere in this book, that apply to all types of distance-based communication, such as disinhibition, hyperpersonalization, etc., all the theoretical knowledge becomes irrelevant if the technology gets in the way. You might liken it to drivers' education classes, where you can't really focus on the rules of the road if you haven't yet mastered the operation of the vehicle. Technical issues have a way of coming to the foreground. Once everything is working smoothly, the technology fades into the background. You don't have to think about turning the steering wheel after a while. You just think "left" and your car goes left. The same thing can happen with computers, believe it or not. You don't think "click and drag," you just think "move." Many counselors and clients we've encountered haven't reached that point yet, so it's crucial to address technical concerns in any kind of training. The extent to which technological issues affect the outcome of counseling is an empirical question. We hope psychotherapy researchers will quickly take on the challenge of exploring the role of technology in online therapy.

GETTING STARTED—THE BASICS

So let's get started. You're a mental health professional sitting in your office. Maybe your office is in a building, maybe it's at your house, maybe it's on a university campus. It dawns on you that online counseling might be a good fit for your needs and interests and you want to give it a try. What do you need? Here's a quick checklist of 10 important things:

Minimum Requirements
1. A Computer
2. An Internet connection
3. A Web browser

Additional Options
4. An email program
5. A chat program
6. A videoconferencing program and webcam
7. A website
8. A domain name
9. A Web-hosting account
10. Security software/hardware

COMPUTER

At the very least, you need a computer, or access to one. You should purchase the best computer you can afford, because it will last that much longer before you have to upgrade. However, for the purpose of online counseling, you merely need a computer that is reliable (doesn't crash or quit unexpectedly) and that is able to run the latest operating system of your choice. Macintosh or Windows operating systems are both fine, depending on your comfort level, although Macs are generally easier to set up and maintain than Windows machines. Both the latest Mac and Windows operating systems (OS) make it very easy to use the Internet and network with other computers. Be sure that the computer you purchase has a built-in modem, at least two USB (universal serial bus) ports and an Ethernet port. These will be important for accessing the Internet (discussed in the next section). One of the best things about online counseling is that you can bring your practice with you. If you travel a lot, then you may wish to get a laptop computer. High quality laptops can easily replace a desktop machine and are completely sufficient for online counseling purposes.

INTERNET CONNECTION

Next, you need a reliable Internet connection. Internet connections are provided by Internet service providers (ISPs). The speed of your connection is referred to in terms of "bandwidth." Bandwidth can be thought of as the size of the "pipe" by which data is transmitted to and from your computer to the ISP. For most people, depending on geographic location, connection options include:

Dial-up

A dial-up Internet connection uses your computer's modem to connect at relatively low bandwidth via a standard telephone line. Most people use dial-up service provided by large ISPs like America Online (AOL) and Earthlink, but nearly every telephone company also provides local dial-up access, and there are many smaller dial-up ISPs as well. The advantage of using services like AOL is that they are self-configuring and provide access phone numbers for nearly every city in the world. This is great if you travel, although sometimes it can be difficult to figure out how to dial out of hotel rooms and in foreign countries. Most dial-up services provide unlimited access for a flat monthly fee. A disadvantage of dial-up is that connections are slow and can be dropped if the telephone connection is bad or the service is too busy. You may also encounter busy signals if the ISP is not equipped to handle heavy customer trafffic. Dial-up service is not fast enough for practical videoconferencing if you have an interest in that modality.

DSL (Digital Subscriber Line)

A high-speed Internet service often provided by local telephone companies, DSL is also sold by some of the large ISPs, such as Earthlink and AOL. There are different kinds of DSL setups (you may hear terms like ADSL) that provide different transfer speeds. DSL service requires a DSL modem, generally given or leased to the subscriber, which connects to your computer's USB port or Ethernet port. Although the computer must instruct the DSL modem to make a connection, this is fairly simple and only needs to be done once after the computer starts up. In fact, you can often instruct your computer to automatically make a DSL connection at startup. DSL service is provided through a normal telephone line, but it uses a different channel than voice communications. So you can use a single telephone line for DSL and phone calls at the same time.

Cable Modem

A cable modem works similarly to DSL service but is provided by your local cable company. The same cable that provides a signal to your television provides a signal to a cable modem, which then connects to your computer either via your USB or Ethernet port. Cable modem connections are "always on" and generally don't require you to connect to the service. Because the bandwidths are about the same, there are often discussions about, "Which is better, cable or DSL?" The consensus seems to be that there is no clear winner, and it depends on your particular needs and service providers. A DSL connection is easier to share in a small local network, but cable can sometimes be more reliable (cable service seems to go out less frequently than telephone service).

LAN (Local Area Network)

You would connect to the Internet through a local area network (LAN) if you are working at an educational institution or large business where Internet access is provided by a technology services department. Many hotel rooms are also equipped with high-speed Internet connections like this. Settings are generally fairly simple and speeds are high. You may also hear these connections referred to as T1 or T3 connections. For LAN connections, your computer must have a network interface card (NIC). Generally you can tell if you have an NIC by whether your computer has an Ethernet port, which looks like a slightly oversized telephone jack. In most cases, you will use a standard Ethernet cable to connect from the access point (usually the wall) to your computer. Like cable modem connections, LAN connections are always on, so the Internet can be available 24/7.

Other Options

Other options for connecting to the Internet include ISDN and satellite Internet, but relatively few people use these types of connections. For this discussion, we will also overlook connections via cell phones (WAP) and other handheld devices, but you should be aware that they exist.

A Word about Wireless

Today, many hotels, university campuses, and even coffee shops provide free wireless Internet access using something called WiFi. We won't discuss this too much—suffice it to say that, if you have a laptop, you can get a wireless access card and often access the Internet just as if you were connected to a LAN (though somewhat slower). If you have more than one computer in your office or home, you can share the same Internet connection among them wirelessly at speeds that are slower than wired connections but much faster than dial-up.

A WEB BROWSER

Every computer today comes with a Web browser, or the program you use to access the World Wide Web. We'll discuss the Web later in this chapter. For now, the main point is that you should have a copy of the latest version of either or both of the most popular browsers—Netscape and Internet Explorer—installed and running on your computer. You can download the programs for free. Other browsers exist, but these are, for better or worse, the current standards for which most websites and browser-based services are designed.

With a computer, Internet access, and Web browser, you have the minimum essentials to begin online counseling (email can be accessed via the Web), but there are some other things that can be useful in your work. We'll describe them next.

AN EMAIL ACCOUNT

Every online counselor needs an email address. If you have an ISP then you have an email address (e.g., joetherapist@aol.com). You may, however, wish to get a special email address that you use only for your online counseling work and that you can access via a Web browser. AOL allows multiple screen names per account and if you have your own domain and Web-hosting account (discussed in a following section), you can create multiple email addresses for different purposes (e.g., DrJoe@joetherapist.com, DrBob@joetherapist.com, info@joetherapist.com, billing@joetherapist.com, etc.). You can also get free email accounts (with limited storage) from places like Microsoft's Hotmail (http://www.hotmail.com) and other websites. We'll discuss how email works later in this chapter.

AN EMAIL PROGRAM

If you want good control over your emails, with the ability to organize them by client, add complicated formatting, and filter out junk emails, then you really need an email program. Most new computers come with some sort of free email program, such as Outlook Express (available as a free download from Microsoft) or Mail (Apple's free but powerful email program). Many commercial email programs, such as Microsoft Outlook or Entourage, also have scheduling functionality, which is helpful in managing an online counseling practice. Any email program should be able to retrieve messages from all of your accounts at the same time. You can also use your email program to set up a "signature," a standard message that gets appended to any email that you send. This is very convenient for online counselors, who may wish to have a standard message about confidentiality and emergency contact information.

A CHAT PROGRAM

If you plan to offer realtime text-chat counseling services, a "chat" program would be helpful. This software allows you to communicate dynamically and interactively with other people, comment by comment. Although you can "chat" using the Web, freestanding chat programs generally work better and offer additional functionality, such as the ability to save session transcripts. One notable Web page–embedded exception is LivePerson, which works quite well and is easy to use, although it has fewer chat features than most freestanding chat programs. We will explain how the Web and "chat" work later in this chapter. Chat programs are ordinarily free to download; good ones are available from AOL (AOL Instant Messenger—AIM), Yahoo, MSN, and ICQ.

A VIDEOCONFERENCING PROGRAM AND WEBCAM

If you plan to communicate with clients via videoconference, you will need a videoconferencing program. As of this writing, videoconferencing is not available via a Web interface. Videoconferencing programs send and receive dynamic images (videostreams) between computers across the Internet. Videoconferencing requires a high-speed Internet connection and a webcam on at least one end of the conversation. Webcams are small video-only cameras that are attached to your computer via a USB or Firewire (IEEE 1394) port. Webcams are relatively inexpensive compared with regular video cameras because they don't record video—they simply send the image stream to the computer, which can then record the images or send them over the Internet. A webcam also doesn't require a power source because it receives its power through the computer port to which it is attached. Some popular videoconferencing programs include NetMeeting (part of the newer versions of the Windows OS), iSpQ VideoChat, CU-SeeMe, and iVisit. Some use their own proprietary technology (requiring all users to have the same software) and others follow the H.323 protocol standard. We will explain more about how videoconferencing works later in this chapter.

A WEBSITE

If you want to promote yourself and/or operate an independent or small group online practice, you will want to set up a website. There are a variety of ways to do this. Some options are cheap and easy, others are expensive and/or complicated. (The mechanics of how a website works will be discussed later in the chapter.) With a website, you can set the tone of your practice, customize your clients' experiences with you, and make available whatever materials you like. You can design and maintain a simple and attractive website purely through Web-based site template services, or you can use Web design software (such as Microsoft FrontPage, Adobe GoLive, or Macromedia Dreamweaver) to make a rich and complex site. Of course, you can also hire a Web designer to create and maintain your site. The many ways to use a website are discussed in other chapters in this book, but from the standpoint of technology, you need to determine whether you will use your website purely as a multimedia brochure (providing static information), or as a dynamic clinic with built-in tools to facilitate submission of forms and interactive communication.

A DOMAIN NAME

If you have a website, you will probably want to acquire a domain name. Then, instead of directing potential clients to somewhere like http://members.aol.com/~joetherapist, you can simply send them to http://www.joetherapist.com. In the latter case, joetherapist.com is the domain name. Domain names are distributed by domain registrars—companies such as Verisign and Register.com. Domain names are regulated by the Internet Corporation for Assigned Names and Numbers (ICANN) but you must reserve them through these private registrar companies. As of this writing, the cost to register a domain name is about $35 per year, with discounts for multiyear subscriptions.

A domain name is like a signpost that points to the address of your website. Through your registrar account, you set the registrar's domain name to point to the location where your website files are being stored. Most registrars offer a domain forwarding service that forwards visitors to the actual location of the website. However, if you have a Web-hosting service, you can attach the domain name directly to the site location.

WEB-HOSTING SERVICE

Websites are no more or less than a series of files (text, images, etc.) that can be interpreted by a Web browser and made available to the public. These files need to be stored on a server. In this context, think of a server as a large storage device with a fairly permanent connection to the Internet. Your own computer's hard drive could function as a server, but generally your computer will not be on all the time, nor will it have a very speedy connection to the Internet (by core networking standards). Because real commercial servers are quite expensive, with large and fast storage drives, redundant systems, firewall protection, etc., most small businesses outsource their Web storage to a Web-hosting service. For a monthly fee, a Web-hosting service gives you a large chunk of storage space with access to the Internet. The Web-hosting account can be used for many purposes: websites, file-sharing archives (FTP), streaming media, and email. If you have a website, a Web-hosting account is good because you have much more control over the files than you have with the free website space provided with most ISP accounts. Also, if you have a Web-hosting account, you can easily set your domain name to be connected so that you receive emails at joe@joetherapist.com, for example, and you can distribute the Web space and email accounts among multiple users.

SECURITY SOFTWARE/HARDWARE

Last, but certainly not least, if you're going online you may wish to acquire some sort of security software and/or hardware. A section on security at the end of this chapter will include more specifics, but here we will cover a few basic components that are involved in keeping your Internet-connected computer safe: A router connects to your DSL or cable modem account and makes it possible to share your connection among multiple computers in your home/office. Firewall software, such as Norton Internet Security, BrickHouse, or Black Ice, blocks certain types of information from being transmitted or received by your computer. Firewall functionality is built into most routers. Encryption software, such as PGP (Pretty Good Protection), allows you to encode your private client files and emails to prevent them from being viewed by unauthorized persons.

UNDERSTANDING THE INTERNET

If we define online counseling as "counseling using the technology of the Internet," it makes sense to say that an online counselor should have a general sense of what the Internet is and how it works. We'll give an overview of Internet basics in this section and provide more detail in subsequent sections regarding more specific topics, such as the World Wide Web, email, and other aspects of working on the Net.

WHAT IS THE INTERNET?

The Internet is probably the most complex system ever devised by humans. As such, understanding how it works can be a challenge. Most of us would rather not think about what happens between the sending and receiving of an email, or between typing in a Web address and seeing information on the screen. Fortunately, the Internet is based on a few simple core principles.

At its most basic, the Internet is a collection of thousands of computer networks, all of which have to cooperate and allow data to pass among them using defined communication protocols. The most important thing to understand is that the Internet is not a giant computer run by a giant corporation. In fact, nobody "runs" the Internet or owns it. The Internet is completely decentralized, and it was designed that way from the beginning. However, it wasn't always meant to be available to the public. The idea of the Internet came from the U.S. military, which wanted to create a computer network that would remain stable even in the event of a catastrophe like a nuclear attack against key communication centers. The key to developing such an invulnerable network was to develop a packet-switched network.

In a packet-switched network, data is broken into tiny pieces (about 1500 characters each) called "packets" and the packets are sent along their way. Each packet contains a header that includes (among other things) the sender's address, the recipient's address, and the packet order. When the data arrives at its destination, the packets are reassembled and made available for the recipient to use.

The common languages of the Internet are known as Transmission Control Protocol (TCP), which breaks apart and reassembles data packets, and Internet Protocol (IP), which routes data. Collectively they are known as TCP/IP. This protocol tells packets how to split apart, properly find their way to their destination, and get reassembled.

The IP routes information using "IP addresses." These addresses are expressed as four number separated by periods, or "dots." An example of an IP address might be 192.168.70.3. Because these numbers are difficult to remember, something called a "domain name" was created. Special computers called "domain name servers" translate the domain names into IP addresses, so that when you send something to "apple.com," for example, your computer knows that it should really go to 17.254.3.183.

Domain names are a system of dividing Internet addresses into sensible groups based on their topic area. These areas are reflected in the last several letters of a domain name. The oldest and most common domain names end with .com (for commercial entities), .org (for organizations), .gov (for government entities), .edu (for educational institutions), and .net (for Internet-related entities). Other, less commonly used domains have been created as well, including .biz, .tv, .usa, .uk, and many more. We'll talk more about addressing when we discuss email later in the chapter.

Client-Server Architecture

The software used by the Internet, and used by individuals to interact via the Internet, operates by something called client-server architecture. Because the terms *client* and *server* are used often in discussing Internet-enabled software, it is important to understand what they mean in your work as an online counselor. Programs that reside on your own computer and that use the Internet, such as a Web browser or an email program, are called "clients." Software that resides on your ISP's computer, which delivers website content and emails to individual users on demand, is called "server" software, and the ISP's computer holding that software is called the "server." We'll talk more about clients and servers when we discuss the World Wide Web and email.

UNDERSTANDING THE WEB

Isn't the World Wide Web the same thing as the Internet? In a word, no. Although the Web uses the Internet and the terms are often used synonymously, they are quite different. The World Wide Web consists of millions of electronic documents linked to one another and accessed via the Internet Protocol. The individual documents are called Web pages. Collections of Web pages residing on the same server are called websites.

Web pages are simple text files that are specially written so that they can be interpreted by a Web browser, a client program designed to display interactive and graphical Web pages. The text of a Web page document tells a Web browser where to show images (other files also stored on the server), how to display text (font, color, size, etc.), and what to do when a user uses the mouse to move over or click on a particular part of the page. The system used to write Web pages is called HyperText Markup Language (HTML). Many books have been written on designing effective websites and writing Web pages with HTML and Web-editing programs. For a comprehensive reference on Web design, see Niederst (2001). Castro (2000) provides a straightforward yet comprehensive guide to HTML.

Web pages are accessed using a Web browser, such as Internet Explorer, Netscape, or other client programs. Each Web page has an address, known as a Uniform Resource Locator (URL), which consists of the protocol name, followed by the domain name, followed by the file name, as in this example: http://www.ismho.org/index.html. This URL begins with http://, which tells the browser to interpret the file using the hypertext transfer protocol. ISMHO.org is the domain (in this case, the International Society for Mental Health Online's server). The "www" refers to the particular part of the server reserved for holding website files. The designation before the domain name is also known as the "host name." The "index.html" is the name of the main Web page (browsers automatically seek out the "index.html" file when no file name is specified in the browser). The ".html" is the file extension and tells the browser that the file is suitable for viewing with a Web browser.

If you do create your own website, you'll want to make sure that it is listed in many of the popular Web search engines, such as Google.com, AskJeeves.com, and AltaVista.com. Most of these websites have forms to submit your URL for "spidering." Spidering refers to automated programs developed by the search engines that will comb your site and determine what its content is so that users can be directed to information that is useful to them. You can embed keywords and a description in the code of your Web pages to facilitate this process. A complete discussion of search engine positioning is beyond the scope of this chapter, but Marckini (2001) has provided an excellent text entirely devoted to search engine optimization.

UNDERSTANDING EMAIL

Email (asynchronous text messaging) is the standard mode of communication on the Internet. Chances are you have exchanged many emails by now if you live in an industrialized country or have attended a university in the past 10 years. So we won't go into too much detail here about what email is. You type the person's address in the address area, a subject in the subject line, and the message, formatted how you like, then you press "send." The message is sent via the same TCP/IP protocol that transmits most other types of data over the Net. In this section we'll talk about some of the things that go on behind the scenes of a typical email transmission (what happens after you click on "send").

Let's first differentiate between two types of email transmission commonly used for online counseling. We'll call them *standard email* and *webmail.*

STANDARD EMAIL

Here's a simplified example itinerary for a typical email. Let's say that therapist123@qwest.com sends an email to joe2345@bellsouth.net. First the message is encoded and split into packets. The packets are transmitted to the ISP's (Qwest's) server. The ISP's DNS (domain name server) translates the domain "bellsouth.net" into its IP address (216.77.188.40) and Qwest's SMTP (simple mail transfer protocol) software sends the packets on their way. The packets arrive at BellSouth's mail server (mail.bellsouth.net), which reassembles the packets and deposits the message in the mailbox file in the recipient's account (joe2345). The email remains in that mailbox on the bellsouth.net server until Joe tells his email program to get new mail, at which point it is retrieved, deleted from the server, and placed in the mail database on Joe's computer.

The key points to understand for the purposes of online counseling are that 1) the mail is not transmitted directly from one computer to the other; 2) the mail is not removed from the recipient's server until it is retrieved (and even then only if the mail client tells the server to delete retrieved messages, usually the default setting); and 3) the email is transmitted in plain text and is readable to anyone who has access to the server mailboxes or who cares to snoop on the packets as they travel across intermediate servers. Hackers have developed "packet sniffer" programs to do this very thing.

If you're curious about the path an email took to arrive to you, select a message in your email client program and choose "view header." You will see a variety of information, including IP addresses and domain names of each server involved in the transmission of the message. The header also displays the "reply to" address, which is set by the sender and is the address to which your email will be sent if you click "reply" in your email program. The "reply to" address is arbitrary and is not necessarily the same address as the account that sent the message. Always double-check the recipient's address before clicking "send" on an email.

WEBMAIL

Webmail works similarly to standard email, but it doesn't require an email client program. Rather, all email is retrieved and read via a password-protected website. Many ISPs and free email providers (e.g., Hotmail, mac.com, Yahoo, etc.) allow you to check your email via the Web interface. An advantage of this is that you can check your email from any computer in the world equipped with a Web browser. Disadvantages include a relatively slow interface (delays between seeing messages) and no easy way to store messages for offline reference.

Secure webmail services don't actually send your message anywhere. They require both parties (sender and recipient) to be registered with the service. Then when you send your message, it is made available to the recipient, who has an account on the same server. Because they don't require the installation of any encryption software (they use the encryption built into all modern Web browsers), secure webmail services are an attractive and commonly used option for online counseling. Examples include Safe-Mail.net (http://www.safe-mail.net) and Hushmail (http://www.hushmail.com). When a new message is received, the recipient gets a standard email simply announcing that a new message has arrived. To see the message, the recipient must log on to his or her secure webmail account.

UNDERSTANDING TEXT-CHAT

Text-chat allows you to communicate dynamically with somebody in realtime via the Internet. Whereas email requires that you send a message in a big chunk, text-chat communications proceed line by line, with counselor and client(s) communicating synchronously. Chat has been around a long time (see Chapter 3 for more about the history of chat). As an online counselor, you will likely use chat in one of two ways. Either you will chat with clients via a Web-based chat room or via a separate chat client. Chat systems are typically made up of a few common parts: the chat window (containing a record of all statements, typically time-stamped), the text entry field (where you type in the next snippet of text to send), and the send button (you can usually hit the enter key to send as well). Depending on which system you use, there may be additional options to set the color and style of the text, or buttons to add emoticons (small graphical elements, such as smiley faces used to express emotions).

Web-based chat implementations are typically small programs called Java applets that run right within your Web browser. They usually work on any computer platform, but there may be slight problems if the applet hasn't been tested thoroughly with your operating system. Web-based chat systems are also often slow, with a noticeable delay between typing a message and clicking the send button and the message appearing in the chat window. Web chat systems are nice because they are easily customized and don't require the client to download any additional software. There are many Web-based chat systems available. Some are free (typically with advertisements) whereas others can be quite pricey (including special features, such as encryption). One particularly good Web-based chat system is LivePerson (http://www.liveperson.com). LivePerson works quickly, allows you to monitor traffic on your website, and allows you to receive messages from clients who try to contact you when you're not around.

The more common way to conduct text-chat sessions is by using Instant Message technology. Numerous systems have been developed to allow instant messaging (chatting). AOL, MSN, Yahoo, and ICQ are some of the most common instant message services. Each has its own free chat client that users can download.

Here's how it works (let's say you're using AIM): When you run your chat program and sign on using your screen name and password, the AOL server makes a note of your online status and your IP address. Anyone else registered with AIM can add your screen name to his or her "buddy list." While you are signed on, the server constantly monitors the status of individuals on your buddy list so that AIM will tell you when one or more of your buddies are online and available to chat. When you send a message using your instant message client, the snippet of text travels to the system's server and then is routed to the other party's IP address.

Ordinarily, chats take place between individuals and nobody is able to butt in to your conversation. However, some instant message services allow you set up password-protected virtual chat rooms so that you can have chat sessions with multiple individuals, as with group counseling sessions.

Discussed in more detail elsewhere in this text, emoticons are frequently used in chat sessions so that participants can express emotional tone. One advantage of using emoticons in chat sessions is that most instant message programs support graphical "smileys." That is, when you type :-), it will show up in the text log as ☺. Chat client software typically supports 10 or more different graphical smileys.

While logged in to your chat program, you can set your status to reflect whether you are available for a conversation. Standard chat client software is easy to use and reliable. It even works well with dial-up connections.

UNDERSTANDING VIDEOCONFERENCING

Videoconferencing is like using text-chat, in that communication is conducted in realtime. However, instead of line-by-line text messages, video information is transmitted. There may or may not also be an audio (voice) component as well.

In some ways videoconferencing is like any other form of communication over the Internet. Data is routed in packets from IP address to IP address. But instead of being transferred via TCP, videoconferencing data usually is sent using User Datagram Protocol (UDP), another type of Internet protocol more useful for streaming audio and video media.

Videoconferencing usually requires each participant to use client software (e.g., Microsoft's NetMeeting, iVisit, CU-SeeMe, iSpQ) to log in to the reflector, a central server computer that maintains a log of videoconferencing sessions. The reflector lists all available videoconferencing "rooms" that have been set up by other participants. You can also set up your own room, password protecting it, if desired. Generally, all participants need to be using the same software, unless the software conforms to a particular standard protocol. Some types of videoconferencing software allow you to make a direct connection to another person's computer if you know his or her IP address. This can usually be found in the network settings of your computer. Note, however, that unless you have specifically requested a static IP address from your ISP, you will have a dynamic IP address—a different number assigned to you each time you connect to your dial-up, cable, or DSL Internet service (or at other regular intervals).

To participate in a videoconferencing session, you must attach a webcam and, if necessary, a microphone to your computer. (Some webcams and laptop computers have microphones built into them.) The camera converts the video signals into digital data, which is then compressed and encoded using a certain protocol (often H.323) and transmitted. The transmitted data then is decoded by the other person's videoconferencing software, which displays it as video on the person's screen. Although many webcams connect to the computer via the USB port, you should use a camera that utilizes a faster port if possible (e.g., USB2, IEE1394/FireWire400, IEEE1394b/FireWire800).

Most videoconferencing software allows you to send text-chat message while you see full-motion video on the screen. Furthermore, the software typically allows you to see video images of all participants (including yourself).

UNDERSTANDING FORMS AND DOCUMENT SHARING

Documents, and the sharing of information in a standardized format, are a very common part of counseling. As an online counselor you may wish to collect data from your clients using Web-based forms and you may wish to allow clients to download worksheets and other informational material for their own use as part of the counseling process. The Internet makes it so easy to share data that many face-to-face (f2f) counselors use it to collect and share information with their clients as well.

The best way to share proprietary documents on the Internet is with the Portable Document Format (PDF). You could just create a Web page with information about anxiety or depression or coping with anger, but plain Web pages are easy to copy (via cut and paste), may not be formatted properly (if clients are missing fonts, etc.), and may not print correctly. PDFs, on the other hand, allow you to prepare a document so that it looks and prints exactly right every time. Furthermore, you can lock a PDF so that it can't be edited or printed, if you are concerned about copyright issues. PDFs are now the standard method for distributing tax forms, brochures, electronic books, and instruction manuals. Anyone can read a PDF using Acrobat Reader, available as a free download from Adobe (http://www.adobe.com/acrobat). PDFs are easy to prepare too. You can use Adobe Acrobat or other software (Mac OS X can save documents in PDF format) to virtually "print" your document as a PDF. As PDFs your documents will look to everyone just as they would if they came out of your printer. There's no need for them to have the same operating system or computer program that you used to prepare them (e.g., it doesn't matter whether you used Word or WordPerfect).

When you want to collect information from your clients or prospective clients, Web forms are a good way to do it. Forms are most often used for client-intake questionnaires and other brief assessment measures (see Chapter 11). Forms are built into HTML and, using a basic HTML editor, you can easily create Web pages with edit fields, check boxes, selection menus, and choice (radio) buttons. However, to have the form function properly, you need to have instructions that tell it what to do when you click the "submit" button. This information is generally provided by a CGI script stored on your Web-hosting server along with your website. Without going into too much detail, the CGI script is just a little program that tells the server how to handle the data provided by the Web form. That is, how should it format the data provided, how should it compile the data, and how should it deliver the data. You may wish to have the data emailed to you, or you may wish to have data from completed forms stored on the server for your later retrieval. Most Web hosts provide prewritten CGI scripts to handle form-submission, but you must read their instructions about how to set up your form in order for it to work correctly.

There are a few other options for data collection. Some sites will help you set up and collect data via free Web-based polling services (e.g., http://free-online-suveys.co.uk). As we will discuss in the next section, data submitted by surveys is not secure without SSL encryption, so you may wish to consider using a secure form-processing service, such as Web Form Buddy (http://www.web-form-buddy). Another alternative would be to send your clients a blank, text version of your form via email. They can then edit it in their reply and return it using a secure mail system (Web-based or encrypted email, discussed below).

UNDERSTANDING SECURITY

Because privacy is so important in counseling (arguably even more important than protecting credit card numbers in online purchases), it is important to understand how to use technology to protect your clients' information. In this section we'll discuss security risks and countermeasures.

Debates about online counseling invariably turn to the importance of privacy and the risk of "hackers" having access to clients' secret information. The thing is, f2f counseling procedures are generally not too secure. Most counselors close their doors during sessions, but only a few use sound-masking devices. Most counselors lock their office doors at night, but how many files are left in plain view on a desk or receptionist counter? What would happen in the event of a burglary? We would suggest that not only is security not an added liability for online counseling, but that rather it is one of the main benefits of online counseling. Technology affords us the ability to quickly and easily store records in a safe fashion. With the use of a few simple and inexpensive precautions, Internet communications are also more secure than f2f conversations—nobody can eavesdrop and you don't need a full-time security guard to patrol your office.

Without the simple security measures, there are some serious risks, but if you understand how the technology works then you won't have a problem. It's analogous to knowing that you probably shouldn't do a private counseling session on a crowded bus. The problem is that most Net novices don't know when they are in a private room and when they are in a crowded bus.

The Internet was not originally designed to be particularly secure. Since its inception, however, steps have been taken to improve the Internet for the purpose of things like electronic commerce and private communications.

RISK POINTS

Figure 5.1 shows a basic layout depicting potential risk points in online counseling. By now, you have a basic understanding of how information is transmitted online: it's broken up into pieces ("packets") and the pieces travel from server to server until they reach their final destination. To use an email as an example, it's like taking a postcard and giving it to a postal worker, who then rips it up into a few pieces and hands each piece to whichever postal worker happens to be walking by. Each piece gets handed to postal workers (who may be headed in the direction of the recipient) until they all finally arrive at the individual's mailbox, whereupon they are reassembled and the recipient can read the postcard. In this case, there is no envelope disguising the message, nor is anyone particularly concerned who they hand the pieces to, so long as they are wearing a postal worker uniform. Clearly there are some risks.

Let's think about a typical email, traveling from an online counselor to a client: The counselor writes the email on her notebook computer. She uses a standard email program, such as Outlook, Entourage, or Eudora. The message is sent. First the message is transmitted to the counselor's ISP. Then (in packet form) it is routed across the Internet from server to server to its final destination, the client's ISP. The message (now reassembled) sits on the ISP's server until the client retrieves it, whereupon it is downloaded to the client's computer. The message stays on the client's computer until it is filed or deleted. After it is deleted, the message remains on the computer's hard drive until it is overwritten.

Here are some of the potential risk points:

The counselor's laptop: is the counselor working in private? How is the sent message stored? What if the laptop is stolen?

The message, en route: Who has access to the message as it travels? Could somebody capture all the packets and store them before sending them along their way? What form would the message have?

Online Counseling Security Risk Points

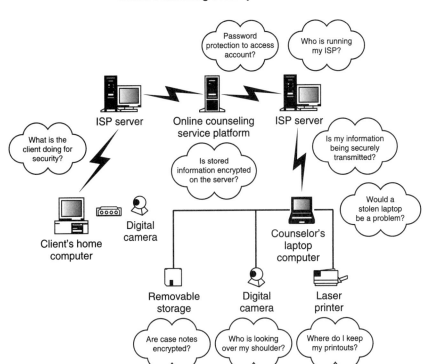

FIGURE 5.1 *Online Counseling Security Risk Points.* In the process of working with clients via the Internet, there are many places where privacy can be compromised. This diagram shows potential risk points that counselors should be aware of as they engage in online counseling.

The client's ISP: Who has access to the client's email box on the server? In what form is the message as it waits to be retrieved?

The client's computer: Who can download the messages? Who else uses the computer? How does the message appear in the client's email in-box? How is the message stored?

Being aware of the risk points gives you the power to effectively implement countermeasures and adopt best practices for secure Internet-based communications.

COUNTERMEASURES AND BEST PRACTICES

Certain security protocols will help protect the privacy of your communications.

Password Protection

Your computer should have some sort of password protection. Every modern operating system allows you to set your computer to require the entry of a password at startup. This is a simple precaution you can use. In addition, you should set your screensaver (also built into most modern operating systems) to turn on automatically after a brief idle period and require a password to turn it off. It's probably not a great idea to share your computer with others if you're using it for online counseling, but if you do, be sure to set up a separate password-protected account for yourself. Windows XP, Mac OS X, and Linux operating systems allow you to do this easily.

For ultimate security, you should avoid writing your password down, but because you have client records that must be accessible in the event that you are incapacitated, we recommend that you write them down and store them in a safe deposit box in case of emergency. Give instructions to a colleague on what to do in case of emergency.

Another word about passwords. Try to make them somewhat difficult to guess! Don't use your name, your pet's name, your kid's name, "password," characters from *Star Wars*, etc. These are easy to guess or figure out using programs that automatically feed in dictionary terms and common passwords. Ideally, you should use a short phrase that is at least eight characters long, including both upper and lowercase and at least one numeral or nonalphanumeric character. One handy way to do this is to pick two words that don't necessarily go together, capitalize at least one and separate them with some sort of nonalphanumeric character like a colon (:). For example: Sigmund:feminist. This password would be relatively easy for you to remember, but relatively difficult to crack by brute force (e.g., using computer programs that guess passwords), although being subjected to such an attack would be unusual unless you were some sort of secret agent or corporate executive (Langer, 2002).

Encryption

It's a good idea to encrypt documents that are private. Cryptography is a very complex science that involves a lot of number theory and mathematical operations that are well beyond the scope of this book but discussed extensively elsewhere (e.g., Garfinkel, 2002). But it is not difficult to implement encryption into your everyday routine, whether you are transmitting or storing confidential information. Encrypting a document involves applying a standard mathematical formula or "algorithm" to the file and a unique "key" so that the contents are mixed up. The mixed-up file can be reassembled (decrypted) by applying another algorithm and key.

There are two basic encryption strategies that you should know about: symmetric encryption and public key encryption. Symmetric encryption is best used for storing documents privately on your computer. The same key is used to encrypt and decrypt the document. It is the most secure method because without the key anyone intercepting the message will have no idea what the file is—it will look like a jumble of random characters. There are many symmetric encryption programs available, and they are even built into most computer operating systems.

With public key encryption, you generate a "keypair"—a set of two keys, one private and one public. You can give your public key to everyone, even post it on your website. Anyone who wants to send you a private message then uses the public key to encrypt the document. Because you have the private key, you are the only one who can decrypt the file.

"Keys" are very different from passwords. They are generally very long strings of randomly generated characters. When you hear about a 128-bit key, that means that there are 2^{128} possible keys that could possibly decode the file. Even if all the computers in the world cooperated, it would take longer than the age of the universe to try all the possible keys (Free Software Foundation, 1999). Here is a sample of what a 1024-bit public key (the author's) generated by the GNU Privacy Guard (GPG) program looks like:

```
Version: GnuPG v1.0.7 (Darwin)
mQGiBDyPlwERBADS5FgRQl+yRHbo0x62fl1OP4/Uq+I2clIrNy4OyGfAiGCN7tFp
jixtjg/5Eeqwh5k5iljI2Wl3J6XykC4jup5+XI7D4mKThavFjc7zvKEH1N7ZTWpd
MZBF5pR/3MPjcGMIyAzFb7TIEaet9O+KPli9yf0fAnumu0zohxLpxjvjVwCgnbhD
PQoSpB9zh5fhHivP8Y9wrukEAL+Xdvuvg4V2amjfr1/sFwfX5GYb6YCbnkilCfwQ
/IzMJOxCyMeHUmqx0dNYpnW5WGadNOLRoK9XUr2luI3Xsglshl/xPS46yEUyOAlp
cPPi9AoOMgJwWSNaJXDya6hocLjwaSa0PsZ+QhtaW2oPsFVNVzSLdthIAVPDmqaI
1dHRA/9GB+mXLe1p8qe6sdm6WYFnURqTKkbBKVSAubN8xvWQHoBP13kv3Syy7aRt
B1K+Euup73GXQM2URACeTqV5XnoGyEw5DUK1BNDUN+7GAnacz8xS/gm0HXT5+CGW
R61XyN/GUqEhvmaZwDsNf9mI5vFizmP7Hrb7GbjaXeH+yBePQLQkSmFzb24gUy4g
WmFjayAoSlNaKSA8anN6YWNrQG1hYy5jb20+iFcEExECABcFAjyPlwEFCwcKAwQD
FQMCAxYCAQIXgAAKCRAE4QFK9kX7Kns4AJ9Q3kP3x44oDvfJ2V7w82LO14ImXQCg
11T2mzW9QUjwGTcd3niFgm/rBYy5AQ0EPI+XIBAEAMIPp1H3YxKtjPlEMxGNnUrQ
MvNHfvaBV9Su8UH3Ikf5tj3f7864diwBhEN6D1mYmwSkVoEONwsyCl9fqhI8o6yM
IYCSLGE57UJZd1ZBgv21sU+F8GPmWXQb4Sd0gUKLWeWmFKtIJThuCvpp/kn09JYH
+CGF3H0LDU09TZALdfVPAAQLA/4m+x6MEV2QP0QesCLNWQ2PWcjCvwJuKed18+59
xcykMyA1iwL/lxxjcCkXUmmBrEWRiMfrwUXAsGw+uZFYqJltChgyx/BA2TTHaAR7
hgpFpbk90+hRtgJCwVQgkdkBYlmGFKHrvDiObAVvC9EkwZEnzVU79HmTBiOnsiWd
sE0HOohGBBgRAgAGBQI8j5cgAAoJEAThAUr2Rfsq19cAnj5qCeOcuZFsTVhfJhD9
H3FYPKLWAJ41Bd/g7YF4OrcVJagLvK2B4F4XoA==
=72Sb
```

Naturally, you don't have to memorize or type in these keys. They are stored on your computer in a key database. You can post your public key on your website, email it in plain text to your colleagues and clients, or list it with a public "keyserver" directory of keys. Anyone with the key can use it to send you an encrypted message that only you can open. Access to your own secret (private) key is protected on your own computer by a typical password of your choosing.

As it turns out, public key encryption is the method built into all modern Web browsers to allow secure communications between your computer and a website. When your browser shows a lock or key in a lower corner (on Netscape and Internet Explorer), you have a secure connection. Basically, the server (e.g., Amazon.com) has sent you its 128-bit public key—your browser then uses that public key to encrypt data (e.g., your credit card number) that you transmit to the server. If that data is intercepted along the way it will be undecipherable to the third party because he or she does not have the secret key. This process is called SSL (Secure Socket Layer) encryption (see Garfinkel, 2002, for more detail about communications layers, etc.).

As discussed above, webmail systems use SSL to allow users to exchange private messages without using any extra security software. Because the messages never leave the server (e.g., Safe-Mail.net), it is sufficient for both parties to enter and read messages right through the browser. Just be sure to log off of your account and close your browser when you finish with the mail so that nobody else can see the messages in your account.

Wiping

As mentioned above, private information that you delete from your computer remains on your computer's hard drive until it is overwritten. Recovery software can easily restore files from a discarded drive (consider this before selling your used computer). You can avoid the possibility of this happening by using wiping software that writes a random series of ones and zeros over your data to be erased.

Firewalls

These days, many of us have computers that are constantly connected to the Internet via a DSL or cable modem connection. Furthermore, many of our computers are connected to large or small networks of multiple computers. Given the proper expertise, sophisticated users can spy on other network computers if the proper precautions are not taken. We recommend that you set up a firewall. A firewall can be software or a hardware device that blocks certain types of information from coming to or leaving your computer. For example, a firewall can be set up to only allow websites, email, and chat data to travel to and from your machine. A full discussion of "ports" and alternative protocols is beyond the scope of this chapter but discussed at length in other sources (e.g., Garfinkel, 2002). You can protect yourself from unauthorized intrusions easily and inexpensively by using software, such as Norton Security (by Symantec), Black Ice, Brick House, or rudimentary firewall systems built into your computer's operating system. Alternatively, if your network has a router between your computer and your cable/DSL modem, then you can set up your router to only allow certain types of data to travel between the Internet and your machine. Ordinarily, computers and routers have default settings set to limit risk, but if you are concerned you might check out some third party firewall software or consider adding a router to your network.

Self-Contained Encrypted Communications Programs

One last thing we will mention is self-contained encrypted communications programs. These are free-standing client programs that securely log into a server and allow chat, email, and file-exchange. One example is a service called CryptoHeaven (http://www.cryptoheaven.com). For a small annual fee, users can access their account and run a small Java application on their desktop that allows them to communicate with 256-bit encryption easily and effectively.

The Weakest Link

Remember that your security procedures are only as strong as their weakest link. You can encrypt all of your data, but if your password is on a sticky note tacked to your monitor then you have a serious limitation. Similarly, you can do everything possible on your end as a counselor, but if your client sends you an unencrypted message there's nothing you can do about it.

COMMON PROBLEMS

One of the inevitabilities of any computer-based endeavor, and online counseling is no exception, is that technical problems can be expected. In this section, we will briefly review some of the more common ones.

NEWBIE PROBLEMS

As we mentioned at the beginning of the chapter, "newbie" is Net-slang for a novice computer user. They are fewer in number as the years go by, but you can expect to encounter people who haven't the slightest idea what they are doing online. Hopefully, anyone who has read this chapter will not be too obviously mistaken for a newbie, but older clients who just started using the Internet will be impossible to miss because of their questions, such as "What's a browser?" and "Does my Web-hosting account come with a phone number to dial in?" Working with newbies will take extra time. They will be easily frustrated by malfunctions and will often be skeptical of what can be accomplished online. However, they are often all the more impressed by the wonders of technology when they work properly.

BROWSER PROBLEMS

Not all Web browsers are created equal. Websites may appear slightly different to Netscape and Internet Explorer. It is wise to test websites with both of these (and probably with several versions) to be sure that everything works properly and looks right to you. Similarly, some Web-based services like email and forms may have slight variations, so if you're using these you might want to test them out on multiple browsers so that you know what your clients will be seeing.

PLATFORM PROBLEMS

Similarly, not all of your clients will be using the same operating system that you use. Cross-platform compatibility is not generally an issue because all modern operating systems are built to handle email, the Web, and many other Internet services. However, be aware that your instructions, or certain security and videoconferencing solutions, may not work on other platforms. For example, some companies (e.g., NetworkPrivacy.com) offer Web services that do not support Macintosh, arguing that Mac users account for only 5% of the market. Although we can't back it up with figures, we would argue that Mac users are overrepresented among online counseling users and providers, given that their user demographics match those of typical online counseling clients (Mac users have higher levels of education and are more affluent, according to a recent Nielsen study).

FULL MAILBOXES

A common problem for counselors and clients alike is the full mailbox. That is, too many messages accumulate in the user's account on the server. As a result, new messages are bounced back to the sender with a cryptic message, leaving them confused. This can be disconcerting to clients who suddenly feel that their link to the counselor has been severed. You should routinely clear your email box of detritus, and set your email program to not leave messages on the server, or to delete messages after a two-week interval.

MISDIRECTION AND MISSING ATTACHMENTS

A common error among email users, especially newbies, is that of mistakenly sending emails to the wrong address. You should always reread your emails and double-check that they are properly addressed and that attachments, if any, are present.

DISCONNECTION

Clients who use dial-up services can be easily disconnected, causing difficulties when doing text-chat sessions. A computer crash can also result in a disconnection. Installing more memory (RAM) in your computer and/or making an effort to not run too many programs at the same time can help prevent this. If a disconnection occurs, you reconnect immediately (if it was your disconnection) or wait for a brief period and your client will probably return. However, the best idea is to have a prestated policy that all clients are given prior to starting work with them explaining what the procedure will be when this happens. Will you still charge for interrupted sessions? In any case, do your best to ensure that your computer is operating smoothly before doing any type of synchronous (realtime) counseling, and encourage your clients to do the same.

FIREWALL PROBLEMS

Finally, be aware that your client's or your firewall, if present, may make it difficult or impossible to access certain websites or to use certain Internet services (like chat). This is most often a problem if the client is trying to connect from a machine at work. As it is, connecting should be discouraged unless absolutely necessary, because corporate policies often stipulate that the company owns any material on the computer, and data is generally backed up on tape drives that are saved indefinitely. Don't keep private information on company computers (unless you encrypt it)! In any case, if you or your client are concerned about firewall problems, you may wish to have a two-minute test chat prior to meeting online for your counseling session.

TECHNOLOGY TRENDS IN ONLINE COUNSELING

Technology is ever-changing. In fact, much of what is written in this chapter will be out-of-date within a few years. It is wise to stay abreast of new technological innovations.

The coming years will see faster computers and faster Internet connections, allowing online counselors the ability to provide bandwidth-hogging services like videoconferencing with ease. But remember, it doesn't matter how much you upgrade your system if your clients don't have access to the same capabilities. This is why videoconferencing hasn't yet taken off in the public sector.

An exciting new development is the growth of virtual reality applications. Already, millions of people are using the Internet to participate in fully-immersive three-dimensional worlds where they slay dragons and search for treasure. Although perhaps less exciting, developers are working on creating similar, more mundane worlds where online counselors and clients can sit in a virtual room together and see three-dimensional representations of each other called avatars. Virtual reality (VR) technology is already being used by counselors working with clients who have phobias (e.g., Rothbaum et al., 2001; Rothbaum et al., 2002). Using a computer and a VR head-mounted display, clients can engage in desensitization or implosion therapy to experience flying in airplanes, riding up glass elevators, or public speaking.

Wireless technology (using the WiFi standard) is growing rapidly as of this writing. More and more computer users are going mobile, and businesses, hotels, and Internet cafes are providing their patrons free wireless Internet access. The implications of this are that more and more individuals will be able to contact counselors no matter where they are, right at the time that they need help the most.

A great way to keep up with new trends in technology is to read computer magazines like *PC World* and *Macworld*, but for a broader view of things to come, we recommend a digital lifestyle magazine, such as *Wired*. Finally, a more scholarly approach to online counseling trends and research can be found in the journal *CyberPsychology & Behavior*.

CONCLUSION

In this chapter, we provided an introduction to the technological underpinnings of online counseling. Having a general idea of how everything works behind the scenes will allow you to be a better counselor and respond appropriately when things don't work exactly as planned. Clearly, this discussion is not anywhere close to exhaustive and volumes have been written on each of the topics above (most of which are incomprehensible to those without a computer science background). We hope you'll use this chapter as a starting point to learn more and to incorporate new technologies into your work so that you can provide the best possible online counseling services.

KEY TERMS

Note: Because this chapter is relatively technical, the key terms section is consequently a bit longer. To ensure technical accuracy, these definitions are quoted or paraphrased from *The New Penguin Dictionary of Computing* (Pountain, 2002).*

Algorithm: A well-defined set of instructions for solving a problem.

Avatar: An animated graphical figure used to represent a person within an online virtual community or shared online game.

*Reproduced by permission of Penguin Books Ltd.

Bandwidth: The amount of information that can be transmitted through a communications channel.

CGI (Common Gateway Interface): A standard interface that enables external programs to be executed from inside a Web server and hence allows essentially unlimited functions to be embedded into Web pages, far beyond those provided by HTML.

Chat (also known as instant message): A conversation between two or more people conducted via networked computer systems by typing messages and seeing immediate responses; takes place in real time.

Client: A computer connected to a network that obtains some resource or service (such as file storage, printing), or email from a server located elsewhere on the network.

Domain name: The name of a particular server or group of servers on the Internet, formed according to the hierarchical naming scheme for Internet resources. For example, in an email address, such as info@ismho.org, everything following the @ constitutes the domain name.

DSL (Digital Subscriber Line): A whole class of digital telecommunication technologies that can offer very fast data rates, up to 50 megabits per second, over the existing copper wires of the analog public telephone system.

Encryption: The encoding of data so that it may be read only by authorized persons.

Firewall: A special type of gateway server that monitors all traffic passing between a local network (or individual computer) and the outside world to prevent security breaches. Firewalls can be self-contained, running independently on a modest PC, they can be software based, or they can be built into network hardware components, such as routers.

FTP (File Transfer Protocol): A client/server protocol used to transfer files from one computer to another over a TCP/IP network. FTP is the principle protocol used to download files from the Internet, and a limited FTP client capability is built into most Web browsers.

HTML (Hypertext Markup Language): The page description language used to describe documents that are to be published over the World Wide Web (www). The HTML description of a document page defines the placement of text and images on the page, and also the hypertext links that lead visitors from this page to other pages on the Web.

Internet: A network of computer networks that now spans the whole world, connecting all the major public, private, and university networks. The Internet permits email to be sent to and from anywhere in the world that has access via an Internet service provider (ISP).

ISP (Internet Service Provider): A company that provides Internet services, such as hosting websites, and usually also sells access to the Internet.

LAN (Local Area Network): A system for connecting many computers together so that they can exchange and share data, where all the computers are located within the same or closely adjacent buildings.

Packet: A generic term for the basic unit of data transmitted across a network.

PDF (Portable Document Format): An electronic document format invented by Adobe. It enables documents containing both text and graphic images to be viewed and printed in a uniform manner on different computer systems, independently of the resolution of the display device.

Private Key Encryption: Any encryption scheme that depends on both parties to the communication possessing the same secret key, as compared to public key encryption methods.

Public Key Encryption: A method of enciphering messages in which all the communicating parties receive a pair of keys: a public key and their private key. The public key may be freely published to all interested parties, but the private key must be kept secret. Any new message is encrypted using the intended recipient's public key, but the message can be decrypted only by using the private key. Hence there is never a need for sender and receiver to exchange their secret keys via a secure channel.

Server: A computer that is designed to provide shared services to other computers on a network, rather than to be directly accessed by users. The most common role for a server is as a file server, to hold data files that can be accessed by many users. Other common roles are print servers, mail servers, and database servers.

SSL (Secure Sockets Layer): A secure communications protocol designed by Netscape that enables encrypted connections to be made over the Internet.

TCP/IP: The protocol upon which the Internet is based. TCP/IP consists of two parts, with IP (Internet Protocol) operating at the network layer to address data, and TCP (Transmission Control Protocol) operating at the transport layer to break up, address, send, receive, and reintegrate data.

URL (Uniform Resource Locator): The string of characters used to identify some resource on the Internet, such as a server, a file, a Web page, or a newsgroup. An example of a URL is: http://www.ismho.org/index.html.

Virtual reality: An advanced form of 3-D graphics that tries to create the illusion of a real three-dimensional space.

Web browser: An application program whose purpose is to request and read pages from the World Wide Web. Examples of browsers include Microsoft's Internet Explorer, Netscape, Mozilla, and Apple's Safari.

World Wide Web (WWW): A set of technology standards that enables the publishing of multimedia documents (which may contain text, images, sound, and video) to be read by anyone with access to the Internet. Using Web browser software running on a personal computer or workstation, users may type the address of a Web page anywhere in the world and see it displayed on their own screens.

STUDY QUESTIONS

1. What is the difference between the Internet and the Web?
2. Who owns the Internet?
3. What are some security risks in online counseling?
4. What is the difference between symmetric encryption and public-key encryption?
5. What are the advantages of PDF documents?

REFERENCES

Castro, E. (2000). *HTML for the World Wide Web*. 4th ed. Berkeley, CA: Peachpit Press.

Free Software Foundation (1999). *The GNU privacy handbook*. Retrieved October 15, 2003, from http:www.gnupg.org/gph/en/manual.html.

Garfinkel, S. (2002). *Web security, privacy, and commerce*. 2nd ed. Sebastopol, CA: O'Reilly & Associates.

Gralla, P. (2002). *How the Internet works*. 6th ed. Indianapolis, IN: QUE.

Langer, M. (2002). *Mac OS X 10.2 advanced: Visual QuickPro guide*. Berkeley, CA: Peachpit Press.

Marckini, F. (2001). *Search engine positioning*. Plano, TX: Wordware Publishing.

Niederst, J. (2001). *Web design in a nutshell*. 2nd ed. Sebastopol, CA: O'Reilly & Associates.

Pountain, D. (2002). *The new Penguin dictionary of computing: An A-Z of computing jargon and concepts*. London: Penguin Books.

Rothbaum, B. O., Hodges, L. F., Ready, D., et al. (2001). Virtual reality exposure therapy for Vietnam veterans with posttraumatic stress disorder. *Journal of Clinical Psychiatry*, *62*(8):617–622.

Rothbaum, B. O., Hodges, L., Anderson, P. L., et al. (2002). Twelve-month follow-up of virtual reality and standard exposure therapies for the fear of flying. *Journal of Consulting and Clinical Psychology*, *70*(2):428–432.

6

ETHICAL AND LEGAL CONSIDERATIONS FOR PROVIDERS OF MENTAL HEALTH SERVICES ONLINE

RON KRAUS

INTRODUCTION

This chapter is written for clinicians, students, mental health professionals and organizations to explain in simple language current ethical issues related to professional work online. Licensed clinicians, who must follow and abide by the existing laws and ethical regulations of their profession, may benefit from additional knowledge about specific considerations that relate to online practice. To ensure familiarity with the ethics regulations, clinicians should log on to the websites of their respective profession and review current regulations online. (A list of sites appears later in this chapter.)

The Internet is a promising new medium that can be successfully used to provide professional services, but it also has limits. It is important to remember that online consultation is not always the most appropriate modality: some people will require traditional, face-to-face (f2f) service at a clinic or hospital. It is important for clinicians to recognize limits of the medium, as well as follow certain rules when offering professional services online to the public. To maintain quality of service, avoid potential complications, and serve the community safely, professionals who use the Internet for clinical work need to know the limitations of online consults, as well as understand ethical and legal considerations that apply to such work. Familiarity and careful compliance with ethical standards will help ensure that clinicians use the new medium professionally and responsibly.

A COMMUNICATIONS REVOLUTION: THE AGE
OF IMMEDIATE ACCESS

The Internet and rapid advances in mobile communication technology in the final years of the last millennium brought about a communications revolution that continues to reshape our lives today. The Internet was initially developed in the United States as a means to preserve secure communications between essential agencies in the event of a nuclear disaster. In the 1990s the Internet was made available for public use. By now, hundreds of millions around the world are connected and the numbers keep growing. In essence the Internet is a global network of computers that are interconnected. The network allows the global community to access, store, process, and transfer vast amounts of data. Never before in history were so many people able to communicate, access information, or find resources with such ease and speed regardless of geographical location. Prior to the days of the telegraph, telephone, and text messages online, scholars waited weeks, months, and sometimes years before a reply from a learned colleague arrived. Today, with the Internet, citizens of the global community are quickly getting used to having easy, immediate, and almost unlimited access to people, information, products, and services online.

The long-term influence of the communications revolution on society may not yet be fully clear, but it is already evident that since the introduction of the Internet to the global community, the public continues to show increasing interest in obtaining information and professional services online. This trend seems especially true when it comes to the public's' interest in the field of physical and mental health (Taylor, 1999).

As a result of the community's interest in professional service and information online, individuals and organizations responded by placing both passive and interactive Web pages on the Internet. Alas, responsible brave pioneers who dared to launch such services into cyberspace quickly recognized that regulations by state boards and guidelines by professional organizations either did not exist or were insufficient to fully address the specific concerns related to the new medium (see, for example, APA ethics statements from 1995 and 1997 on the matter). Although initial studies of the emerging field indicated that therapeutic potential may, indeed, exist (see Chapter 4; studies listed at http://construct.haifa.ac.il/~azy/refindx.htm), there was also the necessity to consider carefully all possible implications of service online. Among the first who wrote about ethics and the provision of clinical services online was the former head of the APA Ethics Committee, Dr. George Stricker from Adelphi University in New York. Stricker's article "Psychotherapy in Cyberspace" (1996) provides a good review of some of the main concerns that online clinicians should keep in mind. Among the issues discussed in the article are: the establishment of a therapeutic relationship and the responsibilities it carries, the need to know the identity of the client, the case of emergency and need to consider in-office care, privacy of online communications, the limits of text-based communications as a treatment modality, and the need to make available to clients the means for dispute resolutions, should such ever arise (see http://www.OnlineClinics.com/main/stricker.htm).

The lack of formal or sufficient guidelines from state and professional associations was probably the reason why private and nonprofit entities were the first to attempt self-regulation. Good examples of such pioneering work to define the dos and don'ts of the mental health dot-com in the United States can be seen online at www.EthicsCode.com, www.ISMHO.org (see recommendations relating to ethics), and the European-based initiative www.HONCODE.org, which provides guidance and certification to health sites. As recognition of the Internet's potential to expand professional services grew, so did the need to regulate the new field and address professional, ethical, and legal aspects. Among such efforts, several leading online health information providers in the United States, including America Online, drkoop.com, Healthwise, Medscape, Healtheon, and WebMD, formed the "Hi-Ethics Alliance" to create consensus on a code of ethics for the medical e-health sector, after the sector had been criticized for lax standards in providing medical advice and in filling out prescriptions online. In 2000 an attempt was made to organize several U.S. agencies to work out collaboratively a set of rules and regulations for clinicians who work online (Rippen and Risk, 2000). More about early ethics initiatives that relate to online work can be seen in G. Eysenbach's article "Towards ethical guidelines for e-health: JMIR Theme Issue on eHealth Ethics," published in the *Journal of Medical Internet Research* in 2000 (see http://www.jmir.org/2000/1/e7/index.htm).

It seems that a few years after the first text-based consults were conducted online, a consensus now exists in the professional community not to ban online counseling but rather to define the limits and learn how to best use the new modality.

WHAT IS ETHICAL? WHAT IS MORAL? WHY IS ETHICAL BEHAVIOR IMPORTANT?

When uncertain about the exact meaning of a new term, my father used to say, get a dictionary definition. Following the good advice, this section will start with definitions of the terms involved. The Oxford Dictionary (Hornby et al., 1971), defines *ethic* as: "science of morals, rules of conduct," and ethical as: "of morals or moral questions." The word *moral*, according to the same dictionary, means that which concerns principles of right and wrong. It thus seems that the term ethics relates to principles of appropriate, correct, and just behavior among members of the human family. Yet now that the terms are perhaps clearer, how does one distinguish between right and wrong? What is the source of our moral and ethical codes? And why would it be wise to follow these principles, anyway?

ETHICS: THE PHILOSOPHICAL AND RELIGIOUS FOUNDATION

Concepts of ethics and morality appeared in many cultures throughout recorded history. Even though various moral codes of cultures are often separated by time, language, religion, and/or geography, it seems that some basic rules of conduct are common to all members of the human family. The oldest and most common source for moral guidance usually comes from a culture's religious scripts. A review of Jewish, Christian, Eastern, and Muslim cultures reveals that the fundamental rule of conduct Moses, Jesus, Buddha, Mohammad, and others teach is that people should treat each other as they would like to be treated themselves. The old saying "Love thy neighbor as thyself" is a message that repeatedly emerges in various scriptures as the most basic religious/spiritual/moral commandment, calling us to behave ethically. The philosopher Immanuel Kant seems to have also arrived at similar conclusions. Below are some quotes about the "Golden Rule" taken from a book called *The Official Rules of Life* (Godin, 1996):

> "Always treat others as you would like them to treat you: that is the law and the prophets." (Christian; from "The Sermon on the Mount," The Book of Matthew)
>
> "What is hateful to you, do not to your fellow man. That is the entire Law: all the rest is commentary." (Jewish; Talmud, Shabbat 31a)
>
> "Hurt not others in ways that you yourself would find hurtful." (Buddhist; Udana-Varga 5:18)
>
> "No one of you is a believer until he desires for his brother that which he desires for himself." (Islamic; from Muhammad's last sermon, Sunnah)
>
> "Surely it is the maxim of loving kindness: Do not unto others what you would have not done unto you." (Confucian; Analects 15:23)

Keeping the Golden Rule in mind is still helpful as guidance in ethical questions that are related to treatment and service issues online thousands of years later. The question one should ask oneself when uncertain about an ethical issue is simple: How would I view events were I the other person? The imaginary shift of oneself into the place of the other, indeed not always an easy task, is one way to better understand the impact of our actions and how these may be perceived.

ETHICS: THE LEGAL SIDE

Licensed clinicians, regardless of training, theoretical background, personal philosophies, or cultural or religious beliefs, are still obligated to follow laws and regulations that govern their profession. In most cases, the agency that issues and regulates a professional license is the clinician's state. To keep a license in good standing, a clinician must know and follow the ethics regulations of his or her state's governing agency when providing professional service to the public. In addition to respecting the state license including the responsibilities it carries, some practitioners are also members of a local, state, national, or international professional association. As in the case of the state license, professionals who are certified members of an association have to be familiar with, as well as adhere to the organization's ethics code. Although a professional organization, such as the American Psychological Association or National Association of Social Workers (in the United States) may deal with a member's ethical violations internally or even take further action if need be, such an association has no authority to revoke a clinician's state license. Simply put, licensed clinicians have to know the regulations of their state and professional associations in order to avoid potential violations and legal risks.

THE PSYCHOLOGY OF BUSINESS: THE VALUE OF TRUST

Psychology has come a long way since Freud first introduced his revolutionary ideas, including those relating to what he named "the Pleasure Principle." Many years later, some of Freud's old concepts still seem valid today. In essence, Freud's Pleasure Principle explains that we are largely motivated by a wish for the gratification of our needs as well as the wish to avoid pain. Borrowing Freud's Pleasure Principle to explain consumer behavior in the modern era, we can understand why customers prefer products and services that are not only gratifying but also reliable. Trust, it seems, is good for business and sales. Consumer trust in a reliable product or service is a good way to ensure, maintain, and increase revenues. The link between trust and sales is a known fact that motivates not only politicians during an election, but also the business and advertisement communities. Such groups invest enormous amounts of money attempting to convince the public that their product or service is reliable and worthy. Indeed, once quality and reputation are established, brand name is created in the public's mind. People prefer the brand name that is associated with a valued and trusted product/service. Keeping ethical principles in mind when serving clients is a good way to create and maintain their trust. Clients, who are satisfied with the quality of the product/service they get, will also help promote the good reputation and future business success of the product/service provider. Recommendations regarding the business aspects of online counseling are discussed in more detail in Chapter 7.

To summarize, justification for ethical/moral conduct comes from various sources, including religious, philosophical, legal, psychological, and business considerations. Regardless of personal philosophy, online professionals need to be familiar with their state's (and/or province's or country's) and, if applicable, their professional association's ethics code(s), as well as carefully adhere to their principles.

WHAT IS PSYCHOTHERAPY?

In most cases, the term "therapy" relates to the process of healing or recovering. Psychotherapy is an interpersonal and personal process that aims to help people better understand and cope with situations, emotions, or perceptions. In essence, psychotherapy is a process of communication and dialogue. The therapeutic dialogue may focus on both intrapersonal and interpersonal issues. For some, psychotherapy may enhance the ability to cope, help identify obstacles to personal fulfillment, allow a search for better alternatives, and/or enable personal growth. Still, it is important to remember that psychotherapy doesn't always produce the same results for everyone.

While mental health professionals strongly believe that there are benefits to psychotherapy, results are not guaranteed and depend on various factors, among which are the individual's motivation, willingness to "work it through," and the feeling that both the process and the selected therapist can really help. Among other important predictors of the success of psychotherapy are the skill, approach, experience, and ability of the therapist; as well as a good match between client and therapist. The question of whether psychotherapy is an effective process has been thoroughly researched (see http://www.apa.org/practice/peff.html) and apparently answered. In spite of the debate and after much investigation over the years, psychotherapy, which includes a wide variety of treatment techniques, methods, and approaches (all of which are not necessarily similar or equally effective), is now considered an acceptable form of treatment for emotional and behavioral problems in Western culture.

It is important to explain clearly the process of evaluation and psychotherapy to a new client, as well as discuss the effectiveness, limits, and available alternatives to treatment. It is considered unethical to promise a client results that one cannot assure. In the same way, clinicians should not tell a client that one method of treatment is superior to another, if such a claim cannot be supported by current research and scientific evidence.

IS IT ETHICAL TO PROVIDE PSYCHOTHERAPY ONLINE?

The question of whether online communications are ethical at all as a form of service mostly stem from the concern that remote communications, such as text or telephone, may be insufficient or less effective than f2f, in-office encounters..

Most psychotherapists believe that nonverbal communication is important to understanding the total message. Nonverbal communication is our body language and everything we communicate besides the spoken word: posture, gestures, dress and appearance, facial expressions, and the like. Nonverbal communication is considered important for us to correctly "read" and understand each other. Since videoconferencing is not yet widely available to the average consumer, the current way most people communicate online is through the written word and over the telephone. As a result, the therapist's ability to "read" a client's nonverbal communication online (consisting of only text or voice) is limited.

Indeed, it may be true that office visits are preferable in some ways to online consults, because the clinician can better assess facial gestures, body language, and the general appearance of a client, and can also offer immediate, concrete help if such is required. Still, initial research seems to indicate that there may not be a significant difference either in the outcome of the treatment or clients' satisfaction when online work is compared to f2f encounters (see Chapter 4). We also know that telephone hot-lines have been serving the community successfully for decades in preventing clients from harm in critical times. It seems that to deny people the ability to locate and communicate with providers of professional help through the Internet may itself be unethical, especially as we already accept and use hot-line services very effectively. While possibly limited when compared to in-office consults, Internet and telephone communications may be helpful to those who require service but cannot or dare not communicate through other means. With the core philosophy of the helping professions in mind, we believe that it is better to ensure that services are offered responsibly and with all ethical considerations, rather than not at all. Being familiar with the contents of this book will allow clinicians and organizations to provide responsible, professional service while avoiding potential hazards.

WHAT CONSTITUTES TREATMENT OR THERAPY?

A therapist–client relationship is usually established when a clinician is contracted to diagnose a condition and recommend treatment. Because of its special nature, not all contacts and communications online fit the definition of psychotherapy, even when they take place between an expert and a consumer. It is important for online practitioners to understand clearly what constitutes therapy as opposed to an educational consult, such as expert opinion. Legally, the responsibility that a therapist has toward the client differs according to the nature of their relationship. A therapist conducting traditional, in-office treatment is usually also expected to act as the "case manager," responsible for assessing the general safety and well-being of the patient in treatment. However, such responsibilities are not required if the professional was contracted, for example, only to conduct an evaluation, give psychological testing, or provide an expert opinion. Clinicians who work online can serve the community in several ways. A passive website, for example, can provide information, educate, and/or recommend techniques/strategies/links for people to use as a source for self-help. An interactive site offers clients means of communication with a clinician, such as by email, chat room, telephone, or videoconferencing. Even when initial contact is made and a client communicates online with a professional, a therapeutic relationship may not yet be established. Clinicians have to decide what type of service they wish to provide online and clearly explain it to potential customers.

ETHICAL CONSIDERATIONS FOR ONLINE PRACTICE

A NEW MEDIUM: KNOW THE POTENTIAL, RECOGNIZE LIMITS, AND INFORM CLIENTS

The Internet and mobile communications revolution provides people with new ways to interact with each other. Today, people around the globe can communicate easily, directly, and immediately via text, voice, and even videoconferencing. Within the past several years, visitors to health and mental health websites have been able to locate and even communicate with various professionals online. Yet, when an individual practitioner or an organization is tempted to simply go online and offer professional service to the global community, it is crucial that they remember that not all clients and/or situations can or should be dealt with online. Some situations require in-office treatment or assessment. For example, it may be inappropriate to use the online modality with a client who poses a risk of danger to self or others. In times of emergency or when there is real threat to a person's well-being, online communications are an insufficient treatment modality. Following are some situations in which online consults are not recommended:

If a client has thoughts of hurting or killing him/herself.
If a client has thoughts of hurting or killing another.
If a client is in a life-threatening or emergency situation of any kind.
If a client has a recent history of suicidal, violent, or abusive behavior.
If a client holds what others may consider unrealistic beliefs
　　(delusions).
If a client sees or hears things that others don't (hallucinations).
If a client is actively abusing alcohol or drugs.

More about the considerations regarding appropriateness of service online can be found at the website of the International Society for Mental

Health Online, in a section called Assessing a Person's Suitability for Online Therapy, available at http://ismho.org/casestudy/ccsgas.htm (Suler et al., 2001).

It is important for online clinicians to clearly explain the medium's limits to visitors and potential clients, as well as advise how and where f2f evaluation and/or help can be obtained in times of need. A responsible clinician must become acquainted with the extant professional literature about online counseling, with particular attention to the effectiveness of treatment and outcome studies. Not only should an ethical clinician know about the medium, current research findings, and limits, but this knowledge must also be shared with clients. Clients should understand the potential risks and benefits of online counseling, in order to make an informed decision. Clinicians should discuss with the client the effectiveness, limits, and risks, as well as point out the availability and effectiveness of alternative treatment. More about the suitability of a client for online services can be found on the ISMHO.org site, in the Case Study Group section (see http://ismho.org/casestudy/ccsgas.htm).

THE POSSIBILITY OF IN-OFFICE CARE AND A CONTINGENCY ARRANGEMENT

When a clinician responds to a request for service online, it is still important to consider the possibility of f2f sessions. Not only could an initial intake (or even continued care) in the actual office be potentially more beneficial, but online clinicians also need to recognize that the f2f modality may be required at some point. Even if a new online client is not experiencing a crisis when making first contact, clinicians should remember that although a client may not actively be in crisis when contracting the service, anyone might sometimes experience an emotionally overwhelming situation that requires more intensive care. Thus, clinicians have to assess the suitability of potential clients for online care and also inform the client that in-office services may be required. A responsible therapist should accept a client into his/her care only if:

(a) both parties agree that the therapist is within reasonable geographical distance from the client and can thus provide in-office care if the need arises; or

(b) both parties agree upon a contingency referral arrangement for cases when in-office care is required.

WHY IT IS IMPORTANT TO KNOW THE IDENTITY OF AN ONLINE CLIENT

One characteristic of the Internet medium is that people can use it to communicate with relative anonymity. One can easily register an email identity and begin communicating through an e-identity, an alter-self online that need not reveal the writer's real name. Much like the experience in a confessional booth, some people actually relish the fact that their listener does not see them or know their identity when unloading sensitive information. In fact, by their nature, online contacts are already known to facilitate more direct, less inhibited communications (Suler, 2002) and, due to the safety that is created by physical distance between the parties, may also be helpful for those who find it difficult to openly discuss intimate or sensitive issues (Budman, 2000). Although online communication and fictional names allow for some level of anonymity when requesting service, it would be problematic for clinicians to therapeutically engage with clients whose identity they don't know. The reason behind this requirement needs to be understood by both clinician and client.

There are two main reasons why a responsible clinician should insist on knowing the identity of the online caller. The first consideration is the client's safety: it is necessary to enable the clinician to offer concrete intervention if/when such is needed. When a therapeutic relationship exists, clinicians are usually obligated to try to protect their clients from harming self or others. At times, clinicians may even have to take active steps to prevent harm, such as contacting the client at home over the telephone, calling a relative of the client, or consulting with other agencies, such as a hospital or an emergency service. To comply with the need to safeguard their clients, clinicians who work online should know who their clients really are so that they have the ability to establish contact with the client (or his or her emergency contacts) through means other than email in times of crisis or danger. The second reason clinicians online need to know the identity of their clients is to avoid dual relationship. Clinicians are usually advised against entering a therapeutic relationship with a colleague or family member because this dual relationship may interfere with the intimate process of mental health treatment. Dual relationships are prohibited for clinicians and compromise the effectiveness of counseling for the client.

DELIVERING CLINICAL SERVICES ACROSS STATE JURISDICTIONAL LINES

The Internet allows people and organizations to post information or availability of services to the public on the World Wide Web. The ease in which people can access information, get services, and communicate gives many the illusion of proximity. It is almost as if cyberspace were a different dimension in which geographic, national, cultural, and other boundaries disappear, leaving many with the feeling that they are citizens of one interconnected global community. And yet, when it comes to the provision of professional services online, clinicians must respect the limitations of their licenses and malpractice insurance policies. Simply put, online clinicians may provide professional care only to those clients who reside in the state(s) or province(s) in which the practitioner is licensed or certified. The reason for that restriction is a legal one: the governing state agency that issues the professional license can only authorize practice in that particular state. Further, in most cases the clinician's professional malpractice insurance is valid only if the clinician practices within the scope of his or her license. In other words, providing service to clients from another state where the clinician is not licensed may automatically violate the terms imposed by the insurer. In turn, the professional malpractice insurance company may not be obligated to cover any legal expenses or damages if a clinician was found guilty of malpractice while serving residents of states where he or she is not licensed to practice. Though the temptation to accept calls online from anywhere does exist, a responsible clinician should not risk being sued in the client's state, where the regulations might be different than in the clinician's state. Traveling to a trial in another state, perhaps hundreds of miles away (where the online client may reside), without the reassuring protection of a malpractice insurance policy is a risk not many would care to take.

So far, recipients of mental health services online in the United States have not complained about unsatisfactory practices by mental health providers. This, however, should not be reason to encourage professional service across state lines. As the modality gains recognition, a case involving practice across state lines online may be eventually brought to the attention of a court. In cases where no better, local alternatives exists, such as for residents of very remote or rural areas, a responsible clinician should remember to explain to clients the limits of the medium in general, and of the inability to have f2f sessions should such be required.

Once clients are made aware of the limits and restrictions, local resources, and alternatives, they still have a right to consult a distant expert, if they so choose and if the practitioner is willing to take the risk. Clinicians and clients should be aware of the difference between communications which are for specific education, referral, or information purposes, and those that can be called therapy or treatment.

One legal way for clinicians online to broaden the scope of their practice is to try to obtain a license in neighboring states. In some instances, states do recognize a license issued by another, a situation often referred to as reciprocity. Obtaining a license to practice (as well as to be insured) in more than one state may be a solution for some clinicians. There seems to be movement toward making a clinical license transferable and valid throughout the United States, but we are not quite there yet. In recent years, much through the efforts of an organization called the National Register of Health Care Providers in Psychology, some provinces and states have adopted a mechanism by which reciprocity (i.e., the recognition of a license from one state as valid by another) is made possible. Unfortunately, it may take years before U.S. clinicians can transfer their professional credentials between all states with the same ease as they can, for example, transfer a driver's license. Until that time, clinicians are recommended to serve clients where they are licensed to practice, or at least recognize the serious risks should they choose not to do so.

UNDERSTANDING RISKS TO CONFIDENTIALITY OF ONLINE COMMUNICATIONS

The World Wide Web is a network of computers that allows storage and transmission of data (see Chapter 5). One of the benefits of the communications revolution is that the public is able to avoid postage when sending messages online. Hard to imagine nowadays, the word *email* was not even a familiar term only a decade ago. As convenient as it is, the wonderful world of email is not all that perfect. For one, an email message is not quite like a letter one puts inside an envelope and slips into a regular mailbox. Email is more like a postcard, which many handlers may view. Experience showed me that no harm was done to my privacy and good reputation even after I sent numerous postcards over the years to friends and relatives. However, great embarrassment was caused when a private note to a girl I loved was read by others for whom it was not intended. In other words, email is not always private and people should try to avoid exposing details that may be embarrassing or damaging. Whereas childhood love notes could cause only limited embarrassment in my junior high school class, similar mishaps online could cause greater harm, because they could be circulated globally.

One simple and often inexpensive way to protect yourself is to download one of the email encryption software packages. Although security systems are never totally perfect, when the client and clinician both use encryption while communicating, privacy is increased. Another way to guard against privacy violations is to communicate using an online counseling platform that already provides an extra measure of privacy for secure chat and email. To maintain ethical service, online clinicians should inform themselves about and advise clients of the potential risks to confidentiality in regard to Internet transmissions.

Although experience shows that many clients do not worry much about confidentiality when using regular email, it is the responsibility of the clinician to explain the limits to privacy of such communications and offer alternatives. Session notes and other documentation gathered online should not be sent to another account or to a supervisor without using the same protection as to the client's privacy. Clinicians who conduct realtime text-based sessions through an existing product should check that the software/ network they are using is designed to maintain privacy, that it includes the ability for encryption, and that records of the sessions are not made or shared by a third party.

The last item discussed is important, because some providers/software/systems do, indeed, keep track of all communications that go through. When evaluating a network's virtual office, or considering which communications product to use, clinicians must be careful to ascertain that records of their sessions and communications will not be made and/or kept somewhere on the system so that privacy is observed. Clinicians can and should take notes as they work with clients. To assure privacy of records, clinicians also have to protect the records after the session. Thus, notes from online (and other) communications should not be kept in the clinician's computer (hard drive), but on a protected disc that can be safely locked elsewhere according to current regulations.

THE LIMITS OF CONFIDENTIALITY

Confidentiality and its limits are important issues to understand for people considering treatment. In general, professional therapists strictly maintain confidentiality. In fact, therapists are required by law, professional regulations, and ethical codes to maintain their clients' confidentiality. Laws, professional regulations, and ethical codes governing exceptions vary by state and profession, but some general information about the limits of confidentiality that may be useful to potential clients includes:

In all states, therapists must report to authorities suspected child abuse or neglect (see www.ReportChildAbuse.com for links and instructions).

In some states, therapists must report to authorities suspected abuse of elders, spousal abuse, and sexual misconduct by other therapists.

If a client poses an imminent risk to self or others, therapists are required to inform those who can assist in managing the risk, including those put at risk by the client, emergency medical service, and/or appropriate authorities.

If clients become involved in certain types of legal proceedings, therapists may be required to respond to demands by an attorney or by the courts for otherwise confidential information about such clients. These proceedings may include, for example, cases where clients place their psychological condition at issue, child custody disputes, civil commitment hearings, lawsuits by a client against the therapist, and court-ordered treatments.

If clients themselves request information about their treatment or their treatment records, or give consent to the therapist to release that information to others, such as to the health insurance carrier or other treating agencies, therapists generally must comply with their clients' wishes.

KEEPING PRIVATE COMMUNICATIONS AND DATA SECURE

By law, clinicians and organizations are now required to keep clients' private information secure and private (see Health Insurance Portability and Accountability [HIPAA] regulations at www.hhs.gov/ocr/hipaa/ privrulepd.pdf) when it is maintained or transmitted online. Thus, when considering a venue or product through which to conduct online consultations, clinicians should make sure that it includes a way to protect the security of confidential data transmissions and storage. Sites and products that allow authorized access with a password usually also mention the level of encryption security that is used. Common for adequate security today are products/sites with a 128-bit encryption level, but some already offer a 1024-bit encryption level and higher. The level of security being developed for secure access and transmission of data is expected to continue to rise. Similar to the need to periodically update psychological testing tools, clinicians online should try to stay current with their security technology. Occasionally updating security features for communications and data will help ensure that privacy is adequately protected. Network-type sites often offer built-in security solutions that include firewall-type protection and other security measures. Good security is usually quite costly, and the price continues to rise in direct correlation with the level of the protective measure's sophistication. Still, experience shows that no security system is completely safe forever, although the security industry is prosperous and works to prove otherwise. An ethical clinician will therefore explain to a client how access to data and communications is protected, as well as acknowledge the limits to even the best security. In general, it may be wise to try to keep as little information as possible in places that may become accessible to others.

WHO COVERS THE COST OF TREATMENT ONLINE?

In October 2001, Medicare (a U.S. federal health program) announced a change of its policy that would allow billing for online videoconferencing consults (even if *not* in realtime) at the same rate as it would for f2f consults (see http://www.openminds.com/IndustryResources/telehealth.htm). Although this was an important move in the right direction, text-based consults are still mostly not considered a reimbursable service by many insurance carriers. As a result, most users of the new medium have to cover the expense of consultation online out of their own pocket, usually with a credit card. Clinicians who provide online consults should clearly explain current reimbursement policies to their clients. Online clinicians should inform potential clients of the current limitations to online care with regard to third-party involvement in, or reimbursement for, online professional services.

It took some time before insurance companies recognized telephone consults as a billable, integral form of patient care activity. Today, time spent on the phone with a patient, with another expert, agency, or family member is recognized as a part of the service. It may not be long before more changes are made to alter existing policies of reimbursement. When more agencies add text-based and videoconferencing consults into what is considered an acceptable modality of service, it is estimated that clients would also be able to get insurance company confirmation for that service as well as do the billing directly online.

QUALITY ASSURANCE AND DISPUTE RESOLUTION

The main reason for ethical rules is to protect the public from harm. Because clinicians are licensed by a governing agency, such as a state certification board, it is that agency that clients may contact in case of a problem. Licensed clinicians must provide accurate information about their credentials, license, training, or certification to clients. In the real office, clinicians or agencies often post such documentation for public view. When clinicians work online, clients still have the same right to know who the provider is, what his or her credentials are, as well as where and how to proceed in situations regarding professional conduct. Responsible clinicians online will post information about their professional standing for the public to view, as well as show links to agencies that govern or supervise their work and license. Display of such links and information will allow patients to conduct further inquiries, in case a dispute about the quality of service, treatment procedure, diagnosis, billing practices, or any other issue cannot be resolved directly between the clinician and the client. In case a clinician is being supervised or consults with another professional or agency, the name and information about that supervising person/agency should also be available to clients. In cases concerning the quality of care, clients have the right to know where and how to apply for a resolution.

RECORD KEEPING

In most cases, clinicians are mandated to make and keep some treatment records of people in their care. Treatment and medical records of clients are confidential. Clinicians are usually bound by professional regulations to respect the privacy of their clients and adhere to certain precautions when handling and keeping treatment records. There should be no difference between the way clinicians keep and safeguard treatment records when communications take place online, over the telephone, or in f2f encounters. Online clinicians maintain records of clients who receive their service online using standard office procedures, (e.g., of such content and detail as are kept in the nonvirtual office).

MASTERY OF THE NEW MEDIUM

In a process similar to that of obtaining a driver's license, therapists must first fulfill certain requirements before they can become licensed to run an independent practice. The first requirement of clinicians-to-be is to demonstrate sufficient academic knowledge by successfully graduating from a recognized institution or program. Further, to be independent practitioners in the mental health field clinicians in most states also have to complete an intensive training program that includes many hours of supervised practice. After completing both the academic and supervised training requirements, clinicians must also pass qualifying tests to be awarded a professional license for independent practice. The long process of education, supervision, and training that therapists are required to complete is designed mainly to ensure that clinicians are well prepared in both theory and practice, and thus qualified to provide responsible service to the public. Even after being licensed, clinicians who face a situation that requires a form of treatment they are not sufficiently trained for are obligated to acquire the needed skill, consult an expert, or refer the client to an expert, so that the best possible treatment is provided.

The new medium of online consulting is similar to a new treatment technique that needs to be mastered. To ensure mastery and understanding of the medium, online clinicians must acquire technical skills, get consultation, or contract to practice under an experienced supervisor prior to providing professional services online.

ISSUES OF PRIVACY: THE HIPAA REGULATIONS

After little or no regulation existed to monitor online operations for some years after the field emerged, the new HIPAA regulations now regulate the ways in which private patient information should be handled when it is delivered and stored online. In essence, the HIPAA regulations require that practitioners and services who handle or transfer patient data online must observe rules of privacy and also inform their patients about the procedure, safeguards, and risks to privacy that may be involved. As a federal initiative probably crafted by skilled attorneys and other professionals, the HIPAA regulations take a global and conservative approach; the regulations maintain that a local state rule, if it protects the privacy of patients better than required by the HIPAA regulations, would supercede the latter. The HIPAA regulations are explained in detail and over hundreds of pages, yet the basic principle of informed consent and observance of the privacy of confidential information is not a new concept for most clinicians. (For more information about the HIPAA regulations, see www.hhs.gov/ocr/hipaa/privrulepd.pdf.)

SUMMARY

Licensed clinicians are obligated to follow their state and professional association's ethics regulations when serving the public. Consultation online is a new medium and regulations in the field are still forming. Careful adherence to existing rules as well as compliance with considerations discussed in this chapter will ensure that clinicians and professional organizations serve the community responsibly. In addition to review of state(s) and professional board(s) manuals, you may also consider exploring some of the following sites:

The American Psychological Association: http://www.APA.org (ethics page at http://www.apa.org/ethics/stmnt01.html)
The American Psychiatric Association: http://www.psych.org
The Ethics Code: http://www.EthicsCode.com
The International Society for Mental Health Online: http://ismho.org/suggestions.html
The American Association of Marital & Family Therapists: http://www.AAMFT.org (ethics page at http://www.aamft.org/resources/LRMPlan/Ethics/ethicscode2001.htm)
The National Association of Social Workers: http://www.socialworkers.org (ethics page at https://www.socialworkers.org/pubs/code/default.asp)
The National Board of Certified Counselors: http://www.nbcc.org (ethics statement at http://www.nbcc.org/depts/ethicsmain
The American Counseling Association: http://www.counseling.org/resources/internet.htm.

Because the field is still forming, clinicians would be wise to continue to monitor the relevant regulations related to online counseling as well as observe occasional updates.

GUIDE FOR FURTHER STUDY AND SOME RECOMMENDATIONS

UNDERSTAND THE REGULATIONS

Online counseling is a relatively new field. State boards, federal institutions, insurance carriers, and professional associations are still evaluating their policies as more data is gathered. Clinicians should therefore understand current regulations as well as occasionally review them, because policies that relate to online consultations are periodically updated. It would be wise to check the regulatory body and/or the professional organization's website for the most updated version of the policies and regulations. Clinicians and organizations should both understand as well as follow the recommended guidelines related to work online.

WORK CAREFULLY AND WITHIN ETHICAL LIMITS

Clinicians must work within the limits of their license and malpractice insurance. In most cases, this means that clinicians limit their online practice to serving clients who reside within their state. Clinicians also should keep in mind that not all situations can be effectively dealt with online and clients may require in-office care or other forms of intervention at some point. Before launching a practice into cyberspace, it would be wise to first become familiar with the current laws as well as adopt and/or display an ethics policy. Clinicians may elect to adhere to existing guidelines, such as those at www.HONCode.org or www.EthicsCode.com, for example, or display their own policy for the public. If a clinician or organization elects to write their own version of an ethics policy, such principles should reflect current professional guidelines.

Before initiating service, online clinicians should prepare various forms and information for clients that would guarantee the clarity of the procedure. Some forms that the online clinician should have include: Informed Consent to Treatment, an Intake form, Patient Bill of Rights, Consent to Release of Information, Treatment Plan, Understanding Limits to Treatment and Privacy Online, and the like. These forms can be sent or shown to potential clients online to reduce the risk of misunderstanding.

LEARN MORE ABOUT THE ONLINE MEDIUM—ITS LIMITS AND BENEFITS—AND EDUCATE CLIENTS

Clinicians continuously expand their understanding and the online counseling field is still growing. Clinicians need to follow developments in the field on a regular basis, so that new discoveries, risks, techniques, or regulations do not go unnoticed. Further, clinicians understand that covering the educational–theoretical component is but the first step to acquiring the skills needed to become proficient in the new medium. Clinicians should review relevant literature and use the links recommended throughout this book for further study. Clinicians should try to stay current with recent research, recommendations, and discoveries. It would also be important to explain the limits and risks involved in online counseling to potential clients.

CONTINUE TO EDUCATE SELF AND OTHERS

Reading this book is one good way to become more familiar with the concept of online counseling. Clinicians who believe in the potential of this medium to improve service, availability, and communication with clients should remember that many in the professional community are still unsure about this form of service. Thus, once clinicians are knowledgeable, they may need to educate others, such as colleagues, supervisors, and administrators, about the benefits and risks involved in online counseling. It is quite possible that patients, who already use email and are known to seek health information online, will need little more encouragement to use the new service than, perhaps, the provision of the clinic or clinician's virtual address. Still, clients, too, will need to be informed and educated about benefits and limits of the medium when such are offered. One of the nice things about work online is that resources are quite easily accessed. The National Institute of Mental Health (NIMH.org), for example, has a patient education page that may serve as a model for individuals and organizations that aim to set such a service. For details, see http://www.nimh.nih.gov/practitioners/patinfo.cfm.

PROMOTE HIGHER STANDARDS OF PRACTICE ONLINE

Since the Internet first started to expand in popularity, many have placed Web pages online to offer services to the public. Some of these sites were or are still wonderful initiatives; some ended up evaporating and/or gave the professional community a bad reputation. Clinicians need to carefully follow their state and professional associations ethics regulations when providing service online. More important, clinicians need to demonstrate professional practice when working online and promote the same for the community.

KEY TERMS

Brand name: A term taken from the business and marketing fields that means a product or company name is known to the public and is associated with a certain reputation.

Case management: A term used in the mental health field that means that a clinician has responsibility for assessing, facilitating, and monitoring the patient's overall functioning.

Dual relationship: A therapeutic relationship with a colleague or family member, for example, would create an undesired situation in which more than one relationship exists. Dual relationships are prohibited for clinicians because they may compromise the effectiveness of counseling for the client.

Confidentiality: A term that means people have a right for privacy when they are receiving health care services. Confidentiality may be breeched by clinicians if clients give written consent to release of information, in case real danger to self or others exist, or if a clinician is mandated to answer to a court of law.

Diagnosis: A term adopted from the medical field, which means that a classification of a condition or disorder was made. Treatment cannot start before a diagnosis is made.

Dispute resolution: The due process by which disagreements are resolved if clients raise grievances against a clinician to a governing agency.

Emergency and crisis situations: In the mental health field, crisis and risk situations are those in which real danger to self or others exist. In crisis situations, clinicians are mandated to take concrete steps to protect clients and others from harm.

Encryption: A way to transfer or keep information after it is coded, usually to increase security and privacy.

Ethics: Principles of appropriate, correct, and just behavior among members of the human family.

Ethics regulations: A code of professional conduct that organizations require their members to know and follow.

Firewall: A term used in the Internet security world that means a host server is protected from unauthorized entries.

HIPAA regulations: Federal regulations that specify how health and mental health should be handled and protected so that patient privacy is maintained.

Informed consent: Describes the process by which a person is being educated about a suggested procedure and gets a fair opportunity to consider it.

Internet: The Internet is a network of computers that are interconnected. The network allows the global community to access, store, process, and transfer vast amounts of data. With the Internet, citizens of the global community have easy, immediate, and almost unlimited access to people, information, products, and services online.

Jurisdiction line: A term that defines the physical boundaries of the legal authority to practice.

Nonverbal communication: Nonverbal communication is our body language and everything we communicate besides the spoken word: posture, gestures, dress and appearance, facial expressions, and the like. Nonverbal communication is considered important for us to correctly "read" and understand each other. Nonverbal communication is important to understanding the total message and does not exist in text-based communications.

Psychotherapy: A term used in the mental health field to describe the personal as well as interpersonal process that aims to help people better understand and cope with situations, emotions, or perceptions. Psychotherapy is a process of communication and dialogue that may focus on understanding and better handling of both intrapersonal and interpersonal issues. Psychotherapy may help people enhance the ability to cope, improve understanding and regulation of emotions, and/or enable personal growth. Still, psychotherapy doesn't always produce the same results for everyone.

State-issued license: An official document issued by a state that certifies that an individual has passed all requirements, including education, training, and supervision, and was found qualified to hold a license to practice the profession.

Supervision: In the health and mental health field, clinicians use the experience of senior colleagues while training and when working to monitor the work or enhance skills.

Therapy: A broad term that usually relates to the process of healing or recovering.

REFERENCES

American Psychological Association (1997). *APA statement on services by telephone, teleconferencing and Internet.* Retrieved November 1, 2002 from http://www.apa.org/ethics/stmnt01.html.

American Counseling Association (ACA). Retrieved August 28, 2003 from http://www.counseling.org/site/PageServer?pagename=resources_internet.

Budman, S. H. (2000). Behavioral health care dot-com and beyond: Computer-mediated communications in mental health and substance abuse treatment. *American Psychologist*, 55:1290–1300.

Department of Health and Human Services, Office of the Secretary (2002). Standard of Privacy of Individually Identifiable Health Information. Federal Register, Vol. 67, No. 157, Wednesday, August 14, 2002/Rules and Regulations. Retrieved August 28, 2003 from http://www.hhs.gov/ocr/hipaa/privrulepd.pdf.

Eysenbach, G. (2000). Towards ethical guidelines for e-health. *Journal of Medical Internet Research, 2* (1), March 31, e7. Retrieved August 28, 2003, from http://www.jmir.org/2000/1/e7/index.htm.

Godin, S. (1996). *The official rules of life: For those of you who thought you'd mastered life's little instructions and learned everything you needed to know.* New York: Simon & Schuster, Fireside, USA.

Health on the Net Foundation (HON). Retrieved August 28, 2003, from http://www.hon.ch/HONcode/Conduct.html.

Hornby, A. S., Gatenby, E. V., & Wakefield, H. (1971). *The advanced learner's dictionary of current English.* London: Oxford University Press.

International Society for Mental Health Online (ISMHO). Retrieved August 28, 2003, from http://www.ismho.org/casestudy/ccsgas.htm.

International Society for Mental Health Online (ISMHO). Retrieved August 28, 2003, from http://www.ismho.org/suggestions.html.

Internet Healthcare Coalition (IHC). Retrieved August 28, 2003, from http://www.ihealthcoalition.org/ethics/draftcode.html.

National Board of Certified Counselors (NBCC). Retrieved August 28, 2003, from http://www.nbcc.org/ethics/webethics.htm.

Rippen, H., & Risk, A. (2000). E-Health Code of Ethics: Policy Proposal. *Journal of Medical Internet Research*, Feb. 29, 2(1), e2. Retrieved August 23, 2003, from http://www.jmir.org/2000/2/e9.

Stricker, G. (1996). Psychotherapy in cyberspace. *Ethics and Behavior, 6*, 169, 175–177.

Suler, J., Barak, A., Chechele, P., et al. (2001). Assessing a person's suitability for online therapy. *CyberPsychology & Behavior*, 4:675–679. (See Correction, 2002, *CyberPsychology & Behavior*, 5, p. 93.)

Suler, J. (2002). The basic psychological features of cyberspace. *The Psychology of Cyberspace* (orig. pub. 1996). Retrieved August 23, 2003, from www.rider.edu/users/~suler/psycyber/basicfeat.html.

Suler, J. (2002). The online disinhibition effect. *The Psychology of Cyberspace* (orig. pub. 1996). Retrieved August 28, 2003, fromhttp://www.rider.edu/users/~suler/psycyber/disinhibit.html.

Taylor, H. (1999). Explosive growth of cyberchondriacs continues. Harris Interactive. Retrieved August 28, 2003, from http://www.harrisinteractive.com/harris_poll/index.asp?PID=117.

Taylor, H. (2002). Internet penetration increases to 66% of adults (137 million). Harris Interactive. Retrieved August 28, 2003, from http://www.harrisinteractive.com/news/allnewsbydate.asp?NewsID=451.

7

THE BUSINESS ASPECTS
OF ONLINE COUNSELING

RON KRAUS AND JASON S. ZACK

Those who are involved in show business know that without the business, there would be no show. In other words, a business must make some cents if it is to survive. This chapter explores some of the economic considerations, potential risks, and business opportunities related to online mental health counseling.

THE INDUSTRY: HEALTH CARE IN THE UNITED STATES

Let us examine the marketplace in which online counseling operates. The health care industry is the single largest segment of the U.S. economy, estimated to generate some $1.5 trillion annually (Itagaki, Berlin, & Schatz, 2002). A study by the World Health Organization, the World Bank, and Harvard University reported that "mental illness, including suicide, accounts for over 15% of the burden of disease in established market economies, such as the United States. This is more than the disease burden caused by all cancers" (Murray & Lopez, 1996).

Clearly, health and mental health care expenses cost the economy dearly and burden the market in many ways, both direct and indirect. Ways to improve the quality of the health care system while at the same time cutting costs have long been sought and are desperately needed. In a recent publication, the Committee of Quality Health Care in America (2001) stated that, among other ways to cut spending while improving access and service, the use of information technology seems to be one of the most promising solutions. Similar conclusions about the benefits of online practice are also expressed by others (Ritterband et al., 2003). After some initial hesitation, it seems that the health care industry now has an official mandate to change with the times and get online. Indeed, as any search engine can show, many organizations, universities, and hospitals are already serving the community via the Net.

WHAT IS TELEHEALTH? WHAT ARE THE BENEFITS OF SERVICES ONLINE?

The market appeal of delivering online clinical services is plain to see. The Internet allows us to communicate with ease, because in cyberspace we "transcend troublesome boundaries like economic status, culture, climate, geography, or even warfare" (Stamm, 1998). When the idea of providing clinical mental health services online was initially explored and considered, several writers in the health and mental health fields referred to the concept by different names. Writers coined a variety of terms like telemedicine, tele-health, e-therapy, cybertherapy, text-based communication, online counseling, and behavioral telehealth, among others. One of the difficulties in trying to learn about the medium is that individuals differ on exactly what online services entail. As is the case when evaluating anything, it is also instructive to consider the potential influence of the disciplines of those writing the definitions in order to get a better understanding of that particular perspective. Stamm (1998) made the following attempt to define the terms and cope with the confusion:

> Arriving at definitions in this emerging field is difficult. Telemedicine is gener-ally the more restrictive of the two terms and refers to the use of electronic com-munications and information technology to provide or support clinical care at a distance (U.S. Department of Commerce, 1997). The broader term, telehealth, encompasses telemedicine and other health care–related activities including health education, administration, and training.

In the world of "telemedicine," mental health care is usually discussed in terms of psychiatry. And because the medical industry is flooded with cash from pharmaceutical companies, many consumers turn to medical-focused websites (e.g., WebMD) for mental health information. Unfortu-nately, this leaves nonpsychiatrists, the bulk of mental health therapists, conspicuously out. Consequently, perhaps, Nickelson (1998) defined tele-health as "the use of telecommunications and information technology to provide access to health assessment, diagnosis, intervention, consultation, supervision, education and information across distance" (p. 527). Moreover, he advocated using the term "behavioral telehealth" when the topic is restricted to the behavioral aspects of health care (as opposed to the more restrictive term "telepsychiatry" often used by the medical community). Whatever term you opt to use, it is important to understand the industry forces involved and the discipline that the term implicates.

Psychologists and other mental health professionals use the Internet to interact with clients in a number of ways. Their work involves myriad activities, including (but not limited to) assessment, psychotherapy, substance abuse counseling, crisis intervention, patient education, case management, and medication support (DeLeon et al., 1991; DeLeon & Wiggins, 1996). Psychologists also conduct research and teach online. Consulting psychologists generally interact with their corporate clients via email and other Net-enabled services. Reports and invoices are emailed, and often payment is collected via Web payment services.

Some states allow clinical supervision to be offered via telecommunications devices (Administrative Rules of Montana, 1995). State and federal laws have begun to provide for reimbursement of direct clinical care conducted electronically (Nickelson, 1998).

Although the infamous dot-com boom and crash early in 2000 affected numerous entrepreneurial industry pioneers, many hospitals, universities, clinics, individuals, and nonprofit organizations continued to expand their online presence. The reasons for this phenomenon seem to include several factors: the growing spread of Internet use; the public's continued interest in getting direct and immediate access online; and the realization by industry leaders that information technology and online services are a cost-effective way to improve the health care system. As with many human activities, the primary motivators are greed and need. Whereas investors are wary of risky ventures like music-sharing and online pet supply stores, consumers will always require health care services, regardless of the vicissitudes of the marketplace.

In a recent Delphi study, a panel of expert psychologists predicted that Internet therapy services would be the second fastest growing mental health development in the next decade (Norcross, Hedges, & Prochaska, 2002). Thus it seems that there is some reason to believe that the growth trend in online mental health is likely to continue.

THE SEARCH FOR HELP ONLINE

We have seen that professionals and organizations are gradually embracing online service delivery, but what about consumers? To see the big picture we may need to take a historical perspective of the Internet. The Internet created a cultural revolution by allowing the public to have immediate and direct access to other people, information, and resources. The popularity of the Internet cannot be denied. Use of the medium has grown rapidly since the Net was made available to the public in the 1990s. According to Mediamark Research, Inc., in 2000:

Approximately 133 million U.S. adults—66% of the adult population—have access to the Internet either at work or home. Of those 133 million, 101 million reported using the Internet in the past 30 days. This means that 50% of U.S. adults, who total 201.7 million, used the Internet in the past 30 days. (See http://www.media-mark.com/mri/TheSource/sorc2001_05.htm.)

Access to educational and professional services online appears to command an equally high degree of public interest:

Fifty-two million American adults, or 55% of those with Internet access, have used the Web to get health or medical information. We call them "health seekers" and a majority of them go online at least once a month for health information. A great many health seekers say the resources they find on the Web have a direct effect on the decisions they make about their health care and on their interactions with doctors . . . Ninety-one percent of health seekers have looked for information about a physical illness or condition and 26% have looked for information about a mental health issue like depression or anxiety. . . . (PewInternet.org)

Taylor (2000) reported that the number of people who went online to search for health care information nearly doubled, to 100 million, from 1998 to 2000. Increases have continued.

Finally, a Louis Harris & Associates company poll showed that 66% of the 66 million adults who accessed the Internet in 1999 also sought information about health care topics such as depression and cancer. Relevant to the present discussion, four of the top ten most searched health topics on the Internet were related to mental health. The 2002 Harris poll also found that nearly 90% of people with Internet access expressed a wish to communicate with their physicians online to ask questions, set up appointments, refill prescriptions, and get test results (Foreman, 2003).

Although different polls produce different statistics, it remains clear that millions of people regularly go online in search for help. The public's need for health and mental health services, and the potential for online communications to benefit them, has not gone unnoticed by people in the health care industry. Since they first learned of the Internet, many clinicians and organizations have begun to offer services and/or information online. Still, as only a small percentage of the total number of providers is active in serving clients online, it seems that the online revolution in health care is but starting.

Although the promise of the new medium seems obvious, it is instructive to consider a few examples of those who tried and failed to capitalize on the online mental health market (e.g., eTherapy.com and Here2Listen.com, discussed in Chapter 3). Several factors contributed to these companies' failure, including unwise budget allocation, difficulties completing the technology platform, lack of a focused goal or business model, and minimal marketing efforts. The expected traffic and resultant revenues didn't materialize as quickly as hoped. Together with the dot-com bust of 2000, these problems caused existing investors to lose trust and pull

out, and made new investors impossible to find. Still, while some online projects withered, other operations have been able to continue and operate
even during the dot-com drought. In fact, reports from clinicians involved
with organizations such as the International Society for Mental Health
Online (ISMHO) suggest that some more modest companies are getting by,
and certain individual clinicians are building and maintaining successful
private practices made up of nearly 100% online clients.

THE NUMBERS: U.S. CLINICIANS/INTERNET
AND INCOME

The appeal of the Internet to both professionals and consumers is clear,
but one should consider the size of the market, opportunities, and risks
before contemplating an ambitious project. Tables 7.1 and 7.2 show data
provided by OnlineClinics.com about the estimated market size and some
details about U.S. mental health providers in 2000.

Taking a cautious estimate only to demonstrate the new market's potential, one may recognize from the tables that even if a small percentage of
client–professional interactions were handled online, a significant market
would exist. For example, if only 10% of clients who seek mental health
professionals or services found these online, it would mean a market of
more than $1.1 billion annually. Further, as direct access can save time,
eliminate the need to travel, and significantly reduce overhead costs, such

TABLE 7.1   Size of U.S. National Market: Mental Health Professionals

	Size of Population in the United States	Average Annual Income	In Private Practice	Gross Annual Private Practice Revenues	Overall Gross Revenues (Billions)	Online
Psychologists	74,000	$ 55,000	57,000	$3.1B	$4.1	70%*
Social Workers	155,000	$ 35,000	Data not available	Data not available	$5.4	70%*
Psychiatrists	40,500	$ 170,000	Data not available	Data not available	$6.9	70%*

Note: In addition to the above, there are also some 25,000 Professional Counselors and
a similar number of Marriage and Family Therapists, who are not always classified as mental
health professionals by state boards, yet they provide similar types of service within a
narrow specialization.

About 57,000 psychologists in private practice provide about 52 million hours of therapy
sessions every year for almost 3.7 million patients. The average cost of a 45-minute therapy
session is $60.

TABLE 7.2   Size of National Market Adjusted to Level of Internet Penetration (70%)*

	Size of Population in the United States	Average Annual Income	In Private Practice	Gross Annual Private Practice Revenues (Billions)	Overall Gross Revenues (Billions)
Psychologists	52,000	$ 55,000	40,000	$2.2	$2.9
Social Workers	108,000	$ 35,000	Data not available	Data not available	$3.8
Psychiatrists	28,000	$ 170,000	Data not available	Data not available	$4.8

*Estimate based on Internet penetration in population with graduate college degree and higher.

services can be offered at better rates, or leave a higher margin of profit with the service provider. If the rate of Internet use continues to grow as it has since about 1998, then up to 20% or more of all client–professional interactions could be done online by 2010. Such services could include selecting a clinician, scheduling a consultation, facilitating communications (email, chat, telephone, or videoconference), processing secure electronic billing, processing third-party payment claims, educating patients, training clinicians, and more.

Despite the potential and concomitant ballyhoo, skeptics continue to emphasize several factors that continue to curb the enthusiasm of optimists, who believe all clinicians will soon operate an office online. First, client participation might be limited by "the digital divide," which prevents many potential clients from having access to service. The other factor is the professional community's resistance to change and fear of the unknown. These two factors deserve some further clarification.

"The digital divide" refers to the inherent inequality of the Internet: While everyone is theoretically able to log on and use the Internet, it appears that the educated and affluent do it more. As a large portion of our global family hops on the "information superhighway," many, in fact, are left behind. Sadly, it is often the most needy who lack the ability, skill, or means to log on and locate resources with the rest of the Internet users. The digital divide basically separates those who have resources, knowledge, and Internet access from those who do not.

Resistance to change within some sectors of the professional community is another factor that may be slowing the growth of online counseling. An integral component of life, change is also somewhat mysterious, as it is both an end of something and a beginning of something new. As it represents the unknown that is yet to come, change is something many tend to resist.

It is quite natural to fear the unknown and thus we usually feel more secure repeating what we have experienced before and is familiar to us. In the United States, there are more than 650,000 professionals in the health care industry and about 250,000 licensed clinicians in the mental health field. In spite of the fact that more than 70% of health care professionals use the Internet (mostly for email, but also for education, shopping, news, etc.), it is estimated that no more than 5–10% of mental health clinicians are using the Internet to serve the public. When discussing the topic of online services that are provided by physicians, Foreman (2003) writes, "Patients are clamoring for it. Many doctors hate the idea." One reason that many clinicians are still uneasy with the new medium may be that they are unfamiliar with it and thus do not yet fully recognize the benefits that come from integrating interactive office management tools into the regular practice. With this handbook and similar publications as a guide for the new industry, it is expected that clinicians will eventually become more familiar and thus less apprehensive about integration of the relatively new medium.

SUMMARY

A tremendous need exists for services, information, and resources online. The public seems especially interested in topics and sites that relate to health and mental health. It appears that the health care industry is coming to realize the potential of online services, because these may improve service and also cut cost. With a gradual, continuous movement toward bringing more services online, the professional community is finally overcoming its initial hesitation to integrate and offer online services.

SETTING UP A PRACTICE ONLINE

REGISTERING A DOMAIN NAME

The most basic step required to set up a Web page online is to register a domain name (see Chapter 5). Domain names were originally managed and registered by a company called Network Solutions, but after some reorganization, dozens of companies are now authorized to offer domain names to registrants. Doing a search of "domain names" on any popular search engine will provide the names of many companies to choose from. It would be wise to shop around, get educated, and compare options before making the purchase. The various registrars of domain names can now compete with each other; thus, the cost of domain name registration remains relatively low—between $35 and $65 annually (depending on the company selling these, promotions, etc.). Another situation arises when one is looking for a valued name that was previously registered by someone and is now resold to the highest bidder. Ever since the days when domain names like Business.com were sold for about $5 million, many were tempted to think that "e- good domain name = e- gold mine." One should be careful to know the market and explore the average price asked on various registries before making a decision to buy. Although some clinicians may wish to buy a domain name that represents their business (such as www.AnalyzeThis.com, for example), others elect to be creative or simply put their first and last name, possibly with their professional title (such as www.DrJoesephSchmo.com). The options can be endless. By now, most distinctive and prized names are sold, held for the highest bidder, used by others, registered to inactive owners, or otherwise unavailable. Still, people should not be discouraged, as creative and thus successful solutions may work when looking to register a unique domain name. Remember the case of Joe Schmo (see above). In our experience, unless you are a big company looking to gain substantial market share, it is unnecessary to spend any more than $100 for a domain name that seems good to you. Another suggestion, however, is to choose a domain name that ends in either (preferably) .com or (second best) .net. Although other suffixes have become available over the years (such as .tv, .us, and .md), these are less likely to be remembered by consumers and colleagues.

THE VALUE OF A TRADEMARK

Once a domain name is registered to a user, annual or periodical renewals become necessary and are important to remember. To make sure a unique domain name is not being copied and/or misused by others, one may consider registering the domain name as a trademark with the U.S. Trademark Office. Such action is now possible online at: www.USPTO.gov.

The one-time registration costs a few hundred dollars, but it establishes ownership and can thus help eliminate later disputes, should such arise. If, for example, you are the trademark owner of www.AnalyzeThis.com, no one in the United States may use a site called www.AnalyzeThat.com, for example, and directly compete with your successful business. In most cases, clinicians who run a private practice do not need to register a trademark for their business or name. However, when setting up a website online, one must take into account the possibility, even if remote, that the site might reach the attention of many more people than a private practice normally would. A trademark registration assures that no other business is allowed to unfairly compete with your practice by using similar marks or names.

BUILDING A WEBSITE: FEATURES, TOOLS, BILLING, AND SECURITY

After registering a domain name, the next step to get online would be the construction of a website. Although websites are not strictly necessary to do online counseling (you could have a private practice that spreads by word of mouth and only communicate by email), they are the standard way that online counselors provide information to potential clients, and market their services. The process of building a website ranges from incredibly simple to profoundly complex, depending on what kind of functionality you want/need (see Chapter 5 for more information on the technical aspects of building a site). Often, Internet service providers (ISPs) or domain registrar companies also sell Web space and the option of using a website-builder tool. Such services make it easy to quickly generate a one- to five-page website even for users who are not professional designers or computer-savvy. Additional tools also allow users to add email accounts, shopping carts, and credit card processing capabilities to the site, if products or services are to be sold.

To ensure the security of billing and privacy of email transmissions, further steps must be taken. For example, clinicians can opt to download a free email security program and recommend the same to their clients, so that email communications are secured (encrypted) for better privacy. When credit card payments online are involved, clinicians need to open a merchant account with a bank account and make sure their domain online obtains a secure socket layer certificate (also called SSL), which assures users that financial activity related to charges on the site is being protected by that security seal/company (for more information on Internet security, see Chapter 5). Another solution would be to use a third-party service to manage credit card processing.

Sophisticated users may wish to design and create original Web pages of their own rather than use the do-it-yourself option offered by registries or professional networks. Regardless of who designs the site, the same considerations relating to security of payments and claims, and privacy of data transfers, must still be observed. Obviously, clinicians who elect to manage a website merely to post information or advertise their service (rather than interact and collect payment online) do not need to be as concerned about security as those who allow interaction and data transfer via a Web interface.

As of this writing, most activity online is done via text (chat or email) and telephone. As more consumers and professionals acquire faster Internet connections through cable or DSL, also called broadband, online interactions will probably include more videoconferencing. If both client and clinician have the capability for videoconferencing, the main issue to observe is the privacy of transmissions, which often depends on the third-party provider of that capability/service. More on the subject is available in Chapter 5.

PROMOTING THE VIRTUAL PRACTICE

Once a website is active online, with secure interaction and billing capabilities, the next task is to make sure the site is noticed and visited by potential clients. When it comes to determining the value of real estate, it is said that the three most important factors are location, location, and location. In the world of Net business, value is measured by three different components: traffic, traffic, and traffic. Millions of Web pages currently flicker in cyberspace, the result of the Internet big boom that started it all. Alas, to get attention from potential consumers in cyberspace, a site must somehow shine. To make an income and serve clients, a practitioner must see to it that visitors find, log on to, and use the site.

Clinicians may consider several ways to promote their website and service. Even those who do not care to spend money on costly marketing campaigns can still find ways to be noticed. First, it is important to submit details about the new site to a few major search engines, because this will get the service listed for potential clients who search the topic. Some search engines allow free entry/registration and one should try to get listed with as many such free services as possible. After all, these are free and may enhance exposure and traffic. Submission to a good spot with the most known search engines will involve a high fee. Some search engines are decent and charge a moderate annual fee. As the saying goes: advertisement pays (but it costs to advertise). A clinician needs to assess his or her budget and, accordingly, decide the best route to proceed. (See Chapter 5 for more about search engines.)

The next thing to consider is writing an introduction letter that will announce your new virtual office to as many colleagues, clients, family, and friends as you can. An introduction note online to all those who are on your email list could be a good way to spread the word. However, it is important to try to avoid sending unsolicited email to those who would not appreciate it (and consider it "spam"). One may consider politely asking recipients to pass the introduction on to others. Printing a new business card with your Web address for distribution to current clients or those who may refer potential clients is another good idea. Some clinicians also elect to be registered with one or more of the professional networks, so that more exposure is achieved from being listed and seen in more than one location as a service provider.

Given the capital, and the inclination to spend it, several other options are available to those who wish to promote their online practice with some initial investment. First, one can pay a large company, such as AOL or Yahoo, to place the site among the first results that appear when a key word is entered. Other alternatives include paid banners, printed brochures, or even consultation with marketing specialists to explore strategies for a media marketing campaign.

OFFICE MANAGEMENT

Once a client is assessed and a recommendation for treatment is accepted, a therapeutic relationship is established. As clinicians are mandated to keep treatment records of their clients, such documentation is also necessary when clients receive ongoing consultation online (see American Psychological Association [APA] Ethical Code). Similarly, clinicians document and report all income from professional activity and continue customary office management practices as with clients who are seen in the office. One-time email consults may not constitute a therapeutic relationship, but any income for such work must be recorded and reported. If you store your records in an electronic database or digital word processor files, consider encrypting or password-protecting all documents. There are many inexpensive programs (including shareware) that will allow you to do this easily. It may also be helpful to know that Microsoft Word allows you to save a file so that a password is required to open and/or modify it.

Clinicians who consider professional work online should make sure they are familiar with any privacy regulations for their state, province, or country, because these will outline the minimal requirements for safeguarding and transmitting clients' private electronic health records. (American clinicians might consider consulting the HIPAA regulations at www.hhs.gov/ocr/ hipaa/privrulepd.pdf.) Some simple suggestions to maintain privacy include:

Do not keep sensitive material available on the hard drive or online but on a securely stored disc.
Use encrypted email or password-protected webmail programs.
Be extra careful about all details before clicking "send."

Digital security is discussed further in Chapter 5.

TRAINING AND PREPARATION FOR THE NEW BUSINESS

To practice ethically and competently, clinicians are usually obligated to be careful when considering techniques and treatment strategies with which they are unfamiliar. As text-based consultation, telephone, and/or videoconferencing is a new practice for most clinicians trained in the traditional face-to-face (f2f) modality, professionals need to acquire the theoretical knowledge, get training, and develop skills before offering to serve the public. One way to start the process is by reading this book and others like it. Careful review of the relevant legal and ethical considerations involved in work online would be another important step to take before services are offered. Getting familiar with both the literature and regulations will ensure that fundamental knowledge is acquired. Another good way to become familiar with the online medium is to join a professional association, so that consultations and dialogue with colleagues in the field can become possible.

To practice and train for online work, one may consider having mock sessions with a colleague, or locating a program/course that teaches that subject. Another option is to go online to donate time and serve the public for free, simply to get some experience. Even if to make referrals only and possibly act as an intake coordinator of sorts, this will still provide some experience to those who wish to get the feel for the field. When training, clinicians should have a clinical supervisor or consider locating an experienced colleague to consult with. Clinicians in training should be careful to represent themselves accurately to clients and avoid making assessments or providing specific treatment recommendations online, as these would suggest a therapeutic relationship. An informed consent form, possibly with the details of a supervisor, would be a good way to assure that clients understand the limits of the interaction when a clinician in training provides services.

NETWORK MEMBERSHIP: BENEFITS AND RISKS

Clinicians or organizations can opt to build a practice online themselves, or they can (perhaps more easily) use an existing platform and join an online professional network (e.g., HelpHorizons.com, Find-a-Therapist.com, AAOP.com or OnlineClinics.com). There are several advantages to registering to work with an online counseling network. Clinicians who join a network can get a virtual office nearly instantly (depending on registration procedures, credential verification requirements, etc.), usually with all features in place for billing and secure interaction. Getting a ready-made virtual office saves the trouble of setting up a Web page from scratch. However, experience shows that there are also some precautions to keep in mind about these networks. As mentioned earlier, several much-ballyhooed online organizations have mushroomed and withered at amazing speed. At times, the announcement to fold was made out of the blue and in at least a few instances clinicians and clients were left desperate to find an alternative platform from which to continue working. One should be careful to join a group that is reputable in the online community and that has clearly stated commitment to quality and ethics. A group that has been around for 3 to 5 years is likely to be more known and possibly also more stable than one that has just gone online recently. It is also important to get a sense of who is running the business behind the scenes. Although clinicians do manage some organizations online, in some cases it is businesspeople who run operations, and clinicians are (or, were, if the operation closed) simply hired to do advise. When selecting a network with which to become affiliated, clinicians should be careful to avoid operations that charge a referral fee or have a fee-splitting policy, because such practice is usually forbidden in the field. One solution has been for networks to add a flat "usage fee," billed either by session to the client (as a surcharge) or monthly to the clinician (as "virtual rent"). Networks that lure clinicians to practice with them at no cost should also be looked at carefully, because experience shows that there are few things in life that are truly free. Because most networks only charge a moderate membership fee, some clinicians elect to register with more than one network. The benefit of multiple registrations is in increased exposure and the ability to have an alternative line to work through. It may, however, be difficult to juggle schedules and referrals from more than one source once a practice begins to get busy.

MALPRACTICE INSURANCE COVERAGE

Clinicians need to inquire with their professional liability insurance carrier if online consults are included as an acceptable modality for service. Because the field and online medium are relatively new, some companies still don't have online consults mentioned on their policies; others already do. Again, membership with an online association may help clinicians get updated information about the current state of the market. If your current carrier does not accept such work (be sure to ask!), it would be wise to get a professional liability policy that does cover this type of practice. Many professional liability insurance companies will cover online activities provided that the clinician practices within the scope of his or her license.

SETTING FEES

When a professional provides services to a client, some form of payment is usually required. In traditional, f2f practice, counselors charge clients by the hour, sometimes adopting a "sliding scale" policy to meet the needs of those with limited financial resources. Practitioners have adopted myriad approaches to charging for online services. There is no "best" or easy way to negotiate fees, but it is still important to openly discuss the issue with clients so that all sides are clear at the outset of your work together.

For example, consider email counseling. Because this modality is asynchronous, the fee can depend on a variety of factors, including length of response (in words), time to read the email, and time to respond to the email. Here are some approaches that are currently used:

Flat rate (e.g., $25) per email with no limit on length (from client or reply)
Flat rate per email, with response no longer than one page
Flat rate per email, with a set amount of time (e.g., 30 minutes) allowed for reading and responding to the message
Special rates for email packages (e.g., $30 each; three for $75)
Flat fee for unlimited emails over a set time period (e.g., 1 week)
First email free

It might seem that synchronous online counseling methods, like text-chat, would simply adopt the counselor's normal f2f rate. However, some therapists choose (or are encouraged by their networks) to offer lower fees in order to encourage business, and capitalize on the fact that online work may have lower infrastructure costs (e.g., office space, no commute, etc.).

DONATING PROFESSIONAL SERVICES

Issues related to payment and financial negotiations are not easy for many. Still, these issues are important to discuss so that misunderstandings are avoided. The APA recommends that its clinical members donate some free service to the community each year (pro bono work). Indeed, many therapists give to their communities, in the form of educational and/or consultation services. Many therapists in private practice also keep a sliding scale policy and try to be compassionate when negotiating a price with a client who is in need. When it comes to online work, a similar attitude can be considered. From a business standpoint, online clinicians generally try to work with their clients just as they would in the traditional office, so that service can be rendered professionally.

CONCLUSION AND SUMMARY

Based on the market projections and interest from consumers and professionals alike, there seems to be great potential in the online counseling business. However, in order to achieve success it is necessary to consider the many options, learn the new market, and study its history. Learning from the mistakes of the past will help avoid repeating these in the future.

KEY TERMS

Behavioral telehealth: A suggested term used to describe mental health related activities and services that are delivered to clients online.

Broadband: A new term coming from the Internet world that means the ability to transfer large amounts of information over short periods of time. The most common consumer broadband connections to the Internet are cable and DSL.

Domain name: A registered address on the Internet, usually the first step that allows users the creation of a website on that domain.

Digital divide: A term used to describe the difference between those with the means to access the Internet and those who cannot enjoy the benefits of modern technology.

Information Technology (IT): A new field that developed greatly because of the growth of the Internet, information technology involves the use of computers and communications online to create, store, display, search for, and use information.

Secure Socket Layer (SSL): A term used to describe the level of security and encryption used to protect information when transferred online. The existence of the SSL certificate on a website usually indicates that the information stored and processed is more protected.

Telehealth: A suggested term used to describe activity related to medical and health issues offered from a distance, such as when services or information to clients are delivered over the Internet.

REFERENCES

Administrative Rules of Montana. Statutes and Rules Relating to Psychologists. §§ 8.52. 606 (2).

Committee of Quality Health Care in America—Institute of Medicine (2001). Crossing the quality chasm: A new health care system for the 21st century. Washington, DC: National Academy Press. Retrieved August 29, 2003, from http://books.nap.edu/books/0309072808/html/23.html.

Dankins, D. H. (1995). Plugging into success: Clinical applications from around the globe. *Telemedicine and Telehealth Networks*, *12*:19–21.

Delaplain, C. B., Lindborg, C. E., Norton, S. A., et al. (1993). Tripler pioneers telemedicine across the Pacific. *Hawaii Medical Journal*, *52*:338–339.

DeLeon, P. H., Folen, R. A., Jennings, F. L., et al. (1991). The case for prescription privileges: A logical evolution of professional practice [Special issue: Child psychopharmacology]. *Journal of Clinical Child Psychology*, *20*:254–267.

DeLeon, P. H., & Wiggins, J. G. (1996). Prescription privileges for psychologists. *American Psychologist*, *51*:225–229.

Foreman, Judy (2003). Doctors resist e-mail system for patients. *Boston Globe*, Feb. 25, 2003, p. C3.

Forkner, M. E., Reardon, T., & Carson, G. D. (1996). Experimenting with feasibility of telemedicine in Alaska: Successes and lessons learned. *Telemedicine Journal*, *2*:233–240.

Grigsby, B. (1997). ATSP report on U. S. telemedicine activity. Portland, OR: Association of Telemedicine Service Providers. Retrieved August 29, 2003, from http://www.atsp.org.

HIPAA regulations. Retrieved August 29, 2003, from www.hhs.gov/ocr/hipaa/privrulepd.pdf.

Itagaki, M. W., Berlin, Richard B., et al. (2002). The rise and fall of e-health: Lessons from the first generation of Internet Healthcare. *Medscape TechMed 2*(1). Retrieved August 29, 2003, from http://www.gotham-ohc.com/html/nw240402.html.

Kavanaugh, S. J., & Wellowlees, P. M. (1995). Telemedicine—clinical applications in mental health. *Australian Family Physician*, *24*:1242–1247.

Murray, C. J. L., & Lopez, A. D., eds. *The global burden of disease and injury* (series). *Volume 1: A comprehensive assessment of mortality and disability from diseases, injuries, and risk factors in 1990 and projected to 2020.* Cambridge, MA: Published by the Harvard School of Public Health on behalf of the World Health Organization and the World Bank, Harvard University Press, 1996. Retrieved August 29, 2003, from http://www.nimh.nih.gov/publicat/burden.cfm (updated January 1, 2001).

McCarthy, P., Kulakowski, D., & Kenfield, J. A. (1994). Clinical supervision practices of licensed psychologists. *Professional Psychology: Research and Practice*, *25*:177–181.

Nickelson, D. (1998). Telehealth and the evolving health care system: Strategic opportunities for professional psychology. *Professional Psychology: Research and Practice*, *29*(6):

527–535. Retrieved August 29, 2003, from the American Psychological Association at http://www.apa.org/journals/pro/pro296527.com.

Norcross, J. C., Hedges, M., & Prochaska, J. O. (2002). The face of 2010: A Delphi poll on the future of psychotherapy. *Professional Psychology: Research and Practice, 33*:316–322.

Norton, S. A., Burdick, A. E., Phillips, C. M., et al. (1997). Teledermatology and underserved populations. *Archives of Dermatology, 133*:197–200.

Office for Civil Rights, U.S. Department of Health and Human Services: Standards for Privacy of Individually Identifiable Health Information. Federal Register. Vol. 67, No. 57. August 14, 2002/Rules and Regulations. Retrieved August 29, 2003, from www.hhs.gov/ocr/hipaa/privrulepd.pdf.

Preston, J., Brown, F. W., & Hartley, M. (1992). Using telemedicine to improve health care in distant areas. *Hospital and Community Psychiatry, 43*:25–32.

Ritterband, L. M., Gonder-Frederick, L. A., Cox, D. J., et al. (2003). Internet interventions: In review, in use and into the future. *Professional Psychology: Research and Practice, 34*(5): 527–534.

Rusovick, R. M., & Warner, D. J. (1998). The globalization of interventional informatics through Internet mediated distributed medical intelligence. *New Medicine, 2*:155–161.

Skorupa, J., & Agresti, A. A. (1993). Ethical beliefs about burnout and continued professional practice. *Professional Psychology: Research and Practice, 24*:281–285.

Stamm, B. H. (1995). *Secondary traumatic stress: Self-care issues for clinicians, researchers and educators.* Lutherville, MD: Sidran Press.

Stamm, B. H. (1998). Clinical Applications of Telehealth in Mental Health Care. *Professional Psychology: Research and Practice, 29*(6):536–542.

Taylor, H. (2000). Explosive growth of "cyberchondriacs" continues. Harris Interactive. Retrieved October 14, 2003, from http://www.harrisinteractive.com/harris_poll/index.asp?PID-104.

Terry, M. J. (1995). Kelengakutelleghpat: An Arctic community-based approach to trauma. In B. H. Stamm (Ed.), *Secondary traumatic stress: Self-care issues for clinicians, researchers and educators* (pp. 149–178). Lutherville, MD: Sidran Press.

U.S. Department of Commerce (1997). Telemedicine report to congress. Available at http://www.ntia.doc.gov/reports/telemed/cover1.htm.

CLINICAL ISSUES IN ONLINE COUNSELING

8

ONLINE COUNSELING SKILLS, PART I

TREATMENT STRATEGIES AND SKILLS FOR CONDUCTING COUNSELING ONLINE

ELIZABETH ZELVIN AND
CEDRIC M. SPEYER

Editors' Note: In any treatment process, it is important to have a sense of direction. In this chapter, the authors present a framework for the overall structure of online counseling. Readers are introduced to what happens across sessions, from the client's initial contact to termination and follow-up.

This broad picture of treatment online describes the essential characteristics of both clients and clinicians who make effective use of the medium. It also presents a flexible view of the structure, course, and pace of treatment. Synchronous and asynchronous modalities offer a variety of opportunities to make the most of client strengths while accommodating the practical needs and preferences of both client and therapist. Treatment structure can range from a single contact to a lengthy course of psychotherapy. The approach may vary from assessment and referral or simple problem solving to full development of a therapeutic alliance, in which transference and countertransference are significant factors in the treatment. Special challenges include the following: incorporating the use of technology, both on a practical level and as a clinical issue when indicated; maintaining confidentiality; facilitating a balance between anonymity and connection; conveying empathy and establishing therapeutic presence in a text environment; and maintaining the client's commitment in a medium where quitting therapy can be accomplished with the click of a mouse. Engagement and contracting must be constantly renegotiated. Flexibility in every area of practice, whether it is scheduling, goal setting, disclosure, or termination, will facilitate the success of online counseling as an innovative way of helping, rather than merely a flawed substitute for face-to-face (f2f) practice.

FIT AND APPROPRIATENESS

Not every competent clinician is a good candidate for online practice. Nor should every client with a computer be encouraged to engage in treatment online. Recent psychology or social work graduates and newly credentialed counselors are advised to develop conventional clinical skills and a body of experience before attempting online work.

WHO SHOULD BE DOING ONLINE COUNSELING?

First and foremost, online practice is for those who love it. If you are deeply skeptical about making emotional connections through the written word in the absence of visual cues, then online counseling is not for you. Being nervous around technology, a laborious typist, or feeling reluctant to explore the Internet are other examples of not being suited to the medium. If you are intrigued but lack experience, try it. Start writing emails to your relatives and friends. Do your best to be emotionally expressive and authentic. Ask colleagues who enjoy chat rooms to recommend a few for you to visit. Or if you are adventurous, surf the Internet and find your own—but be prepared to encounter anything from pornography to thought disorders. Try your hand at instant messaging to get a feel for one-to-one communication in a chat room (see Chapter 5 for more information on how to do these things).

Clinician Characteristics

To be an online therapist, you must be comfortable with the Internet and reasonably skilled on the keyboard, unless you have voice recognition software that you already use effectively. You have to be an expressive writer. The client can be relatively unskilled at putting feelings into words; those beginning f2f therapy often are. As the therapist, on the other hand, you must constantly be modeling text-based expression of emotions. If what you write feels inauthentic to you, it will not convince the client of your authority or integrity, and the therapeutic relationship will be flawed. The best online therapists communicate in text as if the keyboard does not exist. What the recipient gets is simply the presence of the therapist with the same rich personality, mediated by the same boundaries that would be maintained around the professional persona in an office setting.

Flexibility is also essential. If you can only work in a single way or if you believe too strongly in a single approach by virtue of your training and experience, you will not be able to adapt to online work. This field is in a pioneering phase, and its practitioners are still exploring its boundaries. Furthermore, it is developing in a context of skepticism, resistance, and even hostility from various factions. Being an online practitioner involves risk. Client expectations of counseling or therapy are more fluid than in traditional practice. You need to be able to go with the flow.

From a technical standpoint, although you don't have to be a computer virtuoso, you do need to master the tools of the trade (i.e., your computer equipment) and keep it up to date. To deal with glitches, both practically and clinically, you need frustration tolerance. Compared to the mechanics of maintaining a physical office, computer technology is in its infancy. You will get cut off in midsession. You will have crashes just when you're supposed to be online with clients. You will have trouble reaching tech support. You will send clients messages you meant to delete. Consequently, you must have both the skills and the temperament to deal with these situations, your own feelings, and the client's reactions.

Client Characteristics

Clients need to be comfortable on the Internet and with the written word. If a client expresses doubts about typing fast enough, email rather than chat can be recommended. For younger clients, many of whom have grown up with computers, the validity of online relationships tends not to be a treatment issue.

A less identifiable group of clients are those who are shy or inarticulate in direct contact with others, but capable of pouring out their hearts in writing. Critics of online communication fail to appreciate the fact that some people are simply more accessible, even more authentic, in text. Whether the determining factor is the anonymity of the Internet or a gift for writing, cyberspace offers a fertile environment for these individuals to express themselves.

Appropriate Populations and Circumstances

Potential online clients cover a broad spectrum from those who clearly benefit but would otherwise be unlikely to enter treatment to those for whom the appropriateness and effectiveness of online help is still being hotly debated (Stofle & Harrington, 2002). Lifelong computer users form the least problematic pool of clients, of which the first generation, born around 1970, is now reaching an age at which they might be interested in therapy. Those among them who are frequent Internet users are especially good candidates for online help. Another large and varied group are those who have limited access to f2f therapy. These might include clients in rural areas, those without convenient transportation, and individuals who are homebound due to disability, illness, or caregiving responsibilities. There is evidence that stay-at-home mothers are using the Internet in growing numbers (Netsavvy Communications, 2002). In addition, online counseling represents a convenient way to go outside the community for help. This may be an incentive for people such as those who are highly visible in their own community, live in a social environment where accessing psychological help is stigmatized, or personally know all of the available therapists. Online resources also offer access to specialized expertise that may not be available locally. Then there are populations for whom f2f therapy itself is limited. Text-based help may be ideal for clients who are deaf or hard-of-hearing. Clients who are blind or have low vision and use assistive technology have no reason to favor help that offers visual cues. Innovative online therapists are beginning to report, at least anecdotally, some successes with client thought disorders and affective impairments. There are clinicians who maintain that online crisis intervention, even with suicidal clients, appears to be effective in some cases. Proponents of this view point out that such clients may be unwilling to reach out in any other way (Fenichel et al., 2002).

When is Online Therapy Inappropriate?

Individuals whose presenting problems indicate a need for f2f contact must be encouraged to seek those services in their own community. Some examples include clients who express suicidal ideation, reveal a recent psychotic episode, admit to ongoing substance dependence, or display evidence of a thought disorder. Some clients may be attracted to online counseling as a way of seeking help while resisting the necessary treatment. It is important to explore and assess the client's reasons for choosing online help in assessing whether or not to provide it. Online therapists must know their limitations and act ethically. Clients who need medication, a safe holding environment, or specialized treatment should be directed—at times with medical and/or legal intervention—to the appropriate resources. A situation in which it is advisable to refuse treatment can arise during the screening and assessment process, or later on, as the client reveals more background or symptom information. In some cases, a team approach is called for. The online therapist may offer support as the client is stabilized through other means, especially if the client expresses a clear preference for text-based services, and is unlikely to connect with an f2f therapist for ongoing work. However, if the client resists referral or refuses clinical contracting that the therapist deems essential, it is important to set limits and be prepared to terminate the therapy. An example would be a client with a history of severe depression who will not agree to be evaluated for medication and refuses to provide the therapist with contact information.

LENGTH OF TREATMENT

While contemporary f2f treatment models have diverse treatment lengths (from one-session crisis intervention to traditional long-term psychoanalysis), online therapy offers a fresh perspective on the duration of treatment. Mental health treatment online is a relative latecomer to an Internet culture inhabited by young people who are computer-savvy, but not necessarily knowledgeable about therapy. The expectations of online clientele may be different than those seeking traditional therapy. Online practitioners need to examine their preconceived ideas regarding treatment structure, duration, and methods. Factors such as how the therapist presents him or herself on a website involve unconscious assumptions and reactions to being approached for help. One clinician may receive and respond to hundreds of requests for advice or direction without pay, while another engages almost every client referred to in long-term treatment via weekly chat. The importance of pay and continuity may vary not only with the therapist's treatment philosophy and clinical approach, but also with regards to whether the online practice is a primary career or a sideline.

Short-Term Treatment

Both the nature of the Internet and the expectations of its users lend themselves to short-term modalities. Treatment may consist of single session consultation, crisis intervention, assessment and referral, or brief psychoeducation and motivational counseling. The brief duration may be a stated condition of the service as in an employee assistance program (EAP) model.

Internet users who contact a counselor as they surf the Net are not necessarily looking for a therapeutic relationship, even on a short-term basis. They may know nothing about therapy. They may expect a Dear Abby or Dr. Freud or anything in between those two extremes. Often they do not expect to have to pay for feedback. Counselors need to think about what services they request a fee for and what, if anything, they are willing to offer for free. The fine line between resistance and real financial issues is even finer online than in f2f therapy, because insurance is usually not available.

In theory, severe and immediate crisis is best dealt with f2f. In practice, as the population of lifelong Internet users grows, an increasing number of people in crisis will reach out for help online, some of them anonymously. There continues to be ongoing discussion among mental health professionals about the ethics of responding to a crisis online (Fenichel et al., 2002). Clinicians doing online crisis intervention may need to intervene competently if the client refuses to seek local help. The skills to intervene, as well as knowledge of resources available online for clients in immediate need, are crucial. Clinicians may also need information and support on short notice.

Brief treatment may be conceptualized as assessment and referral, with a stated goal of connecting the client with f2f help if needed, or as psychoeducation and motivational counseling. The latter suggest greater faith in the validity of the online intervention itself and may lead to referral either f2f or online, depending on the nature of the problem and the client's circumstances. In addition, brief intervention may be seen as complete in itself, motivating clients to cope better on their own.

The Four-Email Exchange Model of E-Counseling

This brief text-based treatment model, developed for use in EAPs, uses principles of motivational interviewing, brief solution-focused therapy, and narrative approaches to effect change within a limited period (Speyer & Zack, 2002). The process of focusing on feelings, thoughts, and sensations is facilitated for both counselor and client by bypassing f2f self-presentation. Both have more of an opportunity for introspection as they communicate. Similarly, witnessing, or taking a step back from their internal dynamics to gain perspective, is enhanced by the act of "getting it down in writing." As text-based externalization occurs, the client is also internalizing the "voice" of the counselor as a reflection of his or her own inner wisdom. Each email is conceptualized as a microcosm of the overall process, which stresses the client's own strengths, resources, and potential for increasing self-awareness. This short-term model acknowledges but does not delve deeply into the historical nature of problems.

In the first email, the counselor conveys a sense of connection, safety, and containment to help the client cope with present, pressing concerns. The client's particular way of handling psychological pain, conflict, or crisis is normalized through reframing the problem as something the client is in the process of overcoming, either by focusing on underlying strengths or witnessing its grip from a healthier distance. By paying close attention to the client's text—as well as by "reading between the lines"—the counselor is able to refer to it to compliment the client's ability to cope with the difficulty.

In the second email, the difficult and often distressing circumstances in the client's life are revisited with respect to the core issue. The client is put in charge of the rules, myths, patterns, or emotional habits related to the issue and is encouraged to perceive him or herself as having choices. Emphasis is shifted from burden and blame to the client's strengths, gifts, and blessings. The counselor can direct reinforcement, bridging, and task-setting aspects of case management at the person behind the problem. The client is motivated and empowered for self-help through readings and resource material, homework assignments, or behavioral coaching. If the client is resisting the positive interpretation of what he or she perceives as problems or liabilities, the counselor can prescribe the symptom, use paradox, and focus on readiness levels rather than progress and growth.

The third email confirms and validates positive changes in the client's perceptions and behavior, helping the client plan actions beyond the treatment, create a vision of new possibilities, and embrace the tasks, actions, and attitudes it will take to make significant changes. The counselor must anticipate client resistance to change. In the third exchange, the counselor virtually mines the text of the client's previous message for material to be used for remotivation. Methods that foster therapeutic movement include positive tracking, relabeling, humor, externalizing the symptom, metaphors, identifying underutilized resources, creative misunderstandings, active wondering, and normalizing ongoing issues in the context of expected difficulties.

In the fourth email, the counselor summarizes and validates client progress against a background of unconditional positive regard for the person. In addressing unresolved issues, the counselor emphasizes the corrective emotional experience that has been set in motion and, when indicated, refers the client to some form of follow-up treatment. The goal of self-reliance is reinforced through referrals to self-help resources, such as websites, online or print books and articles, and online or f2f support groups. This final exchange emphasizes internalization of the therapeutic "voice." The counselor withdraws by deferring to the authority of the client's own wisdom and experience.

Long-Term Treatment

Long-term treatment can be a rich source of healing and growth for the client and satisfaction for the skilled and dedicated therapist, just as f2f therapy can. Assuming both therapist and client have the verbal and technical skills to handle text and synchronicity well, therapy in a chat room can be remarkably similar to psychotherapy in an office.

The process begins with engagement, contracting, goal setting, and the development of the therapeutic alliance. An extended phase of ongoing work, including transference and countertransference issues, may follow. Treatment is best ended with a deliberate process of termination. Differences between the online process and office practice will be discussed later in this chapter.

TREATMENT STRUCTURE

When the clinician is trying to engage the client in ongoing treatment, the structure of treatment from initial contact to termination resembles that of f2f psychotherapy. Some aspects of treatment are specific to online work, because of constraints and peculiarities of the cyberspace environment, as well as the way users are accustomed to relating to it. For example, it may be necessary to set ground rules by stating explicitly that the client is expected not to multitask, for example, read or watch TV, during a therapeutic chat.

Initial Contact

Clients may make the first contact in a variety of ways. They may find the therapist's website listed on a search engine or directory, see it advertised in print or online, or come across it as a link on another site. They may select the therapist's profile from a panel on an online clinic or network website, based on a search for specific specialties or personal characteristics, or based on the therapist's narrative in text, audio or video, or even his or her photograph. Like f2f clients, they may be referred by colleagues, other clients, or personal friends and acquaintances of the therapist. In each of these cases, potential clients usually email the therapist, state their problem briefly and either request an appointment or ask for more information about how the therapist works.

Making the first contact by instant message is unique to the Internet. The user is surfing the Internet, sees an offer of help that is available immediately—an instant message feature on the therapist's website or a live intake or immediate counseling feature of a clinic website—and impulsively decides to check it out. Email, too, is frequently used in this spontaneous way. Online counselors must learn how to assess and deal with brief communications, often anonymous except for an email address, saying anything from "I need to talk to someone right away" to "My wife is having an affair. What should I do?" A therapist who is suited to online work can develop good intuition about the emotional tone of text communications. It can be a challenge to distinguish between spam and a genuine cry for help.

Stating clearly that a fee will be charged for counseling will discourage the frivolous or mischievous. The counselor, however, must still decide how he or she chooses to deal with requests from troubled individuals who were not expecting to pay and may not have the means to do so. Some therapists are willing to respond without charge to spontaneous queries, offering brief but substantial support and information. Therapists who want ongoing clients must respond with education about the process and interventions that foster engagement.

One reason clinic sites are attractive to therapists is that the clinic takes care of obtaining contact information. In a direct initial contact, especially in realtime with a drop-in, the potential client may be turned off if the focus is solely on obtaining identifying data. The anonymity of the Internet could be the determining factor in being willing to seek help at all. Because of the legal and ethical risks involved, few therapists want to work completely anonymously. From a business standpoint, there is no way to enforce payment from an anonymous client. There is also the danger that a technical glitch will develop. Without contact information, the therapist may be suddenly cut off from the client with no way to reconnect. The timing of the request for contact information is therefore crucial, as is the timing of any discussion of payment. Screening and assessment must also be skillfully timed to promote engagement.

The clinician's challenge in the initial contact is to obtain enough contact information for follow-up in case of a sudden glitch or computer crash; conduct enough screening to assess appropriateness and fit, market his or her services by communicating qualifications and skill; begin the process of engagement through active listening and empathy; and establish his or her authority and therapeutic presence through text alone. Orientation to the technology must also be provided. If a password-protected chat room will be used, the procedure for entering must be discussed. If the client is not an experienced chatter, some tips on chat techniques, such as putting feelings into text or emoticons, indicating when a response is complete, and dealing with overlapping communications, may greatly increase the client's comfort level online. The therapist may want to offer backup contact information, such as an instant message feature, an additional email address, and/or a phone number, in case the therapist's or client's Internet connection or computer crashes during the session. Therapists who work online need to invest in reliable backup, such as an additional computer or a dedicated phone line, in case their high-speed cable or digital subscriber line (DSL) goes down during practice hours.

Beginning Treatment

Because it is so easy to quit therapy online, engagement and contracting may be a far more extended process online than in office practice. Online clients tend to have more ambivalence about committing to therapy. Consequently, therapists must be prepared to educate clients about the therapeutic process and actively encourage them to keep coming back, while allowing them the flexibility they may need in scheduling appointments. Since flexibility of scheduling is one of the Internet's strengths, many clients will never settle into a traditional fixed weekly appointment. Therapists must become comfortable with this feature of online work and be prepared to accommodate the client's individual needs. They would do well to reframe this flexibility as an opportunity to work with clients who have irregular schedules or are frequent travellers. This may mean practicing at times when they might not be able to get to their office yet are available to conduct an online session in a convenient location.

As therapists gain experience online, they will become skillful at eliciting as much assessment information as possible at the beginning, even with uncommitted clients. As in f2f practice, the client's presenting problem is a good place to start developing the therapeutic alliance, contracting with the client and setting goals the client is motivated to work toward. At every session, the therapist must continue to probe for biopsychosocial information and additional identifying data, as well as issues that the client does not readily volunteer.

> Dana began chat therapy to explore her sexual orientation without jeopardizing her position in a conservative community. At each session, she expressed difficulty "opening up" on cue at the scheduled time. After five sessions, she instant messaged the therapist one evening, saying she wanted to talk. The therapist agreed to an immediate unscheduled session, thinking that allowing the client to be

spontaneous would foster engagement. In the course of their talk, the client said: "I wasn't going to come back at all. In fact, we wouldn't be talking now if I hadn't had a few beers."

The therapist's task was to encourage the client to remain in treatment while setting a ground rule that the client could not, in the future, have a session if she had been drinking. She also began to assess the client's alcohol use, which turned out to be problematic and became a major issue in the treatment. Contracting at this early stage was limited to abstinence during sessions and the client's agreeing to listen when the therapist offered information about the effects of alcohol use or reflected connections between her drinking behavior and its adverse consequences. Finally, the therapist now had new information about requests for unscheduled sessions from this particular client. From then on, she was very careful about such requests, allowing an unscheduled chat only when she deemed it therapeutic.

With email therapy, contracting may include issues of structure and commitment, such as the frequency and length of emails, how quickly the therapist responds, and to what extent brief email communications interspersed between longer ones are allowed without charge. Both client expectations and the therapist's limits must be considered with respect to answering these postscripts. If therapists do not establish ground rules from the beginning, they may find the client considering them available on 24-hour call, seven days a week. In most cases, this is neither therapeutic for the client nor acceptable to the therapist. Some clients, in addition to lengthy emails, want to send the therapist songs, poems, and extracts from their journals via the Internet. Therapists need to consider these requests not only from a treatment perspective but in terms of their own boundaries.

The assessment process, not only initially but throughout the beginning phase of treatment, must include the possibility of referral. For a variety of reasons, f2f treatment, services within the client's community, and adjunctive services such as couple counseling, psychopharmacology, or therapeutic bodywork may be indicated. The therapist's assessment skills and professional ethics must guide all such recommendations. At the same time, the experienced online therapist will not undervalue the power of online treatment to help all kinds of clients.

Ongoing Treatment

Because it is so easy for the online client to leave, engagement must be actively maintained during the ongoing phase of treatment. The therapist can contribute to engagement by strengthening the therapeutic alliance, keeping the focus on the client's stated goals, and being proactive about scheduling. The latter is especially important with clients who do not necessarily email or chat at a fixed time on a weekly basis. If the therapist responds promptly to client emails, the response may elicit another email within a day or two, creating a pattern of frequent, clustered communications. If the services can be purchased in batches, as some clinic sites offer them, it is helpful to remind clients when the prepaid emails or chats are running out. The therapist can set the next chat appointment at the end of the preceding chat and confirm the time by email shortly before the session. Compared to the f2f process, some therapists may find it more difficult to keep online clients coming back while working through negative transference. Therefore, more supportive interventions may be called for online. Responsiveness on a nonclinical level can also help maintain engagement. For example, the therapist can reply briefly but supportively to between-session emails and direct the client to adjunctive information and resources on the Internet.

The boundaries between clinician and client are not quite the same as in f2f practice. Clients tend to be proactive in searching for references to the therapist, sometimes even before beginning treatment. Search engines will reveal all aspects of the therapist's presence on the Web, including any personal websites, as well as activities and information that a fairly traditional f2f therapist would be unlikely to disclose. Clinicians need to decide how they want to handle involuntary disclosures. It may be possible to reframe them as an opportunity to connect with clients in innovative ways. For example, online clients who discovered that their therapist was a published poet began to talk about creativity issues in treatment. Furthermore, the insight and acceptance conveyed in poems on such universal themes as family, love, and death seemed to increase the therapist's authority in clients' eyes as someone with wisdom to impart.

Contracting

Contracting about the structure of treatment and the extent of counselor availability is a process that continues in the ongoing phase of treatment. Perhaps even more than f2f clients without prior therapy experience, online clients must be educated about the nature of the therapeutic relationship and the process of therapy. Some new clients expect the therapist to give advice or provide solutions. Others assume that the conventions of casual chatting apply.

The therapist may need to monitor the impact of real life and the client's f2f social systems on the client's attitude to treatment. For example, one therapist belatedly discovered that a client was allowing family members to read the therapist's emails. Their comments and reactions were reflected in the client's changing attitudes toward therapy and the therapist.

Contracting for short-term and long-term goals may be an extended process. When new issues emerge during the course of treatment, new goals must be set. As short-term goals are reached, new objectives may be identified on the way to the client's vision of optimal functioning, mental health, and happiness. Problematic use of alcohol, for example, is even less likely to be an initial presenting problem than in general f2f practice. But once it is identified, it must eventually be addressed in the interests of therapeutic progress (Zelvin, 2003; 2001).

Relationship Distortions

Transference and countertransference issues must be identified and managed in online work, much as they are in f2f treatment. Idealization of the therapist arises more readily because clients can project their fantasies in the complete absence of visual and auditory cues. The limitations of text-based communication may foster idealization of the client on the therapist's part as well. On the other hand, a devaluing client can find a ready object not only in the therapist but also in online therapy itself. Negative countertransference may manifest itself as reluctance to read or answer emails or as defensiveness if the client expresses skepticism or ambivalence about working online.

> Dr. Green had two email clients with similar presenting problems. He enjoyed treating the client who wrote: "I really appreciate your words. . . . Thanks for helping me through this painful time." In contrast, he felt negatively about the client who wrote: "I don't agree at all that I need to express my anger. . . . I don't always agree with your feedback."

It can come as a shock to online counselors when they realize that some clients not only save and reread their emails, but also may copy and paste in order to quote them verbatim in their replies. Sometimes the vulnerability counselors feel about their words being recorded without their control can be a trigger for countertransference.

Intersession Communication

In managing the flow of treatment, counselors must consider how they want to deal with intersession communication and interruptions in treatment. Brief discussions about scheduling, occasional requests for immediate support, and technical problem solving can all take place online or on the phone. Some therapists will want to set boundaries, for example, by prohibiting instant messaging or by asking clients not to monitor the therapist's online activity by putting his or her screen name on a buddy list. Depending on therapist preference, the Internet or the phone may be considered the best medium for crisis intervention. It is best for therapists to set norms about these interactions in the beginning and provide several different ways to contact them. When technical glitches occur, as they inevitably will, alternative forms of communication, follow-up, and reassurance can be presented as ways of strengthening the connection between therapist and client. Vacations and other therapist absences can be dealt with as a clinical issue, just as in f2f practice. However, online therapists with laptops have the option of continuing to meet with clients while they are away from home. Some may choose to take a vacation from chat sessions but offer the option of email to provide continued support. Clinically, it may be better for one client to maintain the connection and for another to accept the limit setting represented by the therapist taking a break. Personally, the therapist must balance continued income against time off as a component of mental health and burnout prevention.

Varying Modalities

Over a prolonged period of treatment, online practitioners have the opportunity to consider the merits of varying the treatment modality: synchronous and asynchronous, Internet and telephone, or online and f2f. Some clinicians take full advantage of the Internet's capabilities by encouraging clients to use graphics in their chats and emails to enhance self-expression and even to create their own websites as an ego-building exercise or journey of self-discovery. Although client empowerment may be a goal, therapists will nonetheless want to maintain clinical control of the treatment. Impulsive changes in scheduling, treatment modality, or any other element of the treatment may be discouraged, although the client may suggest changes worth exploring if they have a sound clinical basis. If adjunctive services are warranted, they should be planned within the context of the ongoing online therapy. Therapists would be wise to obtain the client's permission to communicate with any concurrent providers, such as psychopharmacologists or alternative health specialists. These practitioners may need to be proactively informed that the client is already doing "real therapy" online.

Termination

As in conventional practice, termination takes place when client and therapist reach a consensus that treatment goals have been achieved and that the client can function optimally, coping with new issues and feelings as they arise without ongoing dependence on the therapist. In online therapy, it has to be emphasized (even more than in f2f practice) that it is not a good idea to leave treatment impulsively. When there is no ongoing process of education about the nature of therapy and no contract of client commitment, there is nothing to stop the client from ending treatment prematurely and abruptly. If the payment procedure involves the client renewing the commitment by paying online, in advance, for each session or batch of sessions, the client can leave simply by not making the next payment.

To forestall premature termination, the therapist must begin teaching the client the value of closure well before any question of ending arises. Clients sometimes break a contract to spend time terminating within the therapy, but they are more likely to participate in the process if the contracting has taken place. Whenever the client expresses a desire to leave, whether prematurely or appropriately in the therapist's opinion, the therapist can negotiate a suitable period to review the treatment process, assess achievement of goals, and plan how the client will deal with issues, feelings, and support resources after therapy has ended. This process sometimes helps a client see that it is not yet time to leave. It may also help the therapist accept that a conclusion has been reached, at least at the level the client is currently willing to explore.

Follow-Up

As part of the termination process, follow-up needs to be discussed, as well as circumstances in which the client may return for a brief consultation or another course of treatment. Both client and clinician may have agendas, expectations, or both that must be expressed in order to ensure they are not in conflict. Misunderstandings can be averted through clearly stated ground rules for further communication. Both client and counselor will continue to appear online; therefore, posttreatment boundaries need to be established. For example, the therapist may reiterate that the client is expected not to track his or her presence online through a buddy list or attempt social contact via instant message. Conversely, the therapist may want to indicate that the door is open if the client chooses to continue therapy later or asks for help in a crisis. The fees for such services, if any, need to be discussed at the time of termination. Some online therapists offer free support groups on their websites, either as self-help or facilitated chats or message boards. These services may be offered to terminating clients as a form of aftercare.

SUMMARY

Clients must be fluent and expressive writers, as well as comfortable on the Internet, in order to benefit from online counseling. Clinicians must enjoy text-based communication and deal competently with computer and Internet technology to be a good fit for this work. Appropriate clients for short-term and long-term work may include those with access or mobility problems, those seeking anonymity or services outside their community or region, and the generation who have grown up with computers and take relationships on the Internet for granted. Treatment structure online resembles the structure of f2f therapy in having a beginning phase, a period of ongoing work, and a process of termination. Engagement, contracting, and goal setting, ongoing assessment, and dealing with transference and countertransference are all features of online treatment as they are in f2f therapy. Special challenges include engaging clients who may not expect to pay for "advice," maintaining the therapeutic relationship in spite of the ease of leaving therapy online, dealing with glitches without discouraging the client, balancing the client's need for anonymity and the therapist's practical and ethical need for identifying and contact information, developing text-based communication skills that foster the therapeutic relationship, and adapting to the flexibility and range of communication that are among the Internet's greatest assets.

KEY TERMS

Assistive technology: Technology enabling people with disabilities to use computers and other high-tech devices, such as voice recognition software and Braille keyboards.

Asynchronous: Not occurring simultaneously. Online, asynchronous communication is any time-delayed mode, such as email or message boards, that allows participants to compose and read their messages at times convenient to them without reference to the availability of the recipient or sender. Also, *nonsynchronous*.

Backchanneling: Communicating privately with another individual via email or instant message behind the scenes of an online group forum in which both are visibly participating.

Bridge line: A telephone number that can be dialed by anyone up to a designated number of individuals to participate in an individual or phone session or a conference call.

Buddy list: A list or database of frequent contacts whom the user can easily access by instant message or ascertain to be online.

Bulletin board: A website-based group or conference in which messages are posted asynchronously, usually in chronological order, for participants to view and respond to on the site. Also, *message board* or *forum*.

Chat: A public or private synchronous dialogue or group discussion online, usually adhering to conventions of Netiquette such as the use of abbreviations and emoticons; also, any communication that takes place in a chat room.

Chat room: A software-based or Web-based feature of the Internet in which a synchronous dialogue or discussion can take place, consisting of a message window in which the sender posts messages and a screen on which the text of the discussion appears.

Client-centered therapy: An approach to therapy, first developed by Carl Rogers, involving empathy and nonjudgmental reflection of the client's statements and feelings.

Countertransference: A projected perception of client qualities or problems that triggers unresolved personal issues for the therapist.

Employee Assistance Program (EAP): A professional consultation, counseling, and referral service for employees, who receive confidential help with personal and professional concerns as part of their company's benefit package.

Encryption: A technical method of ensuring online security by having data from messages encoded in transit in a form that can be read only by the intended receiver. The receiver of the encrypted data must have the appropriate decryption software, or it may be built into a chat room or other website feature used by recipients.

Face to face (f2f): In person, as in interactions that take place in physical space as opposed to cyberspace.

Forum: A Web-based message board; also, a regularly scheduled chat.

Instant message: A synchronous online communication between two individuals, accessed from personal computer screens independent of any website.

Instant messaging: One-to-one text-based communication by instant message, usually unscheduled.

Listserve: A method of online group discussion in which individual email messages are distributed to the email addresses of all group members simultaneously. Group membership is controlled at a central location online. Also, *mailing list.*

Motivational interviewing: A therapeutic method of eliciting information in which the client is helped to find self-validated reasons to commit to behavior change.

Narrative therapy: A therapeutic approach that involves working with the client's presentation of a problematic situation by recounting the events or "re-authoring the story" from a positive or therapeutic perspective.

Realtime: Elapsed time in which synchronous communication takes place. For example, a half-hour chat or phone conversation starting at 6 PM Pacific Time and 9 PM Eastern Time takes place in realtime.

Solution-focused therapy: A short-term approach to therapy that involves building on client strengths and successes, thereby turning client attention away from preoccupation with symptoms and toward treatment goals.

Splitting: A defense mechanism in which the client plays one person off against another. For example, splitting involving an online therapist and an f2f therapist may be a way of expressing resistance to treatment.

Synchronous: Occurring simultaneously, or in realtime. Synchronous communication online, such as instant messaging or chat, is a "live" interaction in which delays depend only on the respective typing speeds of the participants and the speed of the browsers processing the communication.

Telepresence: A subjective feeling of being "with" someone, or in their presence, that increases the intimacy of electronically mediated communication regardless of physical distance and lack of visual cues.

Therapeutic alliance: The psychological bond between therapist and client that facilitates client growth by allowing for both emotional support and constructive confrontation in an atmosphere of unconditional acceptance.

Transference: The tendency of a client to ascribe importance, motivation, and intentionality to the therapist, who is unconsciously perceived as a "stand-in" for significant figures in the client's life.

STUDY QUESTIONS

1. Describe the personal and professional characteristics of a clinician who you think would make a good online counselor.

2. Under what circumstances would you decide not to ask for contact information from a new drop-in client during the initial session? Discuss.

3. Create a brief text-based intake form that will elicit information about alcohol abuse from someone who does not consider drinking a problem. Decide whether this screening would be synchronous or asynchronous, and give your reasons.

4. Write an opening paragraph in response to the following first message from a client, in which your sole purpose is to establish text-based rapport.

> I am in a terrible bind. I am a senior salesperson with a very good company. I have been there for 12 years and have built a great career.
>
> Two days ago, I got a wonderful promotion but the new job is in another city. I rushed home with the exciting news and my wife and two teenage daughters told me I could go if I wanted to but they are staying. I am so upset. I do not know how to handle this nonsense.

5. Under what circumstances would you refer each of the clients described below out, and to whom (e.g., f2f psychodynamic psychotherapist, psychopharmacologist, etc.)? Which of these clients would you work with online, primarily or adjunctively? What modality and time frame would you recommend? Give your reasons.

   a. Client is a 39-year-old married woman with three children who works part-time in a supermarket. Her presenting problems are weight gain and a desire for more sex in her marriage. She reports that her husband is under stress at his job and occasionally loses his temper. On those occasions he has called her a fat cow and has shaken her but has never hit her.

   b. Client is a 47-year-old single man who has been unemployed for the past 18 months, since his employer of 15 years downsized. He reports difficulty sleeping, loss of appetite, and feelings of low self-worth. He is having trouble staying motivated to look for a job and watches television as much as 10 hours a day. He has infrequent contact with family and states that he has no friends. Three or four times in the past month he has had thoughts that he is a failure and would be better off dead.

   c. Client is a 35-year-old single mother who seeks help in dealing with a teenage son who is in trouble for truancy and vandalism. She reports that her father was an alcoholic and she is worried that her son will become one too. She states that she smokes marijuana daily because it takes the edge off her anxiety about her son, but she does not think it is a problem.

6. Taking the point of view of a journalist, write two paragraphs reviewing the phenomenon of online therapy. In the first, outline the limitations of text-based communication in the "devil's advocate" position of pointing out the drawbacks. In the second, describe how the use of the medium can enhance therapeutic effectiveness in remarkable ways.

7. What is the difference between the synchronous and asynchronous modes of online communication? Which one do you prefer and why?

8. What are some aspects of Internet behavior that an online therapist has to watch out for? What kinds of client orientation and ground rules would you establish to protect yourself?

9. What are some of the strategies involved in managing termination in an online case?

10. What online options could you offer a client who was seeking help for agoraphobia on the Internet?

REFERENCES

Barak, A. (2003). Personal communication.

Colón, Y. (2004). Technology-based social work practice in end of life care. In J. Berzoff & P. Silverman (Eds.) *End-of-life care: Textbook for social workers.* New York: Columbia University Press.

Fenichel, M., Suler, J., Barak, A., Zelvin, E., et al. (2002). "Myths and realities of online clinical work." *CyberPsychology & Behavior,* 5:481–497.

Henderson, C. (2001). Armageddon averted: People power 2001. Asia Pacific Management Forum. Retrieved January, 2001 from http://www.apmforum.com/columns/orientseas26.htm.

Netsavvy Communications (2002). Moms click with the Internet, averaging more time online than teens. Retrieved from http://sellitontheweb.com/ezine/news0574.shtm.

Speyer, C., & Zack, J. S. (2002). E-Counseling: A 4-Session model. MAX International Co., Ltd., Tokyo, Japan. (English version available from JSZ Behavioral Science, Inc., P.O. Box 331339, Miami, FL 33233).

Stofle, G. S., & Harrington, S. (2002). Treating addictions on the Internet: Can it be done? A dialogue. *Journal of Social Work Practice in the Addictions,* 2(2):85–92.

Suler, J. (2000). Hypotheses about online psychotherapy and clinical work. *The Psychology of Cyberspace.* Retrieved July, 2000 from http://www.rider.edu/users/suler/psycyber/workinghyp.html.

Zack, J. S., Kawanishi, Y., & Uchii, D. (2002). Developing online counseling for Japan: Challenges and realities. Poster session presented at the meeting of the American Psychological Association, Chicago.

Zelvin, E. (2001). Assessing Alcohol Abuse in Online Clients. *Issues of Substance,* 6(2):1, 3.

Zelvin, E. (2003, in press). Treating Addictions in Cyberspace. *Journal of Social Work Practice in the Addictions,* 3(3).

9

ONLINE COUNSELING SKILLS, PART II

IN-SESSION SKILLS

GARY S. STOFLE AND PETER J. CHECHELE

Therapy is easy to do poorly, but quite difficult to do well.
—Gary S. Stofle

Editors' Note: In this chapter, the authors discuss the nature of online counseling, as it occurs *within* sessions, introducing readers to skills that can be used in asynchronous (email) counseling and synchronous (realtime chat) counseling. Clinical examples are also provided.

Specific skills are needed to successfully provide therapy to clients using the Internet, whether in a chat room or through email exchanges. Although some professionals believe a completely new paradigm and skill-set need to be created for online treatment (Childress, 1998), we have the successful experience of adapting face-to-face (f2f) skills and techniques to online interactions. This adaptation is the focus of this chapter. The range of these skills include five broad categories:

- Engagement skills
- Sessional contracting skills
- Teaching/training/modeling skills
- Supportive confrontation skills
- Sessional summary skills

People bring the same types of problems and issues to therapy whether in an online or an f2f setting. F2f therapy has been shown to be effective

(Seligman, 1995), but up to this point therapy online has not been conclusively studied. However, we do know that some people who will not access f2f therapy will access therapy online.

It is essential for therapists to have a good deal of experience in f2f therapy (in addition to online-specific skills) for them to provide effective treatment online without the benefit of nonverbal cues. This absence of nonverbal cues can definitely create a barrier to understanding and processing information sent either by the client or the therapist. Excellent communication skills are essential for this type of work because of the absence of so much information used in f2f therapy. Practical skills such as good typing, grammar, and spelling are needed to make this form of treatment work.

Skills from the five broad categories will be discussed in the context of both chat and email therapy. This chapter was created by the collaboration of both authors; one (Stofle) is experienced in chat room therapy and the other (Chechele) is experienced in working with clients using email. Each skill area is divided into chat and email to facilitate comparison and contrast between these two primary and most-used modes of working online.

ENGAGEMENT SKILLS

CHAT

All the clinical work starts with engagement. All engagement activities online occur solely through the use of the typed word and must continue throughout the session from beginning to end. Although this might make the task of chat room therapy seem daunting, it is so only for those who (1) have never done it, (2) lack ability to communicate effectively using only typed words to create a sense of connection with another, or (3) are new to the very process of providing therapy services to clients. It can actually be quite simple to type words that demonstrate the therapist's care and concern for the client or potential client.

Empathy in either f2f or online therapy is an excellent way of building rapport with a client. When the client sees that you are paying attention to what is being said and accurately understand the communication, the client feels listened to, respected, important, and, as a consequence, engaged.

The example below illustrates two points: accurate empathy as a means of engaging a client in a first session and also the need to "fill in the blanks" based on the therapist's knowledge and experience with the issues the client presents. The single asterisk (*) indicates points in the session where the therapist put forth a hypothesis for testing with the client. The double asterisk (**) indicates points in the session where the client confirms the hypothesis.

Client: if anyone shows interest in me I find all kinds of faults in them because I feel like I'm

Client: not worth someone actually liking me

Therapist: *at the same time, I bet you are very kind towards others.

Client: **I always do for others before myself. I can't seem to say no to anyone

Client: especially when my mom always wants to borrow money, then I end up resenting her for always

Client: asking me after she's blown hers

Therapist: *and you get mad at yourself as well, heh?

Client: if i get the courage to tell her no she ends up mad at me & won't speak to me

Client: **yes i do

Therapist: *so then you give in and give her what she wants.

Client: **yes even if it leaves me without any until I get paid again

Therapist: that's not fair to you.

Client: no but at least it keeps her happy & speaking to me

Therapist: the work ahead for you boils down to one sentence:

Therapist: you need to learn how to take better care of yourself.

Client: I know but just don't know how

In this example of a first session, the therapist's understanding of co-dependency and the issues children face growing up in an alcoholic home enables him to predict, often with a high degree of accuracy, the issues these clients face (Woititz, 1983). The therapist was able to tune in to what the client was saying and thereby make a connection.

EMAIL

Engagement in email therapy with a client begins with the subject line of the email you send to your client. All users of email programs over a period of time learn to quickly scan the subject line of those tens and possibly hundreds of emails one can get in a day's time. It is the first thing the client sees and as such needs to appropriately gain the client's attention.

The subject line provides an opportunity to encapsulate the heart of the discussion thus far. It is also a very succinct and direct way to have the client consider a reframe of an issue, the details of which will be provided in the email itself. A brief, humorous message in the subject line might be able to communicate your care and concern for the client.

Here is an example of an email reply to a client that works at both engaging the client and at the same time educating him about the online therapy process:

Dear Tom,

Let me begin by welcoming you . . . I've read over what you have sent me and there seems to be a lot going on here that may require a bit of back-and-forth dialogue for us to sort all this out. I hear that you are having some problems with opening up with women and feeling ok about expressing your intimacy for another person, and we'll certainly take a closer look at this. Because you've never been in any sort of therapy before let me give you a little idea as to what we'll be doing here. In many respects what I do in my office face to face (f2f) is similar to what I do online with my clients. Namely I strive to help my clients in the following ways: (1) Helping my clients better understand themselves through questioning them about their beliefs and behaviors; (2) asking them about their personal history as it relates to the problems in question; (3) determining what your strengths are and who you can count on for support; (4) figuring out what things need to change in order for you to get back on track; and (5) strategizing with you ways we might tap into your strengths and support system to move you in this direction. Does all this make sense? I suggest that we contract for a month of unlimited email support so that we can begin this process. After the 30 days we will evaluate how we are doing and if additional work is needed. I believe we'll be able to make quite a bit of progress in a relatively short period of time. If you have additional questions feel free to ask. . . .

I'm looking forward to your reply and to the opportunity of working together!

Peter

SESSIONAL CONTRACTING SKILLS

CHAT

At the beginning of each chat session, the therapist and the client need to develop a plan of action for work together during that session. This plan helps the client address the issues that bring him or her into treatment and is based on a simple logic:

a. Through an honest assessment of the client's issues made possible through engaging in therapy with a competent therapist,

b. the client's issues can be worked on directly in therapy and then

c. the client gets better.

It is the responsibility of the therapist to ensure this sessional contracting happens as soon as is appropriate in the session. It is very easy, both for the client and the therapist, to get distracted, particularly in a chat session. At times, the therapist has to motivate the client to work on issues in a session. An example of this is:

Client: I'm okay
Therapist: did your week get any better after we last talked?
Client: yeah . . . I guess so . . .
Therapist: where should we start tonight?
Client: I don't know . . . I don't think I feel much like talking. . . . I feel kind of like.
Client: like I'm tied up . . . on the inside.
Therapist: well, there's quite a value in sticking with that and talking anyway.
Client: why?
Therapist: because it's a valuable skill to learn how to talk when you don't want to,
Client: oh
Therapist: because that's precisely the time you need to.

Client: oh
Therapist: talk about the tied up feeling.
(pause for about two minutes – a long time in a chat session)
Therapist: ok?
Client: about what?
Therapist: about what you are feeling inside.
Client: I kind of feel like I have no control over anything right now.

At this point the client and the therapist went into an in-depth exploration of the client's feelings and her difficulty in managing them. This was a primary focus of the client's online therapy and was very difficult for the client to face. The sessional contracting focuses the session and keeps the work on track.

Another example is below:

Therapist: I thought we would work on some treatment planning tonight if that's ok with you.
Client: thank you, . . . ok
Therapist: so, let's start by naming the issues/problems that you want to work on.
Therapist: we've talked about you growing up in an alcoholic home.
Therapist: and being involved with people with alcohol problems.
Therapist: but what do you see as the specific problems?
Client: some are, I can't be able to do things I want to do
Client: if I think it will upset someone I won't do it
Client: It doesn't seem like I'm living my own life
Therapist: talk some more about not being able to do what you want.
Client: an example, this past weekend I went to meet someone for the first time
Client: everyone in my family was very upset with me for it, but I had fun until I got home
Client: I feel like I let them down. don't know if I will do it again, but I do want to
Therapist: you let them down because they were unhappy with you?
Client: yes
Therapist: can you give me more of the details about this? was it like a date?

As more details came out, the client was completely accurate in saying "it doesn't seem like I'm living my own life" because she was completely wrapped up in pleasing her parents although her parents don't seem to have her best interests at heart and the client is in her 30s. (Over the course of her treatment, she was able to establish emotional independence and move out of her parents' house.)

EMAIL

The opening paragraph is the part of the email where the therapist can prepare the client for comments that are in the body of text below. It can also be used to summarize the central issue of the email or to get the client thinking of leading edge issues. Below is an example of how the email therapist clearly narrows the focus of the interaction to a workable size:

Dear Debbie,

Wow, when I asked you to tell me a bit about your history, you certainly were not at a loss for words. My reaction was one of being overwhelmed with the enormity of your story. My guess is that this may also be the way you're feeling . . . overwhelmed and full of emotions. There was so much I wanted to respond to but I've decided to narrow our discussion down to what I believe are the major themes of your email. These are: (1) Mourning the loss of your childhood, (2) having to always be the "good girl" and feeling like your needs, thoughts, or feelings never really mattered, and (3) never really knowing what a normal family feels like and how to have healthy relations with those around you today. Would you say these are the big three? If I missed something please let me know . . . I think over time we'll begin to see how all of these are interconnected and how changes in one will ultimately affect all. We'll be spending a good part of our time talking about this. One thing that I won't have to worry about here is you being at a loss for words.

Peter

THERAPY/TEACHING/TRAINING SKILLS

The primary purpose of all therapy is to help clients improve their ability to function effectively in reality.

CHAT

At the risk of stating the obvious, therapies that use the written word as an integral part of the f2f therapy process lend themselves to online, text-based adaptation. The use of text-based homework assignments in Cognitive Behavioral Therapy is an example.

Rational Emotive Behavioral Therapy (REBT) focuses on challenging erroneous beliefs the client has that impact the client's ability to function effectively and cause uncomfortable feelings (Edelstein, 2002). This type of treatment lends itself to online work as well because of the opportunity to use text to directly challenge the false beliefs the client has in the here and now. As stated elsewhere in this chapter, when a client expresses a belief about reality that is not accurate (e.g., I shouldn't feel this way), the therapist can simply state: "That's not true—you should feel whatever way you feel." This simple challenge can have the effect of turning the client's world upside down in a positive way immediately. The client often does not respond for a period of time to this challenge as they think about it. This pause causes the challenge to remain on the screen and that reinforces this potential new belief. In f2f therapy, when you challenge an erroneous belief, the words are said and the client starts an internal process of thinking about those words. However, unless the challenge is written on a blackboard or on a computer screen in the office, the external process is limited to the therapist repeating the challenge over and over (which could be awkward).

Chat lends itself to an interactive bibliotherapy process that is simple and straightforward: The client brings up an issue—the therapist provides information, options, and skills training in regard to the issue, along with links or referrals to other documents and sources of information—and the client then can consider new behaviors, practice them, and change.

This following chat session transcript is about a client who had great difficulty letting people know what was going on with her. She was in a situation where she was attacked by an online friend and initially didn't know how to respond or whether she was going to respond at all. She finally wrote a detailed email to him letting him know how his behavior affected her:

Client: i think it got the point across
Therapist: did you send it?
Client: yes
Therapist: how did you feel?
Client: good
Therapist: :0)
Therapist: I was remembering some of our work together in the past,
Therapist: where you've had relationships online end
Client: yeah
Therapist: and how difficult it has been.
Client: yeah
Therapist: the other's response to you doesn't seem to fit with your behavior.
Therapist: do you know what I mean?
Client: no
Therapist: well, if you were flaming someone all day . . . it would make sense for them to say,
Therapist: don't email me anymore.
Therapist: but you're not doing that kind of thing.
Client: no
Client: i think that's why it hurts so much
Therapist: right . . . it's like you are a victim of prejudice.
Client: yeah
Client: but you know what
Therapist: what?
Client: we're talking again . . . and he admitted that he acted "somewhat childishly" :o)
Therapist: wow. . . . that's pretty wild.
Client: yeah
Therapist: did you share your discomfort with him?
Client: discomfort about what?
Therapist: his behavior.
Therapist: did you tell him how hurt you were by the things he said?
Client: well . . . not at the time . . . (this was a few weeks ago), but just the other day i sent him an
Client: email and told him that i didn't feel as safe to share things with him as i used to
Therapist: wow. . . . that was important to do!
Client: and he said that if it had been reversed . . . he would feel the same
Client: so he understands
Therapist: you treated him in a manner that was full of grace.

Therapist: :0)
Client: well . . . i'm not sure that was the motive of my heart
Client: :o(
Therapist: what was your motive?
Client: i wish i could say that though :o)
Client: i think it was because i just don't like people not to like me
Therapist: maybe there's a fine line in between the two. . . .
Therapist: the "people pleasing" is something that will be very difficult for you to shake.
Client: yeah
Client: i know
Therapist: it's part of being an ACOA [Adult Child of an Alcoholic].
Client: really?
Therapist: yes.
Client: i didn't know that
Therapist: you are evaluated on your performance, so you better perform well.
Therapist: and if you can't please people, they will leave.
Therapist: (even though, for the most part, they don't)
Therapist: this guy was going to, though, heh?
Client: yeah
Therapist: so, it brings up a lot of uncomfortable feelings.
Client: gosh . . . yes
Therapist: you know we can talk about these things?
Client: yeah
Therapist: good.
Client: i didn't realize i was feeling stuff
Therapist: all day, every day.
Therapist: I'm proud of you that you seem to be facing some of these feelings with him.
Therapist: I think it was important for you to tell him your decrease in trust
Therapist: in him.
Client: yeah . . . it was kind of weird
Therapist: how so?
Client: because i never told anyone that before
Client: it's like telling someone, "ummm, i don't like you as much"
Therapist: yes it is . . .
Therapist: and that's hard to say, but sometimes we have to say it.
Therapist: much better than pretending, hiding, running, or any number of things we do.
Client: yeah . . . i guess so . . . i'm just used to doing those things. . . . it's easier
Therapist: easier in the short run, harder in the long run.
Client: lol [laughing out loud] i guess so
Therapist: don't take my word for it . . . you'll see.
Client: lol
Therapist: how are you feeling now?
Client: lol i don't know how to answer that . . .
Therapist: fill in the blank after I feel _____.

This client continued to have problems identifying and expressing feelings, but made very specific progress related to her increased understanding of feelings management and the risks she took to try out new behaviors despite her discomfort.

EMAIL

The therapist must be focused and directive in brief email therapy. Decisions on when to lead the discussions and when to follow depend on the treatment goals and the current direction of the topic being explored. New subject matter should only be addressed if it sheds additional understanding and a possible solution to the central issue at hand. The clients will let you know if your interventions/interpretations are responsive to their issues by their response to the following questions:

1. Did they ignore the interpretation?
2. Did they change the topic?
3. Did the tone of their reply give indication that your interpretation was on target?

Therapies that use metaphor, story, and journaling are well suited for adaptation to email therapy. Therapies that use information are also easily transferred to the Internet. Books, articles, and Web pages that are relevant to the client's issues quite easily supplement work in the therapy session.

The following is an example of email therapy that uses an interactive journaling process with the client. The purpose of the interactive journaling is to help the client face up to issues related to self-esteem (note: the therapist's words are in italics):

> *Growth is painful . . . and we are vulnerable while it is occurring by vulnerable I mean when you're in the process of changing you're very "emotionally loose" and you need to take care not to expose yourself to people or situations that might hurt you.*
> Has anyone told you today how good you are at your work?
> *I don't hear it enough. . . . I'm no different than anyone else; I want to be appreciated for who I am and what I do . . . thank you, I'm glad you feel this work beneficial.*
> "Nothing" I ever did was acknowledged as good. There was only focus on what I did that was wrong. Never praise. (Rejection and no worth)
> *It's difficult to have any self-esteem when all you got from your mother was criticism . . . it's no wonder you find praise hard to accept.*
> My mother was always telling me, in anger, that if my so-and-so father cared about me he would pay the child support he was supposed to.
> *sounds like she wanted to take out his irresponsibility on you. I don't know how you felt about your dad at the time but this kind of comment didn't aim to endear him to you.*
> I could go on and on . . . but I hope you get the picture.
> I think I've fought hard to make myself worthy. Of course it's sometimes in a sick way . . . over-doer, over-accomplisher, people-pleaser, take on more than I can handle, etc. . . .
> *it is tiring trying to continually "measure up" . . . when will people just accept you for the wonderful person that you are?*
> . . . it was many years of rejection from the person whom I wanted to acknowledge me, but couldn't. A person whom I wanted to love me, but never felt she did. Yes, I think I do need to grieve this and then hopefully heal.

As pathetic as all this is ... there is a sense of joy within the sadness, because I know there is hope that I can get through this, with your help. For too long I've done things the same way but expected different results ... maybe now I can begin to do things differently ... to obtain better results ... break through my own limitations.

... *you are on your way*

SUPPORTIVE CONFRONTATION SKILLS

CHAT

Chat is an ideal place to be direct with the client regarding behaviors that need to change. As noted previously, challenging a client's erroneous core beliefs can be accomplished quite well in text-based therapy. As the client is working with the therapist in the chat room, the client's thinking and beliefs are the focus of the interaction. The therapist can directly and powerfully challenge erroneous beliefs and at the same time provide specific support for the client in the here and now. Here is an example of a belief challenge:

> *Client:* so, my mother used to tell me that I was wrong for feeling bad about my situation.
> *Therapist:* that's not true. You are not wrong for feeling bad.
> *(pause for three minutes, which is a long time in a chat session)*
> *Client:* what?

As discussed earlier in this chapter, when there is a pause in the chat session, the words stay in exactly the same place on the screen. This cannot be replicated in f2f in the same way as online. If you put something up on the board in your office, the client will look at the board, but will also look at you and other things. In online therapy, the only thing the client can look at regarding your interaction is the screen and the words on it. When the words stay on the screen for an extended period of time, it gives time for the message to be reinforced for the client—it increases the impact of the message. After the client responds, the therapist can explain further, flesh out the new ideas and the new thinking:

> *Therapist:* it's not true. You feel whatever you feel. No one can tell you what you should or should not feel.
> *Therapist:* feelings are facts. We are entitled to feel whatever we feel, even if it doesn't make sense.
> *Client:* I've never heard that before. I thought you should only feel certain ways about things, and if you didn't, you were wrong.
> *Therapist:* no.
> *(pause)*
> *Therapist:* you feel whatever you feel.

Appropriate confrontation of clients requires a sense of timing that can be developed only with experience in providing therapy over time. This sense of timing, both in deciding when to confront a client's beliefs and in the individual interventions themselves, cannot be taught, only experienced.

Chat is also an ideal forum for the use of Motivational Interviewing skills. The central concepts of Motivational Interviewing are quite adaptable to text-based therapy: respectful treatment of the client; allowing the client to make the ultimate decisions about his or her participation in treatment; and using reflective listening skills (Miller and Rollnick, 1991). Reflective listening (talk/listen/reflect) is adapted and changed to reflective text interaction (type/read/reflect). An example of reflective text interaction follows in a portion of a chat interaction that starts after several treatment options have been discussed:

Therapist: that's what treatment is about.
Client: without causing so many other problems
Therapist: you need to hear there will be some problems as you get better.
Therapist: (just like there are problems right now).
Client: I've seen that with the way my sister acts towards me now since I said everything has
Client: had an effect on me
Therapist: right.
Client: I don't understand why it affects me so much but not her
Client: the same things happened to her, except for my father talking to her that way.
Therapist: I don't know. Sometimes people divorce themselves from their feelings.
Therapist: It's a way of coping.
Client: I just feel silly that it's affected me this way after so long
Client: that it didn't bother me sooner instead of later
Therapist: feelings are real. and no one can tell you that you should or shouldn't feel a certain way.
Client: even though everyone seems to think they can
Therapist: right . . . they just don't understand how it works.
Client: i guess not
Therapist: so many people don't understand how to deal with their feelings.
Therapist: yet, it's so much a part of everyone's life.
Therapist: do you have friends?
Client: that's true because I don't know how to deal with the way i feel now either.
Therapist: right.
Client: not really
Client: I have some friends but none that I feel comfortable talking to
Therapist: we each need at least one person we can talk to on a feelings level.
Client: all of my friends that I felt comfortable enough talking to have gotten married & moved out of state.
Therapist: that must be sad for you.
Client: it is & very hard because I don't really have anyone to get out & do things with & then it's
Client: so hard for me to go out & meet new people
Therapist: are you in a relationship now?
Client: no. just ended one about two weeks ago
Therapist: what happened?

Client: basically what I said earlier. He acted like he liked me for who I was so I tried to find

Client: something wrong so I couldn't like him

Therapist: and you did.

Client: yes

Client: from things like we didn't like the same things, he never wanted to do anything, I ended up

Client: always having to pay my way & usually his also, that was the hardest thing for me to deal with

Therapist: you pay the way for enough people already.

Client: i felt like if i didn't then he wouldn't like me either

Client: or i couldn't never get him to do anything

Therapist: hmmm. what kinds of things do you like to do?

Client: movies, going out to eat, going to hockey games

Client: reading, dancing

Therapist: do you do those things?

Client: occasionally

Client: i was going to hockey games all of the time, until my mom & step dad adopted one of the

Client: players & started acting like they were more of a family than we were

Client: it made me sick to look at & listen to them so I've got to where I don't hardly go

Therapist: you must have felt pretty uncomfortable.

Client: uncomfortable & like we didn't mean as much anymore because she was always talking & doing

Client: for them & not paying any attention to us at all

Therapist: us meaning you and your sister?

Client: if we asked her a question we had to ask 3 different times for her to even hear us

Client: me & my older sister

Therapist: it makes sense for you to not want to go.

EMAIL

Using the client's own words in your reply can help the client feel heard. Along with feeling heard, this mirroring of the client's language helps to facilitate closeness.

A mixture of conversation and confrontation seems to work well with text communications. If the tone remains too conversational it may confuse the client about the nature of the relationship and collude with client defenses around avoiding material needing to be addressed. Being too confrontational may cause the client to terminate the therapy prematurely. The following is an example of the therapist working to balance support and confrontation with a woman having difficulty dealing with her young children acting out after a divorce:

Dear Annette,

Keeping busy is one way to avoid having to deal with all the feelings you are having now . . . at least your house will get clean! And although it's good to distract yourself every now and then to take your mind off of all this, be careful not to just "brush it all under the carpet." Talk to your children and assure them that Mommy and Daddy still love them and that it's not anything they did that has lead to your separation. Listen to their questions and allow them the opportunity to express their sadness. And most of all don't forget to take some time for yourself. Talk with you soon.

Peter

SESSIONAL SUMMARY SKILLS

Summarization is used in online therapy for the same reasons it is used in f2f therapy:

1. The summary keeps the client focused on the work of therapy.
2. The summary provides encouragement and acknowledgment of the client's progress in therapy.
3. The summary provides the client with a clear sense of what work needs to be done.
4. The summary can condense the principles of the learning in an easy-to-use, easy-to-remember manner.

CHAT

Here is an example of the end of a chat session where summarizing skills are used to bring together all the issues discussed in a session:

Therapist: so, do you want to summarize tonight, or should I?
Client: ah, I don't know . . . why don't you do it? :o)
Therapist: ok. ;0)
Therapist: here goes. . . .
Therapist: you talked tonight about how upset you were at your boss . . .
Therapist: you said he doesn't consider you or your needs when making out the schedule for the week.
Therapist: you talked about feeling taken advantage of,
Therapist: and you said you didn't like that feeling and you feel it a lot.
Therapist: we talked about making your needs known to your boss in an appropriate manner.
Therapist: you said you are not quite there yet, but are making progress.
Therapist: (I agree that you are making progress! ;0)
Therapist: you told me you plan to continue with your feelings diary because
Therapist: you see it as helping you see the impact others have on you and
Therapist: your feelings. . . .
Therapist: did I get it right?
Client: yep . . . that's about it. . . . you must have paid attention. ;o)
Therapist: yep.

EMAIL

The following is a good example of summarizing a client's progress in the therapy process and is both encouraging and appropriately challenging at the same time:

Dear Barbara,

You don't know how good it makes me feel to read your words. It really is magical what can happen when people take the time to get to know one another. It saddens me to think how many years you spent looking for connection, to be heard, seen and understood. Through our sharing, I've learned a lot about you and myself . . . thanks. Now it's time to begin letting others in so that they too will have an opportunity to share your world.

Best,
Peter

SUMMARY AND CONCLUSIONS

Whatever the mode or context of therapy, helping people change requires a number of specific skills the therapist must have. The therapist needs to be able to:

- Assess and engage the client in the process of treatment
- Reach an agreement about the focus of the work with the client
- Have a set of intervention skills the therapist can use to help the client get from where they are to where they want to be
- Be able to help the client solidify the changes they make.

All of these things can be and are being done online in both chat and email interactions. Many types of therapy lend themselves to direct adaptation to solely text-based interactions, and although common wisdom would lead one to believe that some other types of therapy are impossible to do online, that has not been proved true.

Evidence is starting to accumulate that demonstrates the potential of text-based therapy (Barak, 2001). Transcripts of chat sessions and email exchanges from a number of different therapists show evidence that a therapeutic relationship has been formed and the therapeutic interaction has had a positive result for the client. (Clinical Case Study Group, 2000). Early research is showing online interventions are comparable to f2f interventions with regard to positive outcomes.

The experience of both therapists and clients, as well as early research, tends to support the following conclusions:

- Certain clients who won't seek f2f therapy can and do seek therapy online.
- Certain therapists who are both interested in online work and are specially skilled have been able to adapt their f2f interventions to text-based therapy.
- As a result, online clients are getting better.

KEY TERMS

Cybertherapy: Therapy that occurs online through either email, chat, or videoconferencing.

Directive versus **nondirective:** In *directive interventions,* the therapist has a plan to move the client toward a particular change in the context of the presenting problem; *nondirective interventions* provide support to the client and allow the focus of the session to be entirely up to the client.

Engagement skills: Establishing a relationship with a client by demonstrating that you have an accurate sense of the client's perception of the world.

Motivational interviewing: A type of therapy developed by Miller and Rollnick that focuses on accurate empathy and respect for the client to help increase motivation for change.

Reflective listening: Primary skill used in motivational interviewing to help move a client toward change.

Reflective text interaction: Using text to reflect back the meaning and the content of the client's communication.

Refocusing: Bringing the client back to the issue at hand, or changing the focus on a topic more relevant that will help the client make changes.

Sessional contracting: Reaching an agreement with the client in a particular interaction about the focus of the work in that meeting or interaction.

STUDY QUESTIONS

1. What are some ways you might use text to facilitate the therapeutic relationship?

2. Can you think of any instances where communicating through text might lend itself to miscommunications? How might you facilitate repairing these errors?

3. What might be some of the positive and negative consequences of the absence of visual/nonverbal cues on text-based communications?

4. What is the purpose of sessional contracting?

5. Why is chat an ideal forum for motivational interviewing?

REFERENCES

Barak, A. (2001). Online therapy outcome studies. Retrieved August 30, 2003 from http://www.ismho.org/issues/cswf.htm.

Childress, C. (1998). Potential risks and benefits of online psychotherapeutic interventions [1999, April 23]. Retrieved August 30, 2003 from http://www.ismho.org/issues/9801.htm.

Edelstein, M. (2002). REBT Therapy. Retrieved August 30, 2003 from http://panicdisorder. about.com/gi/dynamic/offsite.htm?site=http%3A%2F%2Fwww.threeminutetherapy.com %2Frebt.html.

ISMHO Millennium Group (2000). A report from the Millennium Group. Retrieved August 30, 2003 from http://www.fenichel.com/CaseStudy.htm.

Miller, W. R., & Rollnick, S. (1991). *Motivational interviewing: Preparing people to change addictive behavior.* New York: Guilford Press.

Seligman, M. E. P. (1995). The effectiveness of psychotherapy: The Consumer Reports Study. *American Psychologist, 50:*965–974. Retrieved August 30, 2003 from http://www.apa.org/journals/seligman.html.

Woititz, J. (1983). Laundry list for adult children of alcoholics. Retrieved August 30, 2003 from http://www.dmh.missouri.gov/ada/facts/coa.htm.

10

ONLINE COUNSELING GROUPS

DONNA R. BELLAFIORE, YVETTE COLÓN, AND PAUL ROSENBERG

The rapid development of Internet communication has opened new and unexplored means of interpersonal communication and has brought dramatic challenges and opportunities to the mental health community. The potentials of online group counseling on the Internet, as a novel therapeutic medium, are just beginning to be explored. Group counseling venues vary from open membership bulletin boards to small counseling groups using multimedia and voice communication to enrich the therapeutic environment. While unstructured chat rooms can, at times, bring out the worst in human nature, in many support and counseling groups strong alliances and lasting relationships develop. This chapter will review several vastly different types of online settings for therapeutic groups and provide guidelines for therapists interested in venturing into this new area.

SUPPORT AND THERAPEUTIC GROUPS

In 1993 Yvette Colón facilitated an experimental group for Echo, a private virtual community, based in New York City. The Group Conference was conducted in a bulletin board format. Criteria for entry were simple. In the spirit of adventure, people could join the group simply by being interested in an online psychotherapy experiment; those interested were required to make a three-month commitment to participate and sign a liability waiver. The screening process consisted of potential participants supplying the therapist with their real names, addresses, phone numbers, previous groups, and/or individual psychotherapy experiences along with any topics they wished to explore. Once participants were accepted, they would be given a password for access to the bulletin board. The groups were text-based. Topics were posted on the bulletin board. Participants had access 24/7, and were free to post whatever and whenever they wished. The groups were limited to eight participants each and lasted 12 weeks. Based on participant feedback, most felt that the groups had helped and that their online experience had been a positive one. (One-hour synchronous chat sessions were included at the beginning of the project, but they proved to be unpopular and were discontinued.)

Beginning with a small grant, Colón created an online services program at Cancer Care, a social service agency in New York City. This program later became a part of the services offered by this agency to its clients in 1997 and remains in operation today. The groups were held in bulletin board (and later listserv) formats and provided online support groups to cancer patients and caregivers. Information about the groups was posted on the agency's website. Online groups were facilitated by staff social workers. Applicants completed and sent email registration forms to be considered for an appropriate online group. Groups were limited to 12 members. Participants completed an online questionnaire, which included demographics, information on their cancer experience and treatment, support system, and reasons for joining the group.

Participants were required to commit to participate for 3 months and to participate/post at least 3 times a week. Although the groups were designed to be 12 weeks in duration to emulate time-limited face-to-face (f2f) groups, one of the online groups continued for one-and-a-half years. After several years the group was redesigned in a listserv format and participation was increased to 25 members per group. The members enjoyed the ease of participation (via broadcast and private email) but felt that topics were not as well organized. There was also no centralized archive of the group. The focus of these online cancer groups was to enable participants to cope more effectively with illness by discussing concerns, gaining emotional support, and finding appropriate emotional and concrete resources.

The Brief Symptom Inventory (Derogatis & Melisaratos, 1983) was used pre- and post-group to assess the effectiveness of these groups. An informal data analysis of this inventory indicated that participants' psychosocial distress, especially anxiety and depression, lessened over the span of the group. Overall, participants found the online group experience to be a positive one.

In 1998 Donna Bellafiore (DRB Alternatives) began an ambitious project to help those dealing with issues of infidelity. This Web-based self-help group was set up in a bulletin board format and was open to world-wide participation and operated on a 24-hour-a-day, seven-day-a-week schedule. It surpassed expectations when, by 2001, the site was being visited by more than 900 people a day. The site was typically ranked in the top 10 on major search engines on the subject of infidelity. Although many of the participants were regular visitors and found the format beneficial, the site became unmanageable. Because of the sheer number of posts, it became increasingly difficult to enforce group norms and guidelines and, therefore, protect the participants from the disruptive or destructive behavior of a few visitors. In 2001 Bellafiore made the decision to convert the site into a more traditional, membership venue.

The above forays into the online world taught many lessons and demonstrated the need for careful monitoring and control. They also very clearly showed the interest in and need for such groups.

ONLINE VERSUS FACE-TO-FACE THERAPY

Online group therapy should be seen as a part of a continuum of therapeutic services. It may serve as an adjunct to f2f therapy. A therapist may, for example, have a client visit support groups online to explore issues dealt with in traditional therapy. Online therapy groups may also provide an entrée to more traditional f2f therapy. A client who is not ready to visit a therapist may begin with an online experience and then proceed to office-based therapy when he or she has become comfortable with the process. Online therapy may also be primary. Although therapy groups are usually held in person at a designated place and time, there are people who could benefit from a traditional therapy group but are unable to attend. They may be people who live in rural areas with few support services, medically ill patients who are homebound or debilitated by treatment, or caregivers who have significant demands on their time. The Internet has the advantage of bringing people together, while allowing them to remain in their homes. Online group therapy offers a practical, cost-effective option. It maintains privacy and may serve to diminish social isolation, anxiety, and depression.

ONLINE BEHAVIOR

Anonymity is pervasive in online interactions, in groups and in one-on-one encounters. This effect dramatically alters the interpersonal environment by making it feel safe to disclose deep personal feelings. Without fear of being judged or held accountable, a deep level of honesty can be rapidly established. In social relations theory, social distance refers to the disconnection between specific behavior, such as online interactions, and one's offline, "real" life. It is seen as a separate factor that acts in a similar way to anonymity. Together, these factors encourage people to be more self-revealing when they are in online groups. The protection by anonymity and social distance may also trigger disinhibited behavior, because there is a sense of not having consequences from behavior that is normally controlled or edited. The hallmark of the disinhibition effect is the willingness of people to say and do things in cyberspace they would never say or do in the "real" world.

Sitting at the computer in a protected, private world, one is able to focus more closely on inner feelings without being overpowered by the ego's need to "look good" to peers. This allows personal feelings to be perceived more intensely and, accompanied by online disinhibition, enhances the expression of things that might not ordinarily be shared. The perception of safety is something people are keenly aware of and is often stated as a reason people are willing to be more open in online groups. Those with social anxiety disorders who join online groups frequently disclose that they feel comfortable participating in online groups because they don't have to face people in person.

Projective mechanisms seen in online groups, where visual cues, auditory cues, or both are lacking, may be more powerful than in traditional groups. In the online group, one participant creates an image of another participant tailored to fulfill his or her unconscious emotional needs or to manage unacceptable feelings by attributing them to another. Projections can dramatically increase the positive or negative perception of others in the online group setting. Positive perceptions may result in clients displaying overly positive behavior, deferential attitudes, and showing excessive generosity. They may form deep relationships very quickly. This may be dangerous to the more vulnerable client with problems setting personal boundaries. Negative projections may be reduced in highly structured groups but must be managed by the counselor in order to maintain the cohesiveness of the group.

Behavioral change has been noted in three basic areas and may reflect the influence of anonymity, social distance, and projective mechanisms in the online environment:

- Greater willingness to reveal personal information, overvaluation, deferential acceptance, and increased generosity, resulting in rapid development of a sense of closeness with others.
- Intense reactions of anger when slighted, and heightened competitiveness, particularly in less-structured groups.
- Increased sexual communication and flirtatiousness, also more common in unstructured group environments such as chat rooms.

The impact on psychological behavior appears to be most positive in groups where issues are controlled by the presence of a therapist, and where group norms discourage negative responses. A wider range of emotional interactions are observed in online process groups than in the more structured, subject-focused groups.

ONLINE VERSUS FACE-TO-FACE GROUPS

Overall, online therapy and support groups have similar "curative factors" as those noted by Yalom (1995) in f2f groups, including a sense of belongingness and acceptance, a willingness and need to disclose personal information, honesty about feelings toward oneself and other members, interest and acceptance of others, good will and support of the group, personal importance, and a sense of stability and hope for its members.

The basic tenets put forth by Yalom for f2f groups have also been found to be true for online groups:

1. Instillation of hope
2. Universality
3. Altruism
4. The corrective recapitulation of the primary family group
5. Development of socializing technique—imitative behavior
6. Interpersonal learning
7. Group cohesiveness
8. Catharsis
9. Existential factors

Members of online groups seek to get the most out of their experiences. They also support other members of the group, feeling that, as part of the group, they are tied to the outcome of the entire group.

In the first study of its kind, Barak and Wander-Schwartz (1999) compared online unstructured process group therapy using password-protected synchronous (realtime) text chat with an f2f traditional process group. Their findings, although based on a sample too small to reach significance, clearly suggested that synchronous online text-based process groups appeared to have similar psychodynamics compared to traditional groups. Their study found that the online group developed openness slightly more rapidly than the f2f group. In this study, transcripts of each group were saved and analyzed. Barak and Wander-Schwartz studied three measures of therapeutic impact: self-esteem, social relationships, and well-being. They measured 10 aspects of group process variables, some of which included expression of feelings, personal exposure, action orientation, anger-aggression, and cohesiveness. An exit questionnaire assessed satisfaction and discharge attitude data. Barak and Wander-Schwartz report:

> ... both therapeutic groups had small, statistically insignificant positive improvement in participants' self-esteem, social relations and well-being, though the virtual group showed slightly more improvement ... the two groups were found to be

mostly similar in perceptions of group cohesiveness, personal exposure, expression of feelings, independence, and order and organization. Members of the [I]nternet group, however, reported higher levels of aggression, action orientation and therapist support and control. (1999)

The exit questionnaire showed that both groups had similar levels of satisfaction with their group experience. Barak and Wander-Schwartz state that the Internet therapy group reported that "anonymity was a major factor in their readiness to open up" (1999).

They noted a phenomenon that appears to be common in Internet-based therapy: although the virtual group "felt emotionally close to one another, they were not particularly interested in actually meeting the other group members." Barak and Wander-Schwartz relate the therapist's observation that the virtual group was similar to traditional groups and that along with "common therapeutic group factors she noticed—such as cohesiveness, catharsis, leadership, disclosure, support and aggression—she recognized much faster processes of interpersonal relationships, reflected in such various aspects as love and dislike, aggression and support" (1999).

This well-organized study documents the effectiveness of online group therapy and the similar psychodynamics to traditional groups. It also demonstrates the unique quality of online therapy and the power and importance of anonymity on psychological behavior in groups: because people feel safe being open and self-disclosing, closeness develops more rapidly. However, this "virtual intimacy" has a shallow level of interaction to it, because group members routinely do not show an interest in meeting other members in person. It may be that group members, who find their online group experience important and helpful on some level, realize the limitations of their virtual relationships and do not want to burst the "therapeutic bubble" of their positive online experience.

Bellafiore's large bulletin-board self-help group, which had an open membership and could not be as closely monitored as smaller process groups, demonstrated greater differences in group behavior than that noted in other more controlled groups. She noted that some of her participants not only formed tight-knit bonds, but actually formed subgroups at other Web addresses. These smaller groups were committed to moving forward and felt that the larger group was not meeting all of their needs. Members of the subgroups continued to visit the larger site and often invited members of the larger group to join them in their more private groups. Members of at least one subgroup did travel to meet each other f2f. Members often returned to the group and offered the newcomers support to welcome and encourage them through the process of recovery.

PROGRAM DELIVERY

Although synchronous and asynchronous text-based groups are the most common online therapeutic venues, videoconferencing and other multimedia experiences are gaining popularity. As technology progresses and the technical expertise of therapist and client increases, novel approaches are inevitable. There is an enormous diversity in the range of online group therapy options available, and the decision depends on selection criteria, degree of structure, leader expertise, and communication pathway chosen. Groups can range from support groups with little structure to formal process groups and structured, topic-focused, psychoeducational groups. Groups with broad selection criteria, drop-in membership, and minimal structure are often more difficult for the leader to maintain and may lack cohesiveness. Process and treatment groups with restricted membership are usually smaller and more tightly controlled.

Some of the delivery modes available to the group therapist today include:

- Group chat rooms
- Bulletin boards and message boards
- Broadcast email
- Self-help support groups
- Videoconferencing

Therapists have the option of using one of the above options or combining them to deliver a richer, more beneficial program to the client. (See the section on Technology later in this chapter for a more detailed discussion of these service modalities.) There are also online assessment tools available, which can be used to match clients to the mode of program delivery and to assess the viability of the therapy as it progresses. Therapists will also have to develop new assessment tools to clarify which of the environments work best for specific clients.

PROGRAM DESIGN

As with f2f groups, the design of the group will have to be carefully considered before work starts. The purpose of the group must be explained. The appropriateness of the group to the clients must be addressed. Clients must be carefully screened, possibly using a formal screening tool to identify fragile or at-risk individuals. (For examples of screening tools available online, see mentalhealthscreening.org and depression-screening.org.) For text-based programs, reading, writing, and comprehension skills may need to be assessed. Following are some of the issues that will need to be addressed during the design phase of the program:

1. Will this be a heterogeneous or homogeneous group?
2. Will it be a support group, a discussion group, or a therapy group?
3. What technology/delivery systems will be used?
4. How many participants (group size)?
5. How will members be screened for admission to the group?

6. How much facilitator involvement will there be?
7. What schedule will be used for synchronous groups?
8. Will the group be an open membership or closed group?
9. Will it be a worldwide support group?
10. Will this be a time-limited (commitment of group members) or open group?
11. Will group members be asked to sign membership forms and disclaimers?
12. What will the fee schedule be? How will the following group be funded?

Once the above questions are explored, the following policies and procedures must be addressed:

1. Group rules and norms must be carefully considered and published.
2. A confidentiality policy must be written and published.
3. Safety issues and conflict management issues must be addressed.
4. Accountability of the group members must be spelled out.
5. Cultural differences, language barriers, along with the ability to read, write, and comprehend must be addressed.
6. Group members must be assessed for severity of depression and anxiety, suicidal ideation, or past and current suicide attempts with an appropriate screening tool.
7. A termination policy must be written.

Welcome Pages

Welcoming members is important. Written communication—using language that is nonthreatening—sets the tone for the group and helps members feel safe. Especially for the more unstructured online self-help groups, a clear message about the purpose and scope of the group, along with the rules and norms expected of participants, must be presented before participation in the group is allowed. Creating these Web pages can be done from the website from which the group is launched. Here is the text that is displayed on the DRB Alternatives website:

> Welcome. You've likely come to our support group hurting from the pain of infidelity. We appreciate your courage and want you to know that relating to others online can, in time, ease your pain and help you heal. Before participating, please take a moment to learn about our board, paying special attention to Policies and Etiquette Guidelines. The following tips may also be helpful:
>
> • Read all posted messages.
> • Tell your story; ask for advice.
> • Support others by responding, because what you give comes back to help you.
> • Set personal boundaries; "walk away" from provocative or disruptive posts.
>
> If the message board is experiencing conflict during your visit, feel free to "read only" or leave and revisit at a calmer time. Communication often reflects the

heightened emotions of participants at various stages of recovery. Participate only when you feel at ease with the board's climate. We want you to experience comfort and healing rather than more turmoil.

Board Policies

All participants must be 18 years or older.

While DRB Alternatives, Inc. maintains the right to enforce its policies, we are not responsible for the content and postings or information members share with each other. As site owner and manager, DRB Alternatives, Inc. reserves the right to monitor this community and to delete outdated and incongruent messages.

We do not keep a library of messages. As with any face-to-face group, members bear the responsibility for protecting their boundaries.

TECHNOLOGY

Professionals interested in conducting therapy in cyberspace must be familiar with the various formats available to them. They must have the technical knowledge to install and operate the software programs, and they must also understand the Internet and email programs. Therapists must also educate themselves on the computer basics necessary for facilitating online groups, including troubleshooting certain technical problems, as well as editing, saving, and deleting messages. Consulting with Internet experts, who can explain the technology currently available as well as emerging technologies, is also important for therapists interested in maintaining a viable online clientele.

VIDEOCONFERENCING

An example of one of the newer technologies being employed in online counseling is videoconferencing. Previously, cost and technical difficulties prohibited its use as a medium for therapy. Recently, however, new and more affordable hardware and software has become available. Videoconferencing allows the group leader to be visible to all members of the group, allows members to speak directly to one another, and also allows the use of concurrent text-based communications. Multimedia presentations, such as video clips and slide presentations, also serve to dramatically enrich the experience of therapeutic groups on the Internet.

Here is a summary of the features used in the "eGetgoing.com" groups, which have been delivering group treatment for substance abuse since January 2001:

- *Full Duplex Audioconferencing.* Audioconferencing permits multiple group members to talk directly to each other and their counselor as if on a conference call together. As in traditional conference calls, several users may speak at once.

- *IP Videoconferencing.* The image of the counselor is transmitted from his computer to the group in realtime. Clients are not visible to the group or the counselor to protect anonymity.
- *Breakout Rooms.* A backup counselor is available should a client need individual attention during group session. Breakout rooms can also be used to separate the group into smaller discussion groups.
- *Evaluations and Polls.* At various points, clients are asked to respond to questions relevant to counseling to evaluate the stage of change and other relevant issues. Data collected is stored in the individual client's database. Information can be used to assess and write reports on client progress.
- *Pre- and Post-Group Assessments.* Information gathered from clients pre- and post-group are graphed and used as an evaluation tool and are posted to the client's homepage.
- *Whiteboard.* The whiteboard is a screen on which clients can write text messages or draw pictures. These words and images are visible to the entire group. This allows text communication to occur during verbal discussion. The counselor can also use the whiteboard to show slides, which can elicit written or drawn responses from the group.
- *Feedback Options.* There are several mechanisms used for feedback. Clients can press "yes" and "no" buttons on their computers to answer questions. They can "raise their hands" by pressing a button; this will place them in a numbered sequence for attention by the counselor. Whiteboard messages and an "applause button" can communicate support. Clients and counselor can send private messages to each other.
- *Multimedia applications.* Slides and videos are presented to the group. To provide rich content rapidly so that all group members can watch videos concurrently and independent of the speed of their modems, several CD-ROM disks are supplied to group members. These disks carry the agendas for each group session and contain the video vignettes that have been filmed to demonstrate relevant content or present issues appropriate for the group.
- *Individual Client Personal Homepages.* Clients sign into the group through a Personal Homepage that is password protected and encrypted (as are all communications throughout the entire treatment program). Attendance, self-esteem, and sobriety data are posted on the client's Personal Homepage. Homework assignments, online assessments, and intergroup mail are all posted on this page.
- *Personal Journal.* A confidential personal journal is available on the client's Homepage.
- *Homework Assignments.* Counselors assign homework via the client's Personal Homepage and respond privately between sessions about the homework.

Rosenberg (2001 internal reports) describes favorable results for substance abuse groups using videoconferencing. Videoconferencing allows the presentation of a format for group treatment that closely emulates traditional groups. Verbal interactions, even the ability to have more than one person talk at a time, resemble f2f groups. A striking feature of this approach is the impact of having the counselor's face visible throughout the group, which seems to significantly enhance group cohesiveness and individual commitment to the group. Clients routinely report that they have a sense of direct communication from the counselor, as if the counselor were talking directly to them. This personalizes the online group experience, because clients feel emotionally connected with the counselor. Even at low bandwidths, the appearance of the counselor's image is powerful.

Counselors choosing this mode of therapy delivery will have to develop a professional on-screen persona, learn to talk directly to the camera, and stay aware of the level of participation of each group member, while simultaneously reviewing private messages from group members. They will also have to remain aware of the group's agenda while facilitating the spontaneous discussion going on in the group. Many counselors have found this challenging at first, but most have readily adapted and even enjoy the multitasking involved in leading this type of group.

A WORD OF CAUTION

As in many areas of cyberspace, new treatment options available through the Internet have thorny legal implications. Old laws, which are structured to protect the public within the bounds of individual states, are suddenly outmoded as state, national, and even international boundaries vanish in the World Wide Web. Laws covering online counseling are changing rapidly and vary from state to state and country to country. For example, at this point, it may not be legal for psychologists, psychiatrists, or social workers to provide Internet psychotherapy to an out-of-state client. Even intrastate treatment may be questionable. Laws governing Internet therapy are gradually maturing and may eventually keep pace with the unstoppable development of Internet treatment. For now, it is prudent for professionals to be aware of the possible legal complications inherent in Internet-based therapy.

CONFIDENTIALITY

Although confidentiality of the group member must be scrupulously maintained, it is necessary for the group leader to have the pertinent information needed to assure that there is a proper "fit" between the participant and the group. Although most groups use "handles" or screen names during group sessions, it is necessary for the therapist to maintain an accurate list of the real identities of the participants. In many cases, identification will include names, addresses, phone numbers, as well as any clinical diagnoses or other information pertinent to participation in the group. In some cases, information such as credit card numbers and social security numbers may also be required. If any personal information will be shared (e.g., with other therapists, a webmaster, or a credit card company), it must be with the authorization of the participant. The therapist should also be familiar with confidentiality policies of those with whom client information will be shared. Professionals are ethically (and in many states legally) required to report clients who may harm themselves or others. To help clients understand in advance how reportable issues will be handled, they should be asked to read and "acccpt" an on-screen description of behaviors that will be reported. It must be explained that confidentiality will be broken if a client is deemed to be a danger to himself or to others.

SECURITY

In all groups, secure communication is a concern. Two aspects of security are:

1. Privacy of the group environment (i.e., is it password protected and do members have "handles" or screen names?)
2. The level of security regarding what is being shared by group members to Internet interception (i.e., is the information being encrypted as it is sent across the Internet?)

Although high levels of security may be cost-prohibitive for therapists in private practice, consultation with an expert in Internet security may aid in deciding how much security is available, necessary, and affordable.

The welcome pages of Bellafiore's self-help support group employed the following privacy statement. This statement was presented to potential group members before entrance into the group was permitted, in order to explain that members' privacy was a top priority:

> Protecting your privacy is one of our primary concerns. Please take a moment to review our privacy policy and note that DRB Alternatives, Inc. refuses all media requests for personal stories and/or contact information. We protect our site with the highest security firewalls. Our group is closed to the public's viewing. Your personal stories will remain within the confines of the group.

ACCOUNTABILITY

Because of the anonymity of text-based communication, group members may need to be reminded that they are interacting with real people and that they are accountable for their actions, not only to the group, but also to the therapist.

Group rules and norms must be explicitly spelled out and remedies for disruptive behavior explained. For severe infractions, a termination policy should also be in place and employed when necessary. The leader must have an adequate tracking system and be aware of each member's real name, password, and screen name. This is especially important when it is possible for participants to leave the group, only to return using a different screen name. (Bellafiore notes that returning to a group with a new screen name has been used by at least one of her participants as a way of extricating the participant from a difficult situation within the group.)

HELLO AND GOOD-BYE

The presence or absence of a group member in an f2f setting is obvious, even when those present are not actively participating in the conversation.

Members in online groups must be cognizant that whereas they may enter and exit a group unnoticed, they have a responsibility to tell other group participants that they are present, and also should notify them when they decide to leave their computer. (This includes all absences, whether the participant goes to the kitchen for a glass of water or turns the computer off and leaves the session for the day.) The group dynamic is affected by all members, whether they are taking an active or passive role. Even in groups where the presence of members is noted on the screen, acknowledging one's presence, and even one's reason for leaving, is important to other group members.

Similarly, when members decide to leave an online group permanently, letting others know not only when they plan to leave, but also why they are leaving, is important to the overall progress of the group. Groups where members just disappear may have a feeling of unfinished business or even a feeling of uneasiness about the sudden departure of a group member, who may have become emotionally important to the group.

Bellafiore's experience with her large open membership group and with the smaller, members-only self-help group has shown that members feel it is important to know when and why others are leaving. She has noted that group members often decide to exchange email addresses to continue the relationships started in the group. The following posting is similar to others from members who have decided to leave the group:

> Our membership expires any time now. Originally we thought we'd renew, but we've decided to take a break for a while. Thank you to everyone for sharing your experiences with us. We leave the board with much hope, due to all of your encouragement and advice. I'm sure we'll be back some day.
>
> We are going to miss this contact with others who have "been there." So please e-mail us. We would welcome the chance to keep the lines of communication open with anyone here . . .

CONFLICT

Conflict is an inescapable part of any type of group therapy. Conflicts in text-based online therapy may occur for many reasons but can be due to miscommunication accentuated by the lack of verbal tone and visual clues.

When there is a conflict, it is critical for the leader to become active in the group, not only where the conflict is occurring, but also in other areas of the group. Conflicts require that the leader maintain neutrality, clarify what has been said, elicit more information about the conflict, and mediate between the participants. In some cases, the conflict can be moved to a private area (e.g., a personal chat room or email) for the original discussion to continue.

This strategy is especially useful in online groups where members can easily absent themselves from the conversation when feelings are stirred that make them uncomfortable. Groups can also quickly lose their focus when disruptive behavior becomes contagious. Disinhibition may be a factor when members react with intense hostility to perceived affronts. Clear guidelines are necessary to help group members understand how to appropriately work through conflict. Once the conflict is resolved, there is an opportunity for the leader to open a discussion about handling anger and conflict in daily lives. Ultimately, it is the responsibility of the leader to deal effectively with conflict, providing a level of comfort and safety to group members that will ensure their continuing participation.

CLIENT RESPONSES TO ONLINE THERAPY

Client reactions to online therapy have been found to be similar to those of f2f groups. Rosenberg's experiences with the online support group dealing with substance abuse may provide insight into the online process. Clients reported the most valuable part of the treatment process was the rapport and support they experienced from other group members. The support of the counselor also ranked high in the client's perceived value. Clients reported looking forward to returning to the group beginning as early as the second session.

Group support and rapport continued to grow during the initial third of the program and remained high through the rest of the sessions.

Group members routinely treated each other with deferential respect and esteem. This helped clients rebuild their self-esteem, damaged by their substance abuse. The highly respectful supportive interactions among group members, which developed rapidly, increased clients' desire to return to the group. As their self-esteem grew, so did their motivation to stay sober. Anonymity was cited as helpful in being able to comfortably self-disclose. As one shared a painful issue and another identified with having similar experiences, rapport developed between specific members of the group.

This consistent positive rapport was interpreted as a reflection of anonymity, social distance, and positive projective mechanisms. There was little conflict noted in the groups.

Some clients came to group sessions intoxicated. The counselor positively confronted this and the client was permitted to remain in the group if he was not disruptive. The sense of being accepted and supported had a very positive effect on most clients who made efforts to attend future groups sober.

Bellafiore reports similar findings in her self-help support group dealing with infidelity issues. Some of the positive comments posted on her site illustrate the positive reactions:

> *Group Member 1:* Let me take this opportunity to thank you for this site. To the extent that anything has helped me, expressing my feelings here has been a positive experience . . . While this site is not someone I can talk to face-to-face, it is in fact, a place for many who understand the need to have a venue where one can express one's most sensitive and painful thoughts without criticism . . . It is calming and helpful
>
> *Group Member 2:* I want to thank you for this board. I have been going to counseling for a long time and reading posts on this board has meant more to me. It has validated feelings that I couldn't explain . . . I have learned that there is compassion for everyone on this board because we all understand the pain of betrayal . . .

ROLE OF THE FACILITATOR

As in an f2f group, the online facilitator shapes the group and sets the tone for the group. As mentioned above, the facilitator must also make decisions on the communication pathways to be used, as well as the technologies employed. In text-based groups, the leader's "voice" is the written word. Good writing skills are necessary to communicate not only content, but also tone and mood, which will set the standard for the group. An atmosphere of trust and comfort must also be conveyed in print. Establishing and maintaining a leadership style is important in keeping the group on track.

Bellafiore posts "Guidelines for Responsible Posting." These guidelines set the tone for the group experience on her self-help site, making participants aware that they are dealing with other human beings:

- Validate members' feelings.
- Avoid criticism that is not helpful.
- Ask clarifying questions.
- Demonstrate empathy for members' pain.
- Avoid disclosures that make you feel uncomfortable.
- Consider motives behind your statements.
- Give honest feedback.
- Show kindness . . . it's contagious!

Understanding when to intervene during conflict and how to defuse anger is also essential. The facilitator must be comfortable enough with conflict to deal with it and not take attacks personally. Those experienced in running f2f groups will find the transition to online groups relatively easy. Although converting verbal communication into the written word may take practice and patience.

In text-based online groups, the therapist and group members do not have the visual or verbal cues present in f2f groups. The therapist must "listen" in a different way by paying close attention to language, the way group members write, the ways in which they express themselves when they are feeling well vs. when they are feeling ill or upset. The therapist must be more active and sometimes more directive in the group to make up for the lack of eye contact and body language. If the therapist does not send messages to the group on a regular basis, he or she is considered to be "absent" from the group.

The biggest challenge faced by an online group therapist is the text-based nature of the group environment. The written word, in or out of context of group communication, can be stark and direct. Humor and sarcasm can be easily misinterpreted and feelings can be hurt. In these situations, the psychotherapist must be a strong presence to mediate and guide the group through conflict.

Therapists who have worked in an online setting are usually surprised at how quickly and how much they can learn about clients through the written word. Emotions and feelings become easily recognizable. The therapist can often discern when a client is ill, intoxicated, or depressed, and may even uncover untruths by "reading between the lines." Therapists have discovered that levels of intimacy and trust may be greater because participants feel more comfortable disclosing and discussing their most intimate concerns. In asynchronous communications, clients are able to give the time and thought to their writings, which provide richer and more meaningful responses.

Facilitators of online groups must decide how much time they will devote to the group. The postings from large groups operating on a 24/7 schedule may prove to be impossible to read and evaluate.

After a decade of experience with online groups, many therapists believe that the size of the group is an important consideration that should be considered before a venue is chosen. Chat groups should be small; a maximum of eight participants is ideal. Because of the realtime nature of chat communications, conversations can occur quickly. Having more than eight members at one time will prevent the group from achieving any depth of focus. A bulletin board group can accommodate 12 to 15 members; more would result in too many messages for the psychotherapist and members to read and respond to, and may leave many feeling overwhelmed. A mailing list support group appears to accommodate up to 25 members without losing intimacy and connection.

Online facilitators also function in the role of consultant and gatekeeper. It is the facilitator who decides which of the online technologies will be employed and in what context and combination. It is also the facilitator who admits or denies admittance to new members, removes disruptive or dangerous members, and keeps track of active members. As technology evolves, the facilitator will need to take an active part in making sure the group evolves with it. Therapists considering opening an online group must have the level of expertise and organization necessary for these tasks.

TECHNOLOGY WILL CONTINUE TO EVOLVE

We are living in the dawn of a new era where computer-mediated interpersonal communication is evolving before our eyes. As the cost and size of computers decrease every few months, and the access to bandwidth increases throughout the world, online therapeutic activities will continue to expand into new venues.

Today, technology is providing therapists with the ability to reach people who just a few years ago would have had no opportunity for therapy. For example, even in rural areas, people have the ability to join groups dealing with very specific and focused issues. As new technologies emerge and people become more comfortable with online activities, it is clear that the delivery of health care in general, and mental health care in particular, will be impacted by this technology.

In the future, we can expect a serial port on the computer to wirelessly monitor an individual's psychophysiological responses to the content and process of groups. Devices that measure skin conductance and pulse rate and can enter these data into the computer are coming on the market today. Group members may wear such devices on their fingers, providing group leaders with realtime feedback. These data may be analyzed and displayed to reveal unconscious reactions. In the future, a group leader may be able to observe on a separate monitor a client responding with increased anxiety as another client describes, for example, conflicts with a father, alerting the therapist to explore that client's willingness to share feelings about this issue. These new developments are on the immediate horizon and portend a complex and exciting potential for future group therapeutic experience on the Internet.

CONCLUSION

The Internet, as we know it, was not commercially available until 1990. The World Wide Web was launched in 1991. The phrase "surfing the Net" was coined in 1992, and the White House went online for the first time in

1993. As the Internet continues to evolve, it is impossible to predict the ways in which this and other new technologies will impact the delivery of group counseling. It can, however, be postulated that as technologies advance, there will be therapists who will use these emerging technologies to design and implement ever more innovative ways to deliver group counseling and online support *(Hobbes' Internet Timeline v6.0)*.

KEY TERMS

Asynchronous groups: Text-based online group where participants post responses at any time.

Breakout room: A separate conferencing screen that can be separated from the group in which part of the group can meet, with or without the counselor, for a private discussion and then return to the rest of the group.

Brief symptom inventory: A psychological self-report symptom scale that measures anxiety, depression, and other forms of psychological distress.

Bulletin board/discussion board: A website in which participants can read and write messages at any time that can be read by any other participant. The messages remain for the duration of the group, posted sequentially and usually organized by topic.

Chat group/chat room: A realtime exchange in which everyone is at his/her computer at the same time. A program is used that allows what is typed by one participant to be seen by all the others. At a predetermined time, the members of the group sign into the group using a special chat program so they can communicate with each other.

Curative factors: Factors that influence positive psychological change in groups.

Full duplex audioconferencing: An audio link through which group members can talk directly to each other, just like a telephone conversation.

Listserv/mailing list: A private email group in which each subscriber receives a separate copy, via email, of each message that is posted. Through these messages members can maintain ongoing communication with other list members who share a common concern or interest.

Process groups: Groups where spontaneous interactions occur that may become the focus of the group without a fixed educational agenda and where the leader takes an observational role.

Projective mechanisms: Perceptions from the unconscious that color how others are perceived.

Psychodynamics: Internal psychological forces that determine how people function and interact.

Synchronous groups: Groups that meet together during a specified time period.

Termination policy: A policy about the conditions under which a person can be dropped from a group.

Text-based groups: Online groups based on written text messages, can be synchronous or asynchronous.

Videoconferencing: A program that allows the counselor and others to be streamed onto part of the monitor screen so the group can see them when they talk, much like a remote TV news reporter.

Whiteboard: A screen that can be used to type messages or draw images that is visible to the entire group; slides can be placed on the whiteboard by the leader to illustrate relevant group issues.

STUDY QUESTIONS

1. What contributes to group members being willing to be more self-disclosing online?

2. Disinhibited behavior online may result from what factors?

3. The presence of a therapist tends to reduce what kind of online behavior?

4. When videoconferencing is used, how do clients respond to the presence of a counselor's face?

5. What are the challenges for a counselor running an online group using videoconferencing?

6. What are the important factors in designing an online group?

7. What are the differences between an online group and an f2f group?

8. What is the role of the psychotherapist in facilitating an online group?

REFERENCES

Barak, A., & Wander-Schwartz, M. (1999). Empirical evaluation of brief group therapy through an Internet chat room. Retrieved from http://www.brandeis.edu/pubs/jove/HTML/v5/cherapy3.htm.

Bellafiore, D. R. (2001). DRB's infidelity support group online, White Paper. Available upon request at lcsw@drbalternatives.com.

Childress, C. (1998). Potential risks and benefits of online psychotherapeutic interventions. Retrieved from http://www.ishmo.org/issues/9801.htm.

Colón, Y. (1999). Digital digging: group therapy online. In J. Fink (Ed.), *How to use computers and cyberspace in the clinical practice of psychotherapy*. New York: Jason Aronson.

Derogatis, L. R., & Melisaratos, N. (1983). The brief symptom inventory: An introductory report. *Psychological Medicine, 13*:595–605.

Hobbes' Internet Timeline v6.0. Retrieved from http://www.zakon.org/robert/internet/timeline.

King, S. A., & Moreggi, D. (1998). Internet therapy and self-help groups—the pros and cons. In J. Gackenbach (Ed.), *Psychology and the Internet: Intrapersonal, interpersonal and transpersonal implications* (pp. 77–109). San Diego, CA: Academic Press. Retrieved from http://www.concentric.net/~AStom/Chapter5/index.html.

Rosenberg, P. (2001). eGetgoing White Paper. Retrieved from http://www.eGetgoing.com.

Suler, J. (1996). *Life at the palace: A cyberpsychology case study.* Retrieved from http://www.rider.edu/users/suler/psycyber/palacestudy.html.

Suler, J. (1999). *Psychotherapy in cyberspace.* Retrieved from http://www.rider.edu/users/suler/psycyber/therapy.html.

Velicer, W. F., Prochaska, J. O., Fava, J. L., et al. (1998). Detailed overview of the transtheoretical model. Retrieved from http://www.uri.edu/research/cprc/transtheoretica.htm.

Yalom, I. D. (1995). *The theory and practice of group psychotherapy*, 4th edition, New York: Basic Books, Inc.

11

INTERNET-BASED PSYCHOLOGICAL TESTING AND ASSESSMENT

AZY BARAK AND TOM BUCHANAN

Editors' Note: In the following chapter, the authors describe the many ways in which online assessment tools revolutionize the field. The uses of online assessment for psychological testing, clinical diagnosis, and self-assessment are explored. Advantages and disadvantages, as well as legal and ethical issues that are related to assessment online, are discussed.

Benjamin had been unhappy for a while. He experienced trouble sleeping and had generally felt unhappy and unmotivated. Everything seemed to keep going wrong for him, and there was nobody he felt he could turn to for help. He was troubled by what he was experiencing, and wondered if there was something wrong with him, but it had not occurred to him to seek professional help. One evening, while surfing the Web, he accidentally came across a link to a self-help[1] site that looked interesting. At the site, he filled in a short questionnaire called a "Depression Screening Quiz" and was informed that he might be suffering from clinical depression and should consult a mental health professional about it.

Sangeeta was desperate. She had no idea what was wrong with her—she couldn't get any work done, felt that she was useless, and just spent all night playing computer games and messing around on the Internet instead of writing the report she should have finished last week. On impulse, she typed "am I depressed?" into www.ask.com and followed a sponsored link labeled

[1]http://depression.about.com.

217

"Are You Depressed? You could have a chemical imbalance. Take the self-test and see." This led to a page[2] that seemed to be mainly advertising proprietary remedies. She followed a link to a simple self-test, which presented a list of feelings and instructed her to follow another link if more than a certain number applied to her. She thought they did, so she followed the link to a page that told her she would benefit from buying certain dietary supplements. Now, where was her credit card?

Lars was reading one of his favorite online discussion forums when he came across a message posted by a psychologist halfway across the world, looking for people to take part in a study on online counseling. This involved anonymously filling out some online questionnaires before participating in a course of email exchanges and filling out the questionnaires again afterward to see whether there had been any changes. He thought it sounded interesting, so he emailed the psychologist to let her know he would like to take part.

Dr. Jones, an experienced psychologist with a busy caseload, had just met a new client for a brief initial consultation. As part of her normal assessment procedure, she liked to administer a comprehensive battery of psychological tests (personality, ability, and clinical screening measures). However, this was very time-consuming, so she had adopted a new technique. She gave the client a Web address and asked him to visit it and complete the questionnaires there in his own time. The website Dr. Jones referred the client to was maintained by a test publisher who offered this service to subscribed clinicians. Later that evening, the client visited the site, at his own convenience. When Dr. Jones arrived at work the next morning, she found a full psychological assessment report on the client had been automatically generated and emailed to her. She used it to plan her next session with the client and to define the issues she wanted to follow up in her assessment of his situation.

These (fictional) scenarios are based on materials found on the Internet at the time of writing this chapter, and represent a few of the ways in which people might come into contact with Internet-based psychological assessment procedures. They illustrate some of the potential uses of such assessments, as well as some of the problems that may be associated with their use. The purpose of this chapter is to describe the principles and different techniques of online assessment, the reasons why one might want to do it, and important issues that anyone involved in online psychological assessment needs to be aware of.

There are numerous contexts in which online assessments may take place, and several different types of assessment procedures. In their simplest forms, Internet-based psychological assessments may take the shape of a Web page on which the items of a traditional paper-and-pencil

[2]http://add-becalmd.com/13242.

questionnaire are represented as a computerized form. Respondents may view and complete this form using browser software such as Internet Explorer or Netscape. Having answered all the questions, respondents then typically click on a button that results in their data being transmitted to a psychologist, or being automatically scored and some form of feedback being presented.

Such Internet-based questionnaires may be used for a variety of purposes by a variety of people. A number of different types of questionnaires are used—in addition to simple tick-the-appropriate-box–style instruments—and some assessment procedures have been used that do not rely on questionnaires at all. In the sections that follow, we outline some of the potential uses of online assessments, the types of assessment procedure available, the advantages conferred by using them, and also disadvantages and ethical and legal issues that need to be considered.

PURPOSES OF ONLINE ASSESSMENT

Internet-assisted assessment is used for various needs and purposes, which can be classified into three major categories: psychological evaluation, psychotherapeutic diagnostics, and self-exploration and awareness.

PSYCHOLOGICAL EVALUATION

Psychologists are often asked to evaluate—or assist in the evaluation procedures of—a person's various characteristics, usually in relation to classification or selection processes (Anastasi, 1997). The assessment usually includes factors relating to personality traits, abilities and special aptitudes, attitudes and values, and sometimes special dimensions. The Internet has become a very efficient professional source of assistance to psychologists who wish to engage in evaluation, because it provides continuously updated, rich information about assessment procedures (e.g., tests, assessment centers, interview techniques), as well as online devices that might be used—for free or for a fee—by professionals. Although both information and tools are available offline, the Internet makes them available in a much more accessible way, to any interested professional, at any time of need. In addition, online portals, as well as organizations (e.g., companies, publishers, universities, research institutes) provide ongoing, usually continuously updated information about assessment devices, so that professionals have a quick, convenient way to find what might suit their professional needs, a channel that is much more efficient than traditional resources, such as the *Mental Measurements Yearbook*.

Furthermore, the Internet makes it possible to assess people very efficiently through the use of various computerized procedures, unlike the manual, human-tiring activities used in traditional assessments. Research studies consistently have reported that online testing produces very similar psychological findings when compared with traditional paper-and-pencil testing (see reviews by Barak & English, 2002; Sampson, 2000; Wall, 2000). Online psychological evaluation has been found to be successful in a variety of assessment areas, including various measures of personality (e.g., Buchanan, 2001; Cronk & West, 2002; Fouladi et al., 2002; Kelly & Jugovic, 2001; Pettit, 2002), integrity (Jones et al., 2002a), career- and work-related measures (Gati & Saka, 2001; Gore & Leuwerke, 2000; Oliver & Chartrand, 2000; Oliver & Zack, 1999), online behavior (Riva, Teruzzi, & Anolli, 2003), behavior checklist (Knapp & Kirk, 2003), abilities (Mooney, 2002), and neuropsychological assessment (Schatz & Browndyke, 2002). It should not, however, be assumed that all psychometric questionnaires will provide valid assessments on the Web, or that the psychometric properties of online versions of questionnaires will remain the same as offline versions. Although most of the research to date has indicated that online questionnaires can be valid, there are reports of instances where factor structures and mean scores have been found to differ (see, e.g., Buchanan, 2001; Buchanan, 2002; Buchanan, 2003; Buchanan et al., 2002a; and other work cited later in this chapter). The most appropriate interpretation of the body of work that currently exists may be that online questionnaires can be (and usually are) psychometrically acceptable, but that this must be empirically demonstrated rather than assumed. One should never just place a test online and expect that it will be the "same test" as it was in paper-and-pencil format.

PSYCHOTHERAPEUTIC DIAGNOSTICS

Counselors who wish to take advantage of the Internet might find it very useful to obtain assistance from online procedures when assessment is desired. Clients may be guided to engage in online testing—provided by computer stations at a clinic or at a client's home—at a time of their convenience, without the necessity of paper forms, scoring keys, or test administrators. Clients may take various types of tests—personality inventories, career-interest questionnaires, or intellectual ability tests—through the Web and receive immediate, accurate results. Moreover, the results can be provided simultaneously to the clients' counselors, too. Test results may be linked directly to relevant online information resources, making the results much more meaningful and applicable for test-takers. Counselors may benefit from having their clients engage in online assessment procedures in several ways. First, quite a few counselors may free themselves from the need to administer tests (themselves or through the help of assistants). Second, counselors receive the accurate results just as soon as they are available, directly into their personal computers. Third, automated interpretation, of a single test or of a whole (online) assessment battery, can be provided in many cases, saving time and obviating subjective biases on the counselor's part. Fourth, all scores (or even item responses) can conveniently be saved and archived for any future use.

Online tests may also be used efficiently as mental health-screening devices to identify psychological problems prior to or as an adjunct to medical procedures, which require initial and immediate diagnosis (Hill et al., 2002). Another example of the practical diagnostic use of online assessment is the successful use of an online measure intended to assess a youth's independent living potential (Bressani & Downs, 2002). A special case in exploiting the Internet for effective diagnosis has to do with sex-function problems (Ochs et al., 2002), for which openness and candidness are necessary, but might be jeopardized in a face-to-face (f2f) interaction needed for assessment. Also, Internet communication channels can be used for the delivery of test interpretation. Jones et al. (2002b) showed that interest inventory interpretation can be conducted effectively with test-takers over text chat accompanied with video.

SELF-EXPLORATION AND SELF-AWARENESS

The Internet is loaded with psychological and pseudopsychological tests and questionnaires that anyone may take for free or for a fee: intelligence tests, personality measures, vocational interest inventories, and other psychological scales. People may take such tests for their own self-exploration and self-awareness, to know themselves better, to obtain answers to personal questions, to help themselves in making choices, or just for the sake of curiosity. People may thus obtain psychologically relevant information on themselves in almost any area and, in principle, make good use of this information. These experiences, which are becoming convenient and normative because of the Internet, should be considered human advancement, as they foster career development, personal development and maturity, and decision-making in various areas. Thus, the tests (online or offline) are usually considered an inseparable part of psychological self-help (Tucker-Ladd, 2000). The ease of using the Net, its normativeness, and indeed its excessive use—related to the "Penta-A Engine" (Barak & Fisher, 2002) of availability, accessibility, affordability, acceptability, and aloneness—has brought about a significant increase in the usage of psychological tests for personal purposes, thereby supposedly contributing directly to valuable personal growth. This assertion, however, depends upon tests' validity as well as the test-takers' effective assimilation of the meaning and implications of the results. A good example of the use of online testing for self-awareness was provided by Cunningham et al. (2000), who developed a brief Internet-based self-assessment procedure that provided normative feedback (by gender and age group) to respondents in regard to their drinking habits. Also in drinking assessment, Miller et al. (2002) found that Web-based measures of drinking habits were as reliable and valid as were paper-and-pencil measures.

TYPES AND METHODS OF ONLINE
PSYCHOLOGICAL TESTING

Like traditional psychological testing, online testing is characterized by multiple methods. Naturally, objective testing techniques (see Anastasi, 1997), such as multiple-choice tests, are the most commonly published type on the Internet, because they can mechanically and automatically be scored without direct human intervention. However, despite this clear preference, other testing methods, including projective techniques and the open-ended format, are possible and available on the Net.

The first multiple-choice tests to be published on the Internet were those that measured intellectual abilities and they became very common, apparently because of the right-or-wrong nature of the test items. Several factors should be considered, however, when referring to these tests. First, these tests should be professionally developed, following clear scientific and ethical guidelines and based on common, empirically based psychometric considerations. Many online tests, however, may be amateur, developed and published—without an established professional basis—by anyone who knows how to create a Web page. Second, online tests may be highly technology-enhanced in a way that takes advantage of advanced computer applications, including the rich use of pictures and sound; they may be highly interactive, allow time keeping, and employ complicated scoring techniques; at the other extreme, such online tests might be very simple, using only text, and be scored manually.

Another type of assessment that is common on the Net is that of personality and attitudes. Here, too, using a response format of rating scales (i.e., Yes/No, numerical, or text-based) makes computer-software automatic scoring easy and fast. There are also various levels of sophistication and exploitation of Internet capabilities with these questionnaires. In this case, too, there are quite a few well-established, professional psychological tests published and used online, as well as amateur ones. It sometimes takes an expert to differentiate between professional and amateur tests, hence the problems for lay people are obvious.

More complicated assessment techniques, such as those that require human interaction for interpretation and scoring, can also be found on the Net. For instance, the pictures of the Rorschach inkblot test may be presented at a certain website, and patients may record or write down their responses, which will later be handed in to a therapist. It is also possible, and might be feasible, to conduct such assessments using real-time video conferencing systems, electronically replicating the interactive situation that might have occurred in a traditional setting. A still more advanced method is possible (and yet rarely used): Stories told following exposure to Thematic Apperception Test (TAT) pictures may simply be typed into a predesigned form, under each picture; when test-takers finish writing their stories they submit the form with a click of a mouse. A clinician thus receives a patient's forms through email to enable efficient assessment. Volcani (2000) reported a sophisticated online projective test, based on principles close to the TAT, that proved to be a useful measure of personality. A similar procedure can be used with a sentence-completion test. Drawing software, although widely available, seems unfit for this medium to be used with drawing tests (e.g., draw a person, draw a family, draw a tree), because the user's behavior is not as spontaneous and free as it is in offline testing. Obviously, these types of tests must be private and secure because of clear privacy issues, in addition to copyright considerations. Using a secure, password-protected website seems to meet these conditions to a large extent.

Just as open-ended questions are included in paper-and-pencil tests and questionnaires, they may also be included in online tests and questionnaires. Although their evaluation may be conducted as though they were submitted on paper, digitized materials have the great advantage of the potentiality of being assessed through computer-based procedures (Shermis & Burstein, 2003). Answers to open-ended questions in questionnaires, as well as essays, may be quickly, efficiently, and more objectively scored following preassigned procedures. This method, however, lacks the *qualitative* component of human impression, just as it is still impossible for a computer to rate the quality of artwork.

NONTESTING ONLINE ASSESSMENT PROCEDURES

Although testing online is widespread and appears to be considered to be the most efficacious Internet-related assessment procedure, it is certainly not the only procedure available. Efficient, variegated online communication channels, on the one hand, and the characteristics of the very online environment, on the other, enable other online assessment procedures. These procedures add a unique value to the use of the Internet as an aid in evaluating people and provide a breakthrough in developing distance appraisal.

The Internet may be exploited to conduct assessment interviews, through text only, by using the computer's sound capability (i.e., a conversation involving the computer's microphone and speakers), or through video (i.e., by using webcams). An Internet-based interview is particularly useful when interviewee and interviewer are at a great distance from each other, because travel time and expenses are saved. Telephone interviews for assessment purposes are possible and actually used, too (e.g., Blackman, 2002; Paulsen et al., 1988), although limited in validity (Cacciola et al., 1999; Silvester et al., 2000). Interviewing through the Net has, however, two special advantages: (a) a conversation may easily be saved for further evaluation; (b) the cost is very low. These special advantages may justify online interviews, at least for initial screening or preliminary diagnostics. Emerging video technologies and recently enhanced communication speed make online interviews not only doable but also quite efficient. However, as with online therapy (Maheu & Gordon, 2000; Manhal-Baugus, 2001; Suler et al., 2001), special professional training, adherence to special ethical guidelines, and advanced equipment are necessary to make online assessment interviews efficient and valid. Diagnostic interviewing through the Internet is an exciting method to gather psychological information on a person. As mentioned above, although phone interviews have the critical disadvantages of the lack of eye contact and of observable nonverbal cues, online synchronous video technology might lessen this shortcoming. Research in applying this method in actual assessment procedures (Yoshino et al., 2001) has shown that high-speed Internet communication technology can produce highly efficient, reliable interviews. Still, an interview based on chat or instant messaging is also possible, particularly in cases in which written script—both for analyzing its content and for detecting characteristic online behavior—may be sufficient to evaluate a person (Leung, 2002; Peris et al., 2002). This verbal-only method might at times even be preferred to the use of video communication, because the lack of eye contact contributes to growing personal exposure (e.g., Duggan & Parrott, 2000).

Another method of exploiting the Net for assessment and evaluation purposes has to do with evaluating resumes and biographical information. Because documents can easily be transferred online, it seems obvious that psychologists receive material this way rather than in the traditional, printed manner. Indeed, such attempts have proved useful (e.g., Coffee, Pearce, & Nishimura, 1999). However, other sources of personal information can be included in this category: personal websites, which often contain a great amount of private details and expressions (Döring, 2002); weblogs (blogs)—online personal diaries that record even more intimate experiences; and poems, stories, and artwork published on the Internet. All these sources of highly significant psychological input may be analyzed and evaluated by clinicians for the benefit of a client or for improved professional appraisal.

In addition, the Internet allows assessment of another aspect of people's behavior: observations of interpersonal interactions in both synchronous and asynchronous environments. Based on the premise that people's behavior online more accurately reflects their real personality, because of the online disinhibition effect (Joinson, 1998, 1999, 2001; Suler, 2001), a close observation of people's (text-based) behavior in chat rooms and forums, as well as in instant messaging and email, can provide important psychological information. Although this information is limited in scope and context, it may contribute to better understanding one's interpersonal pattern in a group or dyadic situations. In the context of personnel selection, simulative environments can be created online parallel with observing people's group behavior in a situational test (e.g., McDaniel & Nguyen, 2001; Weekley & Jones, 1999), to evaluate social interactions in a challenging circumstance. Observing behaviors on the Internet may lead to special information because of the unique characteristics of cyberspace that prompt disinhibitions. Thus, online observations in a chat room or a forum may serve as a significant source of psychologically relevant information, perhaps even more valid than interpersonal behaviors in f2f situations. Similarly, group dynamics in online situations (McKenna & Green, 2002; Sassenberg, 2002; Suler & Phillips, 2000) can disclose significant information about people's various personality characteristics that might be important for therapy. A clinician can benefit from observing patients' behavior in online environments, either a chat room or a forum, and in identifying their typical responses. Taking into account the online disinhibition effect, one can strongly argue that this information contributes significantly to the diagnosis of patients.

One caveat here is the idea that the personae people present online might be constructed or contrived to some degree. There has been speculation (e.g., Suler, 2000; Turkle, 1995) that the Internet can be used as a laboratory for identity exploration, and that people may construct or express different selves online. Clearly, this needs to be considered when using the actions of an online persona as a source of data about the person "behind the screen." However, given evidence that people's online personae are likely to be influenced by their "real" personalities (for instance, Buchanan & Smith, 1999, found evidence suggesting that the personality trait of self-monitoring was associated with whether or not people chose to use a "handle" or screen name when posting to Usenet newsgroups), observation of online behavior is likely to be a useful source of information as long as one remembers that the context of the behavior may affect its nature.

ADVANTAGES OF ONLINE PROCEDURES FOR PSYCHOLOGICAL ASSESSMENT

Relative to traditional personal assessment in the context of counseling and psychotherapy (e.g., paper-and-pencil testing), online assessment offers quite a few strengths and advanced features that make it attractive. These advantages—professional and administrative alike—are enabled by the special characteristics of online communication and by technological developments. Nevertheless, they are flexible enough to be amalgamated into traditional counseling (and, naturally, into online counseling). Following is a discussion of several of the principal advantages of online assessment, both those pertaining to testing and those that are related to other assessment procedures.

One of the main advantages of using the Net in general, and for testing in particular, is its elasticity (i.e., flexibility); namely, the absence of confinement related to time and place (Barak & English, 2002; Sampson, 2000; Sampson et al., 1997). In a traditional testing session, test-takers have to take a test in a particular place and at a particular time. This strict condition has now been overcome, because test-takers may take a test at any time and in any place where a computer is connected to the Internet (e.g., equipped, usually, with basic software). Not only, then, can test-taking conditions become more convenient to test-takers, but the test-taker can also initiate taking a test when he or she feels comfortable with this tiring and usually anxiety-provoking activity (e.g., Tseng et al., 1997). Thus, positive personal feelings and sufficient measurement validity are both enhanced. Practically, clinicians may assign eligible tests to patients, by providing them only with URLs. Results could be electronically sent to clinicians' email as well as to patients', as required. Obviously, if necessary, tests might be taken in the clinic, at designated computers, thus saving the clinician or test administrator time. For example, a client may take an online instrument, such as the Keirsey Temperament Sorter II, assessing the constructs of the Myers-Briggs Type Indicator (see Kelly & Jugovic, 2001) for immediate scoring, results, inferences, and referrals to related information.

Another important advantage of online assessment relates to accuracy of raw scoring and standardization conversion. Because these two operations are performed by software, human errors are avoided; hence, the scores obtained are accurate and better reflect test-takers' true scores. This is a clear contribution to the reliability of measurement. For instance, it was found that scoring a simple career-related inventory, such as the Self-Directed Search (SDS; Holland et al., 1994), where just "yes" responses have to be counted and totaled, is affected by numerous human errors (Elliott & Byrd, 1985). A computerized version of the SDS was developed and it eliminated these errors (McKee & Levinson, 1990). However, using an *Internet-based* version of the SDS (at http://www.self-directed-search.com), which liberates the user from obtaining the SDS software, can also easily avoid such errors and consequent erroneous interpretations (Barak & Cohen, 2002).

Another advantage of machine-based scoring of online tests is the speed both of scoring and of obtaining results. With computer-based tests, this stage usually takes a few seconds, with results fed back to test-takers and/or to counselors immediately, saving tension and frustration (Mooney, 2002).

A special advantage relates to saving test-takers' scores, whether for storage for further clinical use or for any kind of research. The use of digital technology enables data to be saved in preexisting and preset software (e.g., Excel) or merely in test-takers' personal files. A therapist thus can retrieve clients' tests—including item responses, raw scores, or normative data—for any clinical use quickly and easily. Moreover, statistical analyses can be done relatively simply and data entry saved.

Still another important advantage of online assessment relates to the test version being up to date. In using an online test, especially if it is at a website provided by the test publisher, we can make sure that the most recent, updated version of any given test is in use, not an obsolete one. Related to this, changes in instructions, scoring, and norms are automatically applied to online tests through the testing software located on a server and do not have to be distributed, learned, and supervised with individual users (Barak, 1999; Barak & English, 2002). This last consideration is an important matter that is commonly overlooked when using traditional testing at a given agency, because the version used is the version at hand.

One last significant advantage refers to assessment methods other than testing. In online interviewing, through commonly used voice- and picture-enabled systems, the advantage is not only that interviewee and interviewer may be at a distance from each other and each at a convenient location; and it is not only that the interview may easily be saved for later inspection and appraisal. Another important positive aspect is that the interviewee's behavior might better reflect his/her true personality characteristics, as mentioned earlier, because of reduced inhibitions. This factor may significantly contribute to the validity of the psychological assessment.

DISADVANTAGES OF ONLINE ASSESSMENT RELATIVE TO TRADITIONAL METHODS

It is clear that online assessment procedures have much to offer. However, there are also drawbacks that must be considered before they are used. One of the questions that bothers many professionals in regard to online assessment has to do with the testing condition. That is, should a test-taker be allowed to take tests while in solitude (usually at home), in contrast to the traditional method that requires the presence of a test administrator (or a psychologist). One set of possible disadvantages, therefore, relates to diminished control over the testing situation.

Psychometric tests are designed to be administered under controlled, standardized conditions. This may well not be the case in Web-based assessments. People might complete assessment instruments under varying conditions: In different locations (e.g., late at night in the peace of their own home, or in the bustle of a busy Internet café), under different physical (e.g., alert, tired or intoxicated, alone or in the presence of others) or psychological (e.g., relaxed, distressed, bored, mischievous) conditions. One has no way of knowing whether any of these conditions apply to a particular instance of assessment. In some applications (e.g., proctored assessments for educational or occupational purposes), one may be able to instruct respondents to complete tests under certain conditions, to use computers situated within a clinic, or to ask them about the conditions under which they completed the questionnaire. In other applications (e.g., mass screening, or on self-help sites) this is not realistic. It has been argued (see Reips, 2000) that this variance in assessment context might lead to *greater* ecological validity. However, if assessment results are to be used for any important purpose, one needs to establish that results have not been affected by this lack of standardization (or that the effect is a systematic one that can be considered when test outcomes are interpreted). Although there is sufficient evidence that online and paper-and-pencil versions of tests can measure the same constructs to suggest that results will usually be valid (see Barak & English, 2002), there are also sufficient indications of (usually small) differences to indicate that this is an issue in need of further research (Buchanan, 2002).

In nonproctored assessment situations, there is also an issue over the identity of test-takers. Test-takers, when alone, may cheat, misrepresent themselves, or even allow others to take a test for them. This is probably more a concern in high-stakes occupational assessments (e.g., cases of assessing of candidates for a desired job, study program, and the like), for which the motivation to cheat is obvious (Bartram, 1997, 1999). In a psychotherapeutic framework, however, this problem becomes redundant, on the assumption that a patient has a genuine desire to cooperate positively with the clinician. The common solution is to allow test-takers to complete tests in a place (and time) of their choosing only if there is no apparent motivation to cheat. Otherwise, online tests may be taken only in a monitored office, whether individually or in groups, or under circumstances where identities can be verified. There are ways in which identity can be established (e.g., social security numbers; credit card details). However, it is an open question as to whether this will affect some of the phenomena alleged to operate in online assessments, specifically, increased self-disclosure due to anonymity (see Buchanan, 2002).

This leads to another set of issues, related to the psychological effects of different testing situations. There is a growing literature on online psychological assessment, primarily related to its use in research and occupational testing. This includes a number of projects conducted with the aim of establishing whether particular online tests were psychometrically and functionally equivalent to offline measures on which they are based. Results from such studies, and extrapolation of findings from the large body of research on computer-mediated communication (CMC), have suggested that certain characteristics of the assessment medium, such as reduced social cues, deindividuation, or changes in where attention is focused, may influence the way people respond to online tests.

CMC research (e.g. Kiesler et al., 1984; Walther, 1996) has indicated that when people interact via computers, their communication may be disinhibited to some extent, and as we have already indicated, this effect appears to extend to online communication (see Joinson, 1998, 1999, 2001; Suler, 2001), hence our earlier suggestion that people's online behavior might reflect their "real personalities" unfettered by normal social constraints.

Disinhibition effects have traditionally been discussed (and researched) in terms of "flaming"—hostile communications—but also seem to influence the degree to which people are willing to disclose personal (and often very sensitive) information. Simply put, people seem to disclose high levels of personal information when interacting on the Internet (Joinson, 2002). There are strong indications that people may reveal more about themselves to an online questionnaire than in an f2f context, although at the time of writing we are not aware of any direct empirical test of this suggestion (Buchanan et al., 2002b).

There is also evidence that people may respond in less socially desirable ways to online questionnaires: Joinson (1999) randomly assigned college-student participants to complete (among other instruments) a social desirability questionnaire either via the Internet or in a paper-and-pencil format. Social desirability scores were lower for the group tested via the Internet. This finding has been interpreted as evidence that people will be less influenced by social desirability concerns when completing online assessments: they may feel free to express socially disapproved aspects of their identities. On the other hand, they may also feel less constrained to provide the information requested by the assessor (Buchanan et al., 2002b).

Possibly as a function of these phenomena (or perhaps of the idea advanced by Bargh et al., 2002, that people are more able to express their "true selves" on the Internet), a number of studies have reported differences between online and offline respondents, who did not appear to differ in any way other than the medium used to assess them, in mean scores on several instruments (e.g., Barak & Cohen, 2002; Davis, 1999; Fouladi et al., 2002; Joinson, 1999). There are some suggestions that this is the case with respect to measures related to negative affect (in that people report higher levels of negative affect when tested online). If correct, this has clear implications for clinical assessment. In any case, it is an issue on which more research is clearly needed.

One of the implications is that normative data should not be used in interpreting scores obtained with online clinical inventories. This assertion is based on the fact that the vast majority of normative data available will have been gathered offline. Buchanan (2003) has shown that using offline norms may lead to very serious errors of judgment about the meaning of a particular score achieved using an online psychological test (e.g., in the case of one set of data presented, use of offline norms would have led to mis-classification of 18% of the sample). Clearly, this objection would not apply to normative data gathered online: in that case, one would be comparing the score of an individual with data from the appropriate population. The difficulty here is the heterogeneity of that population: it is possible that one may be called upon to assess people from different cultures or countries (or even *in* other countries). Will appropriate data be available under those circumstances? In the case of screening instruments (e.g., on self-help sites), how does one ensure that the correct norms are used and correct feedback given to the individual? These issues led Buchanan (2003) to suggest that online tests should not currently be used in a manner requiring use of normative data, and their main utility would be in applications that did not require such comparisons to be made (e.g., monitoring change during therapy, ipsative measures, such as the SDS). This is a situation that is likely to change, as online tests become more widely used; normative data accrues, and the mechanisms that might affect responses become better understood.

Another potential drawback to online assessment is the current lack of regulation and quality control. In the case of standard offline assessment procedures, a number of mechanisms exist to ensure at least a minimum standard of quality and professionalism. For example, in many countries publishers of psychometric tests adhere to standards developed by bodies such as the International Test Commission (International Test Commission, 2001) and require evidence (e.g., a recognized qualification in testing, or attendance at a course run by the publisher) of competence before they will sell a test to an individual. Most people with access to assessment procedures and the opportunity to use them will have had appropriate training, and in most cases will also be members of a professional body with a code of ethics and disciplinary procedures for anyone found to have acted inappropriately.

This will extend in part to online assessment procedures: those involving commercially published psychometric instruments, or employed by trained, qualified therapists. However, a large proportion of the assessments being conducted over the Internet (e.g., via self-help or personality testing sites) do not meet these criteria, and numerous examples of very bad practice can be found (e.g., invalid instruments, data stored without informed consent, misleading information, potentially distressing feedback) (Oliver & Zack, 1999).

Editors' Note: It is important for readers to remember that not all sites and services offering assessment online are the same. Users would be wise to explore and get more information about the sources they are using, with a particular focus on understanding the ways in which information is collected, transmitted, stored, and used.

ETHICAL AND LEGAL ISSUES

Codes of ethical conduct for psychologists typically include some statement to the effect that psychologists should only use procedures that are fit for their purposes. For example, the section of the current American Psychological Association (APA) ethics code dealing with assessment states,

"Psychologists base the opinions contained in their recommendations, reports, and diagnostic or evaluative statements, including forensic testimony, on information and techniques sufficient to substantiate their findings" (APA, 2002). This statement was explicitly reconfirmed in regard to online psychological activities, including online assessment (APA, 1997). This principle applies both to therapeutic interventions (which should be evidence-based and empirically supported) and to assessment procedures (which should actually measure the intended constructs).

Relatively little is yet known about the efficacy of online counseling procedures (see Laszlo et al., 1999; Maheu & Gordon, 2000; Manhal-Baugus, 2001), although emerging studies (see Ström, Petterson, & Andersson, 2000; Andersson et al., 2002) and work presented in this volume add significantly to that knowledge base. Relatively little is also known about online assessment. Despite numerous indications that they can work successfully, factors that may affect the validity of online tests still require much more investigation. In this sense, there is a great burden of responsibility on people conducting online assessments to ensure that their tools are fit for their purposes. Unfortunately, many of the "tests" currently available on the Web are likely to be manifestly unfit for any purpose whatsoever, lacking any evidence of reliability or validity. These include measures developed by (well-intentioned) amateurs who are not aware of psychometric issues, and professionals who are aware of psychometric issues but have not fully considered the possible effects of using a new testing medium. Given that many "end users" of online assessments will be unaware of the quality of the test they are using, this may create problems, especially in the (many) situations where feedback is given to users (see also Barak, 2003, for discussion of a parallel situation with career-related assessments where people may make wrong career decisions on the basis of flawed feedback).

One possible use of Internet-mediated assessments is for self-exploration and personal development purposes: as already indicated there are a wide range of instruments available for this purpose, and the popularity of self-testing websites indicates that people are using them. The primary incentive to take a test under such circumstances is to obtain feedback, which the test-taker may then use for various purposes (including making life decisions).

This makes it very important for people constructing online tests to ensure that the information is accurate, and that it will not have a negative effect on test-takers. Accuracy can only be ensured by using assessment techniques of demonstrable validity and by making comparisons with appropriate normative data if required (e.g., when informing someone how their scores on a screening inventory compare to those of other people). The majority of sites presenting online tests do (appropriately) print a disclaimer of some sort, advising people not to place too much reliance on the test results. However, it is an open question whether such disclaimers have much impact, given the strength of the well-known "Barnum effect." The

Barnum effect is the tendency of people to accept test feedback composed of high base-rate personality traits as descriptive of themselves, even if the feedback is fictional (Anastasi, 1997). Research is required to establish whether people actually do believe feedback from online tests, and to assess whether inappropriate feedback might have any negative effects on their lives. It is also possible that test feedback might have immediate negative effects, irrespective of any action people take based on it. It has been shown that fairly minor mood manipulations in Internet experiments can influence people's emotional states (Goritz et al., 1999). How might people react to feedback indicating that their level of intelligence was "well below the pop-ulation average"? Or that they had a pattern of scores which had some neg-ative implications for their physical or mental health? Or that they had a high score on some socially undesirable construct (e.g., psychoticism)? These issues might have an especially large impact on people with prob-lems or low self-esteem: exactly the kind of people who might be seeking mental health help or information on the Internet.

This observation also applies to use of online tests by psychologists for diagnostic purposes and is a reason why there might be reservations about their unsupervised use. The very taking of a psychological test might itself create a detrimental situation. This may result from the client experiencing stress while taking the test, as well as with an unexpected negative evalua-tion in cases where immediate results are provided to test-takers, which is a common procedure in many tests published on the Internet. Therefore, being an unaccompanied test-taker might potentially be painful and even harmful. A solution to this problem is to use a computer stationed in a clinic to take Internet-based tests, so that immediate support is available. Another possible solution to provide support when needed, even if a test-taker is in solitude, is through the phone or synchronous online communication. Clearly, such support is easier to provide within established therapeutic relationships than in cases of mass-screening or self-help sites.

Issues related to the remote provision of mental health services must also be considered. One of the great advantages of behavioral telehealth is that services can be provided for people in other locations. This is also an area of potential difficulty, especially given the "emergent" nature of Internet law.

In some areas, there are local or national laws relating to telehealth provision. However, there is evidence that a high proportion of behavioral telehealth providers are unaware of (or misunderstand) local legislation that applies to them (Maheu & Gordon, 2000). Maheu and Gordon also found that a high proportion of practitioners provided services to clients in other jurisdictions (in their study, other U.S. states). If one extrapolates this to the (realistic) scenario of people providing assessments to people in other countries, it is clear that there may be legal issues one needs to con-sider. What recourse might a client have in the case of malpractice (e.g., giving misleading or damaging feedback from an online assessment) by a remote practitioner? What legislation applies regarding the secure transmission and storage of data, and access rights to it?

Security of data transmission and storage must also be considered. Much has been made of the "hacker threat," or risk of unauthorized interception of or access to test data by third parties. The extent to which this is a problem is open to debate. On the one side, it is certainly possible. For example, Reips (2002) observes that configuration errors or certain data transmission techniques result in possibly confidential data being openly available via the WWW in the case of online psychological experiments, and that this happens frequently. Given that psychologists constructing such experiments are likely to be among the more technically proficient and "Internet savvy" members of the profession, this is a worrying finding. This may cause a problem for online counseling applications if Maheu and Gordon's (2000) prediction that many therapists, who are not computer experts, will find themselves forced to adopt new technologies is correct. On the other side, the extent to which there really is a problem may be exaggerated. Yes, it is possible to intercept data transmitted via computers. It is also entirely possible—and probably easier for most people—to tap a telephone, listen outside a therapist's door, break the lock to a "secure" filing cabinet, and so on. The risk is therefore probably no greater than in traditional assessment contexts (Barak & English, 2002). We are not aware of any incidents where the "hacker threat" has been anything other than a hypothetical problem, so although it is an issue people should be aware of, it is possible that its practical importance is low.

SUMMARY

The current chapter attempts to cover the wide spectrum of issues relating to Internet-based psychological assessment. No doubt, the Internet has provided psychology with a revolutionary vehicle through which methods of assessment of people—for therapeutic purposes, for appraising a person's suitability for a study program or a job, and for self-exploration—are changing. Thanks to the typical characteristics of the Net—availability, affordability, accessibility, acceptability, and aloneness—its exploitation as a tool that enables efficient testing and assessment is inviting. Perhaps the Internet's central advantages for assessment are its flexibility in terms of time and place, provision of quick and accurate scoring, availability of textual information and Web links pertaining to the nature of the assessment results, central control of updating test versions, and Internet-based nontesting assessment methods. Furthermore, because of the special communication characteristics of people who use the Internet, such as anonymity, invisibility, asynchronicity, and lack of eye contact, human inhibitions diminish; more candid responses may be anticipated as a result, thus elevating the validity of the assessment.

Although online assessment is useful and valuable, there are several precautions that have to be taken as well. Perhaps the most problematic issue is that many amateur tests are published on the Net, and naive surfers cannot differentiate between a professional, validated assessment website and a nonprofessional one. There is some evidence to suggest, as was pointed out, that the measurement of specific dimensions online might possibly be erroneous, and perhaps assessments of some people, or people in certain circumstances, might be biased. We made a special point of the issue of providing assessment feedback online, and of the potential harm this could cause if done badly.

Online assessment is a young area. Many issues and questions are being raised and only a few answers based on empirical research can be given to date. Until knowledge based on much practice and massive research is accumulated, we should be cautious in routinely applying online assessment. Intensive investigations are needed to provide reliable answers to questions regarding basic issues, such as questions related to converting traditional tests to online versions, providing feedback to test-takers online, performing chat-based interviews, using synchronous and asynchronous environments as a means of behavioral assessment, and more. In addition, we encourage raising public awareness and understanding of online tests so people will know what to expect and what not to expect, thus obviating potentially harmful situations. We also call for the training of professionals in Internet-related assessment, to provide them with new and advanced tools, on the one hand, and to make them aware of their shortcomings and limitations, on the other.

KEY TERMS

Deindividuation: A psychological process characterized by reduced self-evaluation and decreased inhibitions in crowd situations.

Disinhibition: Abolition or reduction of psychological mechanisms that govern spontaneous behavior.

Ecological validity: The degree to which findings obtained from research in controlled situations might be generalized and found relevant under other circumstances and more natural environments.

Factor structure: The basic main dimensions or psychological constructs underlying responses to a given test.

Myers-Briggs Type Indicator (MBTI): A well-known, widely used personality assessment test based on Jung's typology of personality.

Normative data: Statistical parameters of a comparison group by which an individual person's test results are analyzed.

Qualitative: Based on subjective analysis and impression rather than objective, measured assessment.

Projective test: A psychological test in which people are asked to respond to ambiguous stimuli (e.g., pictures, unfinished sentences). Responses are interpreted as expressing the desires and needs of the individual.

Psychological assessment: A set of various procedures, including verbal and nonverbal intelligence measures, written and performance tests, interviews, appraisal of group behavior, and more, used to evaluate a person's personality and various traits.

Psychometric properties: Quality of measurement of a psychological test, assessed by several factors, such as reliability and validity.

Reliability: The degree to which a test consistently measures a trait or construct.

Rorschach inkblot test: A projective test in which symmetric ink stains are presented to people who are asked to describe what they see in them.

Social desirability: A general trend of people to do and say things so others value and like them.

Thematic Apperception Test (TAT): A projective test that is based on creating personal stories stimulated by given standard pictures.

Validity: The degree to which a test measures the concept it is supposed to measure.

STUDY QUESTIONS

1. What are the main advantages of online psychological testing over traditional testing?

2. What are the main disadvantages of online psychological testing compared with traditional testing?

3. What practical and ethical problems may be encountered when using online psychological assessment?

4. Other than simple testing, what additional techniques are available on the Internet for the purpose of psychological assessment? What are their pros and cons?

REFERENCES

American Psychological Association (1997). *APA statement on services by telephone, teleconferencing, and Internet.* Retrieved November 1, 2002, from http://www.apa.org/ethics/stmnt01.html.

American Psychological Association (2002). Ethical principles of psychologists and code of conduct. *American Psychologist, 57*:1060–1073.

Anastasi, A. (1997). *Psychological testing,* 7th edition. Upper Saddle River, NJ: Prentice Hall.

Andersson, G., Strömgren, T., Ström, L., et al. (2002). Randomized controlled trial of Internet-based cognitive behavior therapy for distress associated with tinnitus. *Psychosomatic Medicine, 64*:810–816.

Barak, A. (1999). Psychological applications on the Internet: A discipline on the threshold of a new millennium. *Applied and Preventive Psychology, 8*:231–246.

Barak, A. (2003). Ethical and professional issues in career assessment on the Internet. *Journal of Career Assessment, 11*:3–21.

Barak, A. & Cohen, L. (2002). Empirical examination of an online version of the Self-Directed Search. *Journal of Career Assessment, 10*:383–396.

Barak, A. & English, N. (2002). Prospects and limitations of psychological testing on the Internet. *Journal of Technology in Human Services, 19*:65–89.

Barak, A. & Fisher, W. A. (2002). The Future of Internet Sexuality. In A. Cooper (Ed.), *Sex and the Internet: A guidebook for clinicians* (pp. 267–280). New York: Brunner-Routledge.

Bargh, J. A., McKenna, K. Y. A., & Fitzsimmons, G. M. (2002). Can you see the real me? Activation and expression of the "True Self" on the Internet. *Journal of Social Issues, 58*:33–48.

Bartram, D. (1997). Distance assessment: Psychological assessment through the Internet. *Selection and Development Review, 13*(3):15–19.

Bartram, D. (1999). Testing and the Internet: Current realities, issues and future possibilities. *Selection and Development Review, 15*(6):3–12.

Blackman, M. C. (2002). The employment interview via the telephone: Are we sacrificing accurate personality judgments for cost efficiency? *Journal of Research in Personality, 36*:208–223.

Bressani, R. V. & Downs, A. C. (2002). Youth independent living assessment: Testing the equivalence of web and paper/pencil versions of the Ansell-Casey Life Skills Assessment. *Computers in Human Behavior, 18*:453–464.

Buchanan, T. (2001). Online personality assessment. In U. D. Reips & M. Bosnjak (Eds.), *Dimensions of Internet science* (pp. 57–74). Lengerich, Germany: Pabst Science Publishers.

Buchanan, T. (2002). Online assessment: Desirable or dangerous? *Professional Psychology: Research and Practice, 33*:148–154.

Buchanan, T. (2003). Internet based questionnaire assessment: Appropriate use in clinical contexts. *Cognitive Behaviour Therapy, 32*:100–109.

Buchanan, T. & Smith, J. L. (1999). Research on the Internet: Validation of a World Wide Web mediated personality scale. *Behavior Research Methods, Instruments, & Computers, 31*:565–571.

Buchanan, T., Ali, T., Heffernan, et al. (2002a, October). *Psychometric properties of online self-report memory questionnaires: The EMQ and PMQ.* Poster session presented at German Online Research '02, Hohenheim, Germany.

Buchanan, T., Joinson, A. N., & Ali, T. (2002b, October). *Development of a behavioural measure of self-disclosure for use in online research.* Paper presented at German Online Research '02, Hohenheim, Germany.

Cacciola, J. S., Alterman, A. I., Rutherford, M. J., et al. (1999). Comparability of telephone and in-person st(SCID) diagnoses. *Assessment, 6*:235–242.

Coffee, K., Pearce, J., & Nishimura, R. (1999). State of California: Civil service testing moves into cyberspace. *Public Personnel Management, 28*:283–300.

Cronk, B. C. & West, J. L. (2002). Personality research on the Internet: A comparison of Web-based and traditional instruments in take-home and in-class settings. *Behavior Research Methods, Instruments, & Computers, 34*:177–180.

Cunningham, J. A., Humphreys, K., & Koski-Jännes, A. (2000). Providing personalized assessment feedback for problem drinking on the Internet: A pilot project. *Journal of Studies on Alcohol, 61*:794–798.

Davis, R. N. (1999). Web-based administration of a personality questionnaire: Comparison with traditional methods. *Behavior Research Methods, Instruments, & Computers, 31*:572–577.

Döring, N. (2002). Personal home pages on the Web: A review of research. *Journal of Computer-Mediated Communication, 7*(3). Retrieved November 1, 2002, from http://www.ascusc.org/jcmc/vol7/issue3/doering.html.

Duggan, A. P. & Parrott, R. L. (2000). Research note: Physicians' nonverbal rapport building and patients' talk about the subjective component of illness. *Human Communication Research*, 27:299–311.

Elliott, T. R. & Byrd, E. K. (1985). Scoring accuracy of the Self-Directed Search with ninth-grade students. *Vocational Guidance Quarterly*, 34:85–90.

Fouladi, R. T., McCarthy, C. J., & Moller, N. P. (2002). Paper-and-pencil or online? Evaluating mode effects on measures of emotional functioning and attachment. *Assessment*, 9:204–215.

Gati, I. & Saka, N. (2001). Internet-based versus paper-and-pencil assessment: Measuring career decision-making difficulties. *Journal of Career Assessment*, 9:379–416.

Gore, P. A., Jr. & Leuwerke, W. C. (2000). Information technology for career assessment on the Internet. *Journal of Career Assessment*, 8:3–19.

Goritz, A., Batinic, B., Goersch, A., et al. (1999, October). *Induzierbarkeit von Stimmunslangen uber das WWW.* Paper presented at the meeting of German Online Research '99, Nürnberg, Germany.

Hill, B. C., Theis, G. A., & Davison, M. A. (2002). Integration of a Web-based behavioral health assessment tool in clinical medicine. *American Clinical Laboratory*, 21(3):21–25.

Holland, J. L., Powell, A. B., & Fritzsche, B. A. (1994). *The Self-Directed Search: Professional user's guide.* Odessa, FL: Psychological Assessement Resources.

International Test Commission (2001). International guidelines for test use. *International Journal of Testing*, 1:93–114.

Joinson, A. N. (1998). Causes and implication of disinhibited behavior on the Internet. In J. Gackenbach, (Ed.), *Psychology and the Internet: intrapersonal, interpersonal, and transpersonal implications* (pp. 43–60). San Diego: Academic Press.

Joinson, A. N. (1999). Social desirability, anonymity, and Internet-based questionnaires. *Behavior and Research Methods, Instruments, & Computers*, 31:433–438.

Joinson, A. N. (2001). Self-disclosure in computer-mediated communication: The role of self-awareness and visual anonymity. *European Journal of Social Psychology*, 31:177–192.

Joinson, A. N. (2002). *Understanding the psychology of Internet behaviour: Virtual worlds, real lives.* Basingstoke, U.K.: Palgrave Publishers Ltd.

Jones, J. W., Brasher, E. E., & Huff, J. W. (2002a). Innovations in integrity-based personnel selection: Building a technology-friendly assessment. *International Journal of Selection and Assessment*, 10:87–97.

Jones, W. P., Harbach, R. L., Coker, J. K., et al. (2002b). Web-assisted vocational test interpretation. *Journal of Employment Counseling*, 39:127–137.

Kelly, K. R. & Jugovic, H. (2001). Concurrent validity of the online version of the Keirsey Temperament Sorter II. *Journal of Career Assessment*, 9:49–59.

Kiesler, S., Siegal, J., & McGuire, T. W. (1984). Social psychological aspects of computer mediated communication. *American Psychologist*, 39:1123–1134.

Knapp, H. & Kirk, S. A. (2003). Using pencil and paper, Internet and touch-tone phones for self-administered surveys: Does methodology matter? *Computers in Human Behavior*, 19:117–134.

Laszlo, J. V., Esterman, G., & Zabko, S. (1999). Therapy over the Internet? Theory, research and finances. *CyberPsychology & Behavior*, 2:293–307.

Leung, L. (2002). Loneliness, self-disclosure, and ICQ ("I Seek You") use. *CyberPsychology & Behavior*, 5:241–251.

Maheu, M. M. & Gordon, B. L. (2000). Counseling and therapy on the Internet. *Professional Psychology: Research and Practice*, 31:484–489.

Manhal-Baugus, M. (2001). E-therapy: Practical, ethical, and legal issues. *CyberPsychology & Behavior*, 4:551–563.

McDaniel, M. A. & Nguyen, N. T. (2001). Situational judgment tests: A review of practice and constructs assessed. *International Journal of Selection and Assessment*, 9:103–113.

McKee, L. M. & Levinson, E. M. (1990). A review of the computerized version of the Self-Directed Search. *Career Development Quarterly*, 38:325–333.

238

McKenna, K. Y. A. & Green, A. S. (2002). Virtual group dynamics. *Group Dynamics*, 6:116–127.

Miller, E. T., Neal, D. J., Roberts, L. J., et al. (2002). Test-retest reliability of alcohol measures: Is there a difference between Internet-based assessment and traditional methods? *Psychology of Addictive Behaviors*, 16:56–63.

Mooney, J. (2002). Pre-employment testing on the Internet: Put candidates a click away and hire at modem speed. *Public Personnel Management*, 31:41–52.

Ochs, E. P., Mah, K., & Binik, Y. M. (2002). Obtaining data about human sexual functioning from the Internet. In A. Cooper (Ed.), *Sex and the Internet: A guidebook for clinicians* (pp. 245–262). New York: Brunner-Routledge.

Oliver, L. W. & Chartrand, J. M. (2000). Strategies for career assessment research on the Internet. *Journal of Career Assessment*, 8:95–103.

Oliver, L. W. & Zack, J. S. (1999). Career assessment on the Internet: An exploratory study. *Journal of Career Assessment*, 7:323–356.

Paulsen, A. S., Crowe, R. R., Noyes, R., et al. (1988). Reliability of the telephone interview in diagnosing anxiety disorders. *Archives of General Psychiatry*, 45:62–63.

Peris, R., Gimeno, M. A., Pinazo, D., et al. (2002). Online chat rooms: Virtual spaces of interaction for socially oriented people. *CyberPsychology & Behavior*, 5:43–51.

Pettit, F. A. (2002). A comparison of World Wide Web and paper-and-pencil personality questionnaires. *Behavior Research Methods, Instruments, & Computers*, 34:50–54.

Reips, U. D. (2000). The Web experiment method: Advantages, disadvantages, and solutions. In M. H. Birnbaum (Ed.), *Psychological experiments on the Internet* (pp. 89–117). San Diego, CA: Academic Press.

Reips, U. D. (2002). Internet-based psychological experimenting: Five Dos and Five Don'ts. *Social Science Computer Review*, 20:241–249.

Riva, G., Teruzzi, T., Anolli, L. (2003). The use of the Internet in psychological research: Comparison of online and offline questionnaires. *CyberPsychology & Behavior*, 6:73–80.

Sampson, J. P. (2000). Using the Internet to enhance testing in counseling. *Journal of Counseling and Development*, 78:348–356.

Sampson, J. P., Kolodinsky, R. W., & Greeno, B. P. (1997). Counseling on the information highway: Future possibilities and potential problems. *Journal of Counseling & Development*, 75:203–212.

Sassenberg, K. (2002). Common bond and common identity groups on the Internet: Attachment and normative behavior in on-topic and off-topic chats. *Group Dynamics*, 6: 27–37.

Schatz, P. & Browndyke, J. (2002). Applications of computer-based neuropsychological assessment. *Journal of Head Trauma Rehabilitation*, 17:395–410.

Shermis, M. D. & Burstein, J. (2003). *Automated essay scoring: A cross-disciplinary perspective*. Hillsdale, NJ: Erlbaum.

Silvester, J., Anderson, N., Haddleton, E., et al. (2000). A cross-modal comparison of telephone and face-to-face selection interviews in graduate recruitment. *International Journal of Selection and Assessment*, 8:16–21.

Ström, L., Petterson, R., & Andersson, G. (2000). A controlled trial of recurrent headache conducted via the Internet. *Journal of Consulting and Clinical Psychology*, 86:722–727.

Suler, J. (2000). *Identity management in cyberspace*. Retrieved November 1, 2002, from http://p24601.rider.edu/suler/psycyber/identitymanage.html.

Suler, J. (2001). *The online disinhibition effect*. Retrieved November 1, 2002, from http://www.rider.edu/users/suler/psycyber/disinhibit.html.

Suler, J., Barak, A., Chechele, P., et al. (2001). Assessing a person's suitability for online therapy. *CyberPsychology & Behavior*, 4:675–679. (See Correction, 2002, *CyberPsychology & Behavior*, 5:93.)

Suler, J. R. & Phillips, W. L. (2000). The bad boys of cyberspace: Deviant behavior in a multimedia chat community. *CyberPsychology & Behavior*, 1:275–294.

Tseng, H., Macleod, H. A., Wright, P. (1997). Computer anxiety and measurement of mood change. *Computers in Human Behavior, 13*:305–316.

Tucker-Ladd, C. E. (2000). *Psychological self-help.* Retrieved November 1, 2002, from http://www.mentalhelp.net/psyhelp.

Turkle, S. (1995). *Life on the screen: Identity in the age of the Internet.* New York: Simon & Schuster.

Volcani, Y. (2000). The tale of SAGASTM: Bringing apperception tests into cyber world. *CyberPsychology & Behavior, 3*:303–307.

Wall, J. E. (2000). Technology-delivered assessment: Power, problems, and promise. In J. W. Bloom & G. R. Walz (Eds.), *Cybercounseling and cyberlearning: Strategies and resources for the millennium* (pp. 237–251). Alexandria, VA: American Counseling Association.

Walther, J. B. (1996). Computer-mediated communication: Impersonal, interpersonal, and hyperpersonal interaction. *Communication Research, 23*:3–43.

Weekley, J. A. & Jones, C. (1999). Further studies of situational tests. *Personnel Psychology, 52*:679–700.

Yoshino, A., Shigemura, J., Kobayashi, Y., et al. (2001). Telepsychiatry: Assessment of televideo psychiatric interview reliability with present- and next-generation Internet infrastructures. *Acta Psychiatrica Scandinavica, 104*:223–226.

12

INTERNATIONAL AND MULTICULTURAL ISSUES

ADRIAN E. G. SKINNER AND
GARY LATCHFORD

*After all, when you come right down to it, how many
people speak the same language even when they speak the
same language?*
(Russell Hoban, *The Lion of Boaz-Jachin and
Jachin-Boaz*, Ch. 27, 1925)

The first author recently flew from the United Kingdom to the United States. On arrival in the United States purchases were made with credit cards; on return home the bill was on the doormat. While in the United States emails were sent home.

To accomplish these tasks, flights and reservations were made on the Internet, involving companies in the United Kingdom and the United States. A "back office" specialist in Canada, to whom one or more of the banks involved had subcontracted this work, processed the credit card transactions. The emails visited servers in a number of countries making their way to their destinations. On return home it was necessary to query an item on the account—a "local" call made from the United Kingdom was answered by an employee based in Delhi, where the bank had sited its Call Center.

This tale of everyday life in the 21st century illustrates that we now live in the "global village" envisaged by Marshall McLuhan in the 1970s. It is now takes no more effort to communicate with someone across the world than it takes to talk to a neighbor. Many transactions cross international boundaries without the permission or even the knowledge of those involved. Importantly, as McLuhan foresaw, the technology involved has changed the nature of the transaction (McLuhan & Powers, 1992). He would undoubtedly have seen it as inevitable that not only would counseling and psychological treatment be delivered via the Internet, but that these services would be delivered across national and cultural boundaries.

The chapter authors are both English, and work providing psychological treatment in the U.K. National Health Service.[1] This chapter has been informed by the developments in the therapeutic community in the United Kingdom to respond to the needs of a multicultural society, and by the authors' experiences within it.

CULTURAL ISSUES IN COUNSELING

Recent years have seen a clear recognition that ethnicity and culture play a potentially important role in therapeutic relationships, with the publication of guidelines for those providing psychological services to ethnic minorities (e.g., APA, 1993), many insightful works on the mechanisms of action and the potential for racism (Fernando, 1993), and some documents outlining the key areas for training (Patel et al., 1996) and multicultural skills of counselors (Sue et al., 1992).

This short chapter cannot hope to provide a comprehensive summary of this important work; it will focus specifically on the implications for online counseling. Some initial thoughts are necessary, however. First, rather than discuss definitions of different ethnic groups, we would like to encourage you to see culture as something individuals define themselves in relation to. All of us carry the influences of our own culture or cultures. It is important to remember that any discussion of cultural issues is not focused exclusively on the client, but takes account of the culture of the therapist and the interaction that results. To begin with, then, take a look at Table 12.1 before you continue.

The second point to note is that cultural diversity will mean different things to different people in different parts of the world. Mental health services in Northern England may focus on providing an adequate service for those whose ethnic background is Pakistani or Indian, for example, while in parts of the United States the focus may be on Spanish-speaking Americans. Contemplating online counseling, the reality is that the potential juxtaposition of cultures between client and therapist is breathtakingly wide.

[1]The U.K. National Health Service (NHS) is a government-funded organization that provides most health care to U.K. citizens, including running the majority of hospitals. Private treatment is available but regarded mostly as a "top-up" and used only by a minority. Psychological treatment and counseling is also available throughon the NHS as well as in the voluntary and private sectors.

TABLE 12.1   Looking at Your Own Culture

Question 1	How would you define your own culture?
Question 2	What influence does your culture have on you?
	Your religion and beliefs?
	Your choice of food?
	Your choice of partner/friends?
	Your choice of places to live/places to travel to?
	Your sense of security within your society?
	Your experience of discrimination?
	Your reaction to someone with a different cultural background?
	The reaction of those with a different cultural background to you?

How might cultural differences between therapist and client influence the process?

PERCEPTIONS OF THE THERAPIST ABOUT THE CLIENT

Our own culture influences the way we see ourselves and others. In the context of counseling, the therapist may have a stereotyped view of people from certain cultures, may have limited understanding of the experience of the client (e.g., of racist abuse), or may have limited understanding of the role of culture in the experience of physical or mental illness (e.g., the role of spiritual beliefs in coping with a chronic physical illness).

PERCEPTIONS OF THE CLIENT ABOUT THE THERAPIST

The client may have particular expectations of a therapist with a different cultural background, and may be apprehensive or uncomfortable, or fear being misunderstood. In a situation where the client comes from a cultural minority and the therapist from the majority, then the "power" status within the therapeutic context may be skewed. The ability to consult "away" from a local situation may actually encourage people from minority communities to seek help via other means such as the Internet.

LANGUAGE

Most counselors and therapists will have come across situations in which they have seen clients with a different mother tongue. In the majority of face-to-face (f2f) transactions the client will have moved to the therapist's country and neighborhood and will be fluent in the language of his or her hosts. In other situations there will have been linguistic barriers that will have had to be overcome. In areas where there are large numbers of immigrants using the language of their inheritance, then local authorities may have set up special facilities. The success of these enterprises is variable. In northern England, black mental health centers do a good job in providing ethnically appropriate support to the Punjabi- and Urdu-speaking population, but the success of black West Indian mental health centers in London and the Midlands has not protected this population from, for instance, the overdiagnosis of psychotic disorders (Littlewood, 1992; McGovern & Cope, 1991). Even in situations where both participants speak the same language there are ample opportunities for misunderstandings to arise via the regional or national differences. One can imagine the confusion when an English client with an American counselor announces, "I'm dying for a fag [cigarette]" during an online session! In George Bernard Shaw's words, we are "2 nations separated by a common tongue."

The use of the Internet for counseling has, therefore, both potential advantages and disadvantages from a multicultural perspective. The absence of visual and auditory cues might imply that both parties are less likely to be swayed in their judgements by cultural factors. What is less clear is whether this is always a good thing!

THE CULTURAL CONTEXT OF MODELS
OF COUNSELING

Most models of counseling are rooted in Western models of psychology, and this can create problems. Research involving participants from different ethnic backgrounds has not always been methodologically rigorous, leading to common but unsubstantiated stereotypes such as "South Asians are more likely to somatize mental illness." Further, the often implicit assumption is that non-Western models of psychology are inferior. Other authors have placed counseling in a much wider, international context, arguing that all cultures have developed models of healing based on either a medical-physiological, sociopsychological, supernatural, or bodily functional/behavioral intervention, and that in Western societies these have tended to become specialized and distinct (Tseng & Hsu, 1979). It is important to be aware of this context, and open to the experience and beliefs of the client.

THE IMPACT OF ONLINE COUNSELING

Research into the importance of culture in online counseling is in its infancy, and we simply do not have the answers to many questions we would like to ask. It is, however, apparent that the ability bestowed by Internet services may have a profound impact on how people seek counseling and how they experience it.

It is possible that the absence of the visual cues that would otherwise influence people's assumptions of culture (e.g., color of skin) may lead to a degree of cultural blindness. It is also possible, however, that people will rely more on other cues, such as surname. Moreover, the assumptions individuals have about cultures remain, and it is arguable that the risk of misunderstanding can be even greater. It is likely, for example, that online counselors would, in theory, be exposed to clients from a great many unfamiliar cultural backgrounds, well beyond their expertise. Understanding the beliefs, needs, and social context of the client is important, and to achieve this in such a situation would require counselors to acknowledge their lack of knowledge and skills and to be aware of any assumptions they may make. They need to be prepared to listen with sensitivity and to support their work with appropriate study.

It should also be remembered that future developments will inevitably see the widespread introduction of real-time video, which will again alter the cues available to counselor and client influencing the assumptions they make about the other.

Another possibility, of course, is that it may be possible to provide counseling from someone of a similar background more easily than it is at present. For instance, someone of a West Indian background living in London or a Hispanic living in Chicago could conceivably choose to consult a counselor based in the West Indies or Cuba, feeling that they were more comfortable dealing with their problems in this way.

This would, of course, set new difficulties for the counselor, whose potential ignorance of the culture of his or her clients might be replaced by ignorance about their environment instead. Would a black Briton of West Indian heritage receive a better service from a white British counselor who lived in the same town than from a West Indian counselor working in Jamaica?

Finally, consideration of these issues raises an important dilemma. Should counselors take cultural background into consideration in the assessment, mindful that not doing so may lead to ignoring a major influence on the client, or should they take advantage of the medium and strive to remain culturally blind, keeping their client's and their own cultural background hidden so that the biases they would introduce are kept from the experience of counseling? Given the many subtle influences of culture and stereotype, the latter is probably impossible, but we would also like to stress the difficulties inherent in the first option: to really attempt to understand the cultural context of client and counselor is not easy, but we would argue that it is essential.

ETHICS

A number of organizations in the United States and the United Kingdom have produced ethical guidelines about working on the Internet. The

American Psychological Association's guidelines are quite basic (APA, 1997) and caution the practitioner to exercise care in this new medium; its booklet aimed at the actual or potential consumer (APA, 2000) concentrates on providing guidance on assessing the quality of information on the Internet. The ACA guidelines (American Counseling Association, 1999), while making no explicit statement about international practice, make detailed recommendations about issues such as ensuring backup for Internet clients and adhering to "state regulations" that militate against international work. The British Psychological Society's report (BPS, 2001) makes specific reference to potential problems in operating outside national boundaries, and although this report does not recommend "banning" such transactions it does suggest that international users be made aware of specific potential problems. Similarly, the BAC's report (British Association for Counselling and Psychotherapy, 1999) has a number of concerns about Internet counseling that might be made more acute across international boundaries.

The report produced by the International Society for Mental Health Online (ISMHO Case Study Group, 2001) about assessing suitability for Internet therapy faces a number of these issues squarely. Apart from linguistic and cultural concerns the report stresses the need for online therapy to be potentially part of a treatment package; such a package must inevitably be more difficult to assemble across national boundaries. The Group expresses concerns about the effect of concurrent or previous therapy; there are risks that clinicians may have faulty or incomplete understanding of treatments in other countries and cultures. The group is also concerned about cross-cultural practice and recommends that clinicians only practice within cultures with which they are familiar.

Although none of these concerns will necessarily be exacerbated by the presence of an international boundary, this might well occur. What kind of issues may be made more acute across international boundaries?

ISSUES OF SECURITY: THE IDENTITY OF THE THERAPIST

A key area of difficulty for the client obtaining counseling on the Internet is the establishment of the identity and credentials of the person providing the service. How does the client determine that his or her counselor is properly qualified and trained?

These problems also exist in the "real" world, but in the cyberworld they are potentially made more difficult. When we visit the office of a doctor, dentist, or counselor, we are supplied with cues that tell us that we are visiting a properly qualified person. There may be certificates on the wall, the service provider may be sharing premises with other professionals, etc. The cues tell us that the service provider has had their credentials checked by a trusted authority and is who they say they are.

Using the Internet, the client is prevented from making many of these checks. There is no office and no wall of certificates. A number of websites offer "credential checks," such as that offered at Martha Ainsworth's "Metanoia" site (http://www.metanoia.org/imhs/identity.htm). Other websites are less regulated and consist of little more than an advertising service in which therapists describe themselves. Choosing a "credential-checked" therapist will certainly increase the level of protection for a client, but it is perhaps expecting too much for any organization to understand the complexities of a wide variety of therapy professions in numerous countries. It is also difficult to estimate the validity of different "credential checking" processes offered by a variety of websites. Certainly some websites offer advertising space to therapists who do not mention any qualifications, or whose qualifications are not widely recognized. This is scarcely surprising in view of the enormous task they set themselves in making judgments about a variety of professionals from all over the world.

If a client uses a counselor from another country then this problem is therefore potentially much greater. Is the person I am consulting registered with the professional body in his or her own country? What is the professional body in that country?

To illustrate our point, the "qualification" situation in two countries with quite similar traditions and languages (the United States and the United Kingdom) is radically different. The United States has a tradition of state registration of a large number of therapy professions, which both protects the public and oversees the payment of fees by insurers. When U.S. citizens go to a psychologist, social worker, or counselor in the United States, they know that an independent authority governs the professional's qualifications and practices. Using the Internet for therapy would not be problematical for these organizations if the therapist and client came from the same state or country, but might be if the two resided in different countries.

Practicing counseling or psychotherapy in the United Kingdom, however, is unregistered and anyone may call himself or herself a psychologist or counselor. There are a number of counseling and psychotherapy organizations although there is no statutory body. People practicing bizarre treatments can and do set up fine-sounding organizations. Some of these are listed on U.S.-based websites.

This may sound hopelessly disorganized, and to some extent it is. The British Psychological Society has been seeking statutory registration for psychologists for many years and there have been similar attempts by counseling and psychotherapy organizations to persuade Parliament to legislate to control the practice of a range of psychotherapies. To date these efforts have not resulted in success, due in part to disagreements among those wishing to be registered. Lord Alderdice, Speaker of the Northern Ireland Assembly and trained psychoanalyst, attempted to introduce a bill regulating psychotherapy to Parliament in 2001 but failed when the government did not support it; instead, action was sought to register psychologists under existing regulations. Psychologists are to be registered under the Health Professions Council in the next two years.

The potentially harmful effects of this omission are mitigated by the fact that a substantial amount of counseling and therapy in the United Kingdom is organized through the National Health Service (NHS). The NHS only employs or contracts with properly qualified staff, and thus undertakes the credential-checking task. Therapy in the private sector is often on the basis of referral from a family doctor, who will have undertaken the same task.

There are, of course, instances where unqualified or maverick counselors and psychologists (and doctors and dentists) have carried on dubious practices, sometimes for many years. It is not our contention that the international use of the Internet for therapy exposes users to a new risk, just that it increases an existing one.

As can be seen from the above account of United Kingdom events, and the contrast between the United Kingdom and the United States, someone seeking counseling from a practitioner in another country, even when the two countries seem similar in language and tradition, could be quite severely handicapped when judging the qualifications of his or her counselor.

ISSUES OF SECURITY: THE IDENTITY OF THE CLIENT

Just as the client seeking treatment needs to have concerns about his or her therapist, so the Internet therapist must have concerns about the identity of his or her client. Because these transactions are frequently fee-based, the provision of a credit card number provides part of this check. There is, however, no guarantee that the person logging in is the client, although measures can be taken to minimize this problem. There is a risk of a child masquerading as an adult, a male passing themselves off as female, etc. It is not apparent to us that these kinds of risks are any greater across national boundaries, but it does seem as if the insistence of some U.S. insurance or Health Maintenance Organizations on restricting practice to clients and counselors from the same state may protect against this to an extent.

The drawback of such a stance, however, is that it prevents a resident of, say, Utah from benefiting from the expertise of an online therapist in New York, never mind anywhere else in the world.

SECURITY OF THE TRANSACTION

As there are with other types of Internet transactions, there are concerns about the security of counseling transactions on the Internet. Such transactions need to be protected by measures such as encryption. There is, however, no reason to suppose that international transactions would be any more vulnerable than national ones.

ISSUES OF SAFETY: PROTECTION AND REDRESS
OF GRIEVANCE

In an f2f transaction, or with an Internet transaction with a therapist in the same country, the client has a route to follow if something goes wrong. In both the United States and the United Kingdom, the therapist will probably have an employer or professional association with whom to lodge a complaint, and the client has the resort of legal action. It's important to note, however, that the therapist is also protected from groundless or frivolous complaints.

This legal protection largely disappears with international Internet transactions. Many sites state that their service is conducted under the laws of the country in which they are based (http://www.psychologyonline. co.uk). In consequence, a disgruntled client would have to undertake legal action in the resident country of the service, potentially an expensive and confusing task of grappling with an unfamiliar legal system. Interestingly, there are moves toward authorities claiming jurisdiction over Internet transactions involving their residents ("An Act to Amend Chapter 63, Title 40, Code of Laws of South Carolina, 1976, Relating to the Licensure and Regulations of Social Workers," 2002), although it is difficult to envisage a therapist in, say, Australia being prosecuted by the South Carolina authorities. It is also likely that the therapist would claim (perhaps with some justification) that his or her services were governed by the country or state in which he or she were based. In any case, in practice it would be difficult to enforce legislation across international boundaries.

Taking a broader view, it is likely that the question of Internet liability will be addressed first in a more popular area of e-commerce, after which Internet counseling may well be forced to follow whatever precedents are set down.

The other mode of redress for a disappointed client would be to a therapist's professional organization, if he or she is a member of one. Such organizations should be prepared to investigate an international complaint, though this investigation may well be hampered and/or made more expensive and difficult for the client.

However, organizations such as the APA and BPS have extensive investigatory and disciplinary machinery and there is no reason why they should not handle international complaints using the same technology that facilitated the Internet transaction to interview the complainant and therapist.

We are of the opinion that one of the consequences of the Internet revolution may be that these organizations find that they need to be much more cooperative on an international level. One could very well see a future scenario in which the APA asked the BPS to conduct an investigation together if a case involved both United States and United Kingdom participants. Such an enterprise would require a much closer understanding and appreciation of each other's differing cultures, standards, and expectations.

LIMITS OF CONFIDENTIALITY

Situations will arise in which therapists have to consider breaching client confidentiality. For instance, a client may confess to a crime or say he or she intends to commit one. A client may also present with thoughts or behaviors that threaten his or her health or integrity and may, in the extreme, require hospitalization.

For f2f practitioners this problem is familiar (if infrequent) and they have the training, skills, and the local knowledge to cope with the situation. The increased distance between therapist and client would potentially create great problems—whom would the therapist call? Moreover, there may well be different expectations with respect to confidentiality in different cultures.

ACCESS TO SUPPORT

Practitioners of f2f therapy will regularly consult with fellow professionals about clients, almost always with that client's permission. Clients in therapy will often be taking medication prescribed by a psychiatrist or family doctor, and there is usually good liaison with the therapist. If an Internet practitioner becomes concerned about a client's medication or medical care and that client comes from the same country, the problems of distance may well be overcome with the use of the telephone. This would be much less easy across national boundaries where, for example, time zones may impede contact or medications may be differently named. In addition, an Internet practitioner may not have access to information about resources local to the client.

There is significant doubt that an Internet practitioner would be able to exercise a full "duty to protect" his or her client if that client were far distant and operating in a care system about which the practitioner might know little.

MULTICULTURAL COMPETENCE

It is reasonable to expect of an online counselor that he or she will consider the implications of working with clients with different cultural backgrounds, as well as the competencies he or she needs to provide an adequate service (see Table 12. 2 for a concise outline). As we have emphasized, this process begins with counselors increasing their awareness of their own cultural influences and their beliefs about other cultures, and then increasing their understanding of other cultures. They also must focus on the influence of culture on understanding and expression of mental and physical health problems, as well as how culture affects the understanding and expectations of counseling. It involves an acceptance of difference, and an active attempt

TABLE 12.2 Developing Cross-Cultural Skills

1. Increasing self awareness of:
   a. The influence of your own culture
   b. Your assumptions about other cultures
   c. Your feelings about working with clients from other cultures
   d. The potential impact on clients with different cultural backgrounds of your own culture
2. Developing knowledge of different cultures, e.g.:
   a. Acknowledging the importance of the cultural context for the individual
   b. Acknowledging the influence on beliefs about health/mental health
   c. Acknowledging the influence on experience and expectations of counseling
3. Developing culturally sensitive interventions, i.e.:
   a. Respecting individual beliefs and cultural differences
   b. Acknowledging limitations as a counselor
   c. Actively seeking knowledge and advice/supervision

to fill the many gaps in knowledge and skill. We strongly recommend the reader follow up the references given in the present chapter.

"PREPARE TO BE ASSIMILATED!"

Of the messages entered on the e-group run by the International Society for Mental Health Online, a significant proportion concern therapists' worries about practicing abroad or out-of-state. Often informal and formal advice is "Don't do it!" The difficulties outlined above, especially legal uncertainties and problems with funding, have lead to a widely held view that Internet therapy is fine provided it is practiced only within national or state boundaries. See Table 12.3 for a summary of key issues.

However, the decision of whether to offer services across geographical boundaries may not be a decision counselors have the privilege of making for much longer: consumers will exercise their right to choose who to

TABLE 12.3 Opportunities and Threats in International Practice

1. What are the advantages and disadvantages for the client?
2. What are the advantages and disadvantages for the counselor?
3. If you were to offer a service to someone from another country, how would you:
   a. Ensure your qualifications are accepted by the client
   b. Follow the requirements of the law where you and/or your client reside
   c. Take into account the cultural background and context of the client
   d. Plan to deal with a situation in which you became concerned about your client's well-being
4. How do you think that international practice will affect traditional counseling in the future?

consult, seeking out the most appropriate (or cheapest) counselor regardless of national or international boundaries. Market forces may well determine the way online counseling develops in the future.

Editors' Note: Even when the Internet resembles a global bulletin board, where everyone can cross borders with amazing ease to approach an abundance of services or resources, delivery of professional services by licensed clinicians to the public is still governed by state laws and restricted by the clinician's malpractice insurance. Readers are invited to review the ethics chapter in this book (see Chapter 6) as well as visit www.EthicsCode.com for more details about existing recommendations.

SUMMARY

Online counseling is already having an impact and has raised important issues regarding areas such as ethics and security. We have argued that the difficulties in addressing these issues are multiplied when an international dimension is added. Although we have recognized the reluctance of many online counselors to take on clients from other geographical areas, we feel that such a change is inevitable in the future.

Responses to the challenges this creates will inevitably be both organizational and personal. Professional and state organizations need to address the legitimate concerns of current and potential users of these services, ensuring that complaints are investigated and services are regulated.

On a personal level, it is up to all online counselors contemplating work with clients from different cultural backgrounds to be familiar with the issues that may arise, and to ensure that they are equipped with the skills that will enable them to be competent to practice. We have provided a very short introduction to the area, and attempted to raise awareness of the important issues, both practical, such as access to support, and more theoretical, such as the way the medium may affect cultural aspects of the therapeutic process.

We feel that an awareness of multicultural issues is fundamental to all practitioners, but would argue that the opportunities afforded by online counseling again add a different dimension. There is a real prospect of clients seeking out specialists with different cultural backgrounds in different countries, or clients seeking out counselors with similar cultural backgrounds but potentially different understanding of context. In either case, there is potential for confusion in the resulting combination of client and therapist.

One thing is certain, and that is that there is no going back. It is likely that the future of online counseling is one largely without national or cultural boundaries, but one where these will nevertheless impinge significantly on therapy. It is a future of more choice for consumers, challenges for providers, and a great deal of interest for sympathetic observers of this developing scene.

KEY TERMS

Counseling, therapy: Terms used interchangeably meaning the provision of active psychological intervention designed to aid the recipient.

Confidentiality: The agreement not to share certain kinds of information, or information gathered in a specific setting.

Culture: The customary beliefs, social forms, and material traits of a racial, religious, or social group.

Ethics: The principles of conduct governing an individual or a group.

Perception: The interpretation of the utterances and actions of one person by another.

Therapist: A psychologist, counselor, social worker, or any practitioner qualified to provide mental health interventions.

REFERENCES

An Act to Amend Chapter 63, Title 40, Code of Laws of South Carolina, 1976, Relating to the Licensure and Regulation of Social Workers (2002). Code of Laws of South Carolina (Chapter 63, Title 40).

American Counseling Association (1999). Ethical standards for Internet online counseling.

APA (1993). *APA guidelines for providers of psychological services to ethnic, linguistic, and culturally diverse populations.* APA online. Retrieved October 27, 2003, from http://www.apa.org/pi/oema/guide.html.

APA (1997). APA statement on services by telephone, teleconferencing, and Internet. American Psychological Association.

APA (2000). dotCOMSENSE: Report. American Psychological Association.

BPS (2001). The provision of psychological services via the Internet and other non-direct means: A professional report. British Psychological Society.

British Association for Counselling and Psychotherapy (1999). *Counselling online: opportunities and risks in counselling clients via the Internet.* Rugby: BAC.

Fernando, S. (1993). *Mental health, race & culture.* London: Macmillan Education.

ISMHO Case Study Group (2001). Assessing a person's suitability for online therapy, (Vol. 2002): International Society for Mental Health Online.

Littlewood, R. (1992). Psychiatric diagnosis and racial bias: Empirical and interpretative approaches. *Social Science & Medicine, 34:*141–149.

McGovern, D., & Cope, R. (1991). Second generation of Afro-Caribbeans and young Whites with a first admission diagnosis of schizophrenia. *Social Psychiatry & Psychiatric Epidemiology, 26:*95–99.

McLuhan M., & Powers, B. R. (1992). *The global village: Transformations in world life and media in the 21st century.* Oxford University Press.

Patel, N., Bennet, E., Dennis, M., et al. (1996). *Clinical psychology, "race" and culture: A training manual.* Leicester: British Psychological Society.

Roth, A., & Fonagy, O. (1996). *What works for whom? A critical review of psychotherapy research.* London: Guilford Press.

Sue, D., Arrendondo, P., & McDavis, R. (1992). Multi-cultural counselling competencies and standards: a call to the profession. *Journal of Counselling and Development, 70*:477–486.

Tseng, W., & Hsu, J. (1979). Culture and psychotherapy. In A. J. Marsella & R. Thorp & T. Ciborowski (Eds.), *Perspectives on cross-cultural psychology*. London: Croom Helm.

PART

IV

A LOOK TO THE
FUTURE OF ONLINE
COUNSELING

13

THE FUTURE OF
ONLINE COUNSELING

LEONARD HOLMES AND
MARTHA AINSWORTH

Imagine a future in which no one feels embarrassed about seeing a counselor. Imagine a future in which mental health care is accessible to everyone, where competent and caring therapists are so plentiful that no one need travel far to see one. Imagine a future in which emotional health is so valued by society that mental health care has been made affordable and barrier-free.

Is this science fiction? It could be. Science fiction does not so much predict the future as it examines our concerns about the present by projecting them to extremes. Writers often explore issues such as overpopulation, racism, and poverty through science fiction, and could just as well use it to examine ideas about mental health care and Internet communication. Will our vision of the future reflect our hopes, or our fears?

In his short story "The Machine Stops," novelist E. M. Forster imagines a future in which humans live their entire lives in isolation, each person confined to one small, luxurious room. The technological features of the room provide them with every comfort. In this future, people never meet in person; only an electronic communication system connects them with each other, while they remain enclosed in the privacy of their own rooms.

Those who are uncertain about the benefits of online counseling may fear a future like the one Forster describes. They too may fear that Internet communication will depersonalize and isolate us, and thus will have little value for mental health. But our positive experience of the present encourages us to embrace a more hopeful vision for the future. It may be a very long time before mental health care is barrier-free. Until that time comes, we feel that online counseling offers unique possibilities that may even help that hopeful future come to pass.

Imagining a future for online counseling requires one to visualize a complex web of possibilities stretching in many directions. Few strands of this web move in a single, unambiguous direction. Like science fiction writers, we can extrapolate some potential future paths if we assume that current trends will continue. We will attempt this task using our own experiences and the insights of the experts who have authored the previous chapters. Numerous issues, many of which can be neither foreseen nor controlled, create forks in the road. The direction that online counseling will take at these intersections remains uncertain. Even the state of online counseling in 2002 would have been difficult to predict 10 years ago when the World Wide Web was new. The authors of this chapter have been active in online mental health since the early 1980s, before the Internet, as we know it, really existed. Among the first therapists to offer online consultations to the public over the Internet and among the earliest consumer advocates for it, we each envisioned a future for online counseling. Some of our vision has come to pass, and some is still coming to fruition. We both have been surprised by developments that we could not have predicted.

We have no doubt that online counseling will have a future. It is safe to say that people will continue to seek emotional help and advice online, and that mental health professionals will continue providing it. Those of you reading this will have a hand in creating this future. By envisioning some of the possibilities, perhaps we can encourage you to influence the direction the field will take.

PRIVATE PRACTICE ONLINE COUNSELING

We believe that individual psychotherapists will continue to practice online. Some therapists in the United States will open online practices to supplement an income that has been eroded by the growing influence of "managed care" on mental health care. Offering services online on an independent website is a way to become an entrepreneur in an age of big health care corporations. Managed care has stripped many therapists of their autonomy. Providing services online for a fixed fee can be a refreshing break from the sometimes-excessive rules and regulations imposed by managed care companies.

Opening an "online practice" is relatively simple for any therapist to do. Creating and editing Web pages has become as easy as using a word processor. Even a therapist who is an Internet novice can offer services using encrypted email with the help of user-friendly software programs now available. Individual entrepreneurs can easily accept payment online by credit card, using their existing merchant accounts over the Internet, or use economical services that allow such payments even without a merchant account.

The cost of opening and operating an individual online practice on a do-it-yourself basis is also quite reasonable at present, and we anticipate this trend will continue. As of this writing, we calculate that a private practice online counseling website can be created by an enterprising therapist for an initial cost of no more than $350[1] without unusual technical expertise or assistance from a professional Web designer, and can be maintained for less than $30 per month. As innovations continue to make it easy and convenient to create online content and accept online payment, we anticipate that an increasing number of therapists will be encouraged to try it.

To date, nearly all large-scale commercial online counseling ventures have been unsuccessful. Such ventures seemed initially to hold great promise, because they provided individual therapists with a technologically robust online counseling environment at a modest cost. Unfortunately, as of this writing all but one have either gone out of business or have failed even to launch online counseling services. Until a viable business model is found, we believe it is unlikely that large group online counseling businesses will have a significant impact, and that it is much more likely that most online counseling will be offered primarily by individual therapists with their own private online counseling practices.

COMMUNICATION SECURITY

It seems certain that even therapists who do not establish an official online practice will increasingly communicate online between sessions with patients in their traditional practice. As technology becomes ubiquitous it is seamlessly integrated into life. Therapists don't think twice about using the telephone to communicate between sessions, though they often do set limits on such interactions. The asynchronous nature of email adds greatly to its convenience. I can read my email when I want to. Unlike a telephone call, email does not interrupt my schedule.

The fact that therapists are increasingly using email for patient communications raises important questions. Is an email between a client and a therapist part of the official medical record? Should such interactions have the status of "psychotherapy notes," which are accorded a higher level of privacy under regulations of the Health Insurance Portability and Accountability Act (HIPAA), which went into effect in 2003? Should a therapist

---

[1]Start-up costs might include: "WYSIWYG" Web authoring software (Jasc Namo Web Editor, $120), Web graphics software (Jasc Paint Shop Pro, $90), file transfer software (WS_FTP, $40), domain name registration (Verisign, $35/year), dial-up Internet access with Web hosting (Earthlink, $20/month), encrypted email software (ZixMail, $45/year), online credit card payment processing (PayPal, no setup fee), and ISMHO membership ($25/year).

who lists an email address be required to check his or her email on a daily basis? What are the implications of the fact that email can be intercepted under certain circumstances?

Privacy regulations related to HIPAA have several implications for the future of online counseling. For the first time psychotherapy notes have a different status than the rest of the medical record. The verbatim record that is created in online encounters between therapists and patients contains a good deal of sensitive information. The HIPAA privacy rules define psychotherapy notes as "notes recorded (in any medium) by a health care provider who is a mental health professional documenting or analyzing the contents of a conversation during a private counseling session or a group, joint, or family counseling session and that are separated from the rest of the individual's medical record" (U.S. Department of Health and Human Services, 2002). Much of the content of an online counseling session falls under this category, assuming that the online interaction can be considered to be a "conversation."

Does unencrypted email pose too many risks for accidental disclosure of confidential information? If a therapist is required to secure all written notes in a locked filing cabinet, and required to obtain specific additional authorization to release such notes to a third party (beyond a general consent to release information), then what requirements should there be for transmitting such material over the Internet?

All therapists who use the Internet to communicate with patients, including those who offer online counseling to the public, will need to answer these ethical and logistical concerns. Bodies that set regulations for counseling and psychotherapy may require encryption for all online communication, including online counseling, as the technology for it becomes more readily available.

INTERNET AS A COMPONENT OF
TREATMENT PROGRAMS

We predict that online treatment programs targeting specific problem areas will become even more popular. In many cases the Internet will provide only a portion of treatment, with telephone interviews, printed materials, and face-to-face (f2f) sessions also being included. Such programs exist for problem areas such as depression, eating disorders, public speaking, and agoraphobia (Botella et al., 2000; Bouchard et al., 2000). Many of these programs will follow the currently popular model of "manualized therapies." Such treatment programs can contain prewritten educational modules with homework assignments. The Internet will provide an interactive component that would otherwise prove cumbersome. By combining prewritten components with online interactive elements economies of scale can be realized without losing the "personal touch" of individual interactions.

VIDEO AND AUDIO

As more and more consumers upgrade from dial-up to high-speed Internet connections such as ISDN and cable, audio (e.g., voice-over-IP or "Internet phone") and video communication channels will become more popular, to supplement words typed on a screen.

Hospital- and clinic-based telepsychiatry treatment programs already employ high-bandwidth videoconferencing to connect treatment centers and to provide services in rural areas without sending a clinician in person. Telepsychiatry typically begins with an initial f2f interview; in subsequent sessions, the physician at the hospital center connects by videoconference with the patient at a remote regional clinic. Telepsychiatry systems can be used to follow patients after discharge, to provide consultation and training to other health care professionals, or to conduct specific treatment and educational programs. As of September 2002, the Telemedicine Information Exchange (http://tie.telemed.org) lists 70 telepsychiatry programs nationwide, in addition to numerous programs operated by the Department of Veterans Affairs and the Department of Defense.

In contrast to technologically sophisticated telepsychiatry systems, consumers and therapists have been slow to adopt video for online counseling, in part because it is difficult to achieve adequate results with consumer-level technology. Although the addition of audio and video allows online counseling to more closely approximate f2f counseling, privacy concerns may also increase. As a consumer of online mental health services I am likely to be using a computer located in a public area of my home. It is relatively easy for me to hide typed text on a computer screen from curious family members. It is more difficult to maintain privacy when live audio and video are used. By speaking aloud I am inviting others in my house to eavesdrop on my conversation.

Most therapists would prefer to have a visual connection with their patient, but the experience of some online counselors and patients suggests that some people find it easier to discuss intimate subjects when there is no visual connection. Many consumers may continue to prefer the private feel of email and text-based chat to higher-bandwidth communication channels.

A disadvantage of text-based communication is the relative lack of a sense of "presence." It may be especially difficult to have a sense of another human being "present" and communicating with you when using asynchronous email (see e.g., Heeter, 1999). Almost anything that augments text communication can enhance the sense of presence. Chat environments that allow some degree of nonverbal communication (e.g., "The Palace," researched by John Suler, or even Microsoft's "Comic Chat") enhance the sense of presence by adding another visual dimension of communication. A therapist's picture on his or her website also enhances the sense of presence. We expect to see additional attempts to enhance "presence" in essentially text-based communication.

ATTITUDES OF SOCIETY

The future of online counseling will likely be influenced by changes in the attitudes of consumers toward mental health care in general. Despite much positive change, stigma continues to create a major barrier. People who are embarrassed about their need for emotional help may find it easier to seek help online. Negative public attitudes about psychotherapy may continue to inhibit people from admitting a need for help, and inhibit them from approaching either traditional therapists or online counselors.

In the wake of the tragic events of September 11, 2001, mental health agencies estimated that as many as 1.5 million New Yorkers would need mental health help (Sealey, 2001). Yet as of this writing, a year later, only a fraction of the predicted numbers have sought help, even though trauma symptoms are clearly widespread and free counseling is easily available (Alter & Gagnon, 2002). Patriotic bravado appears to be the favored form of "therapy" and admitting to a need for help is not on the agenda for many New Yorkers (Satel, 2002). Therapists who were asked to provide on-site counseling for employees returning to work in the Wall Street area reported that after about two weeks some corporations canceled the counseling services to avoid the perception that there were any problems. "When you swim with sharks," said one therapist, "you can't afford to be wounded." This sudden flare-up of stigma may seem counterintuitive given the context, but it serves as an example of the unpredictability of public attitudes toward counseling.

For those who do decide to seek counseling, increased threats of terrorism throughout the world may increase the popularity of Internet services. People who worry about the possibility of being blown up, contaminated, or irradiated in a public place may feel that it is safer to communicate with their therapist from the relative security of their own home. Taken to extremes, could this result in a world like that envisioned by Forster? It would be easy to sympathize with the worries of those who imagine it.

ECONOMIC ISSUES

The state of the economy in general is a major factor influencing the future of online counseling. During an economic slowdown, online counseling will also slow (even though, ironically, financial stresses may increase the need). When the economy flourishes, online counselors are more likely to do so as well.

Many consumers who seek counseling online do so because managed care organizations and the mental health industry have made it difficult for them to get the care they need. People turn to the Internet for help when traditional systems fail them. If their health insurance does not provide adequate mental health care, and they cannot afford to pay out of pocket for traditional therapy, online counseling may present a less costly alternative. If personal finances are strained, however, fewer consumers will make counseling a priority in their budget—even less expensive online counseling.

As noted previously, the development of consumer-level videoconferencing technology will broaden the appeal of online counseling to more therapists and consumers. However, advances in videoconferencing depend on the availability and widespread use of broadband Internet access. Will enough consumers purchase high-speed service to encourage investors to fund broadband networks and applications? A Pew Internet study reported that as of June 2002, 24 million Americans—21% of all Internet users—had broadband access (Pew Internet & American Life Project, 2002). Although that number had quadrupled since June 2000, subscriber growth had not been as great as had been anticipated, contributing to the bankruptcy of some broadband providers, such as @Home. It is safe to predict that the number of broadband users will continue to rise, although the state of the economy in general will affect the rate of growth. Consumers with less discretionary income may decide not to upgrade to broadband access immediately.

Taking all these factors into account, we must point out that, as of this writing, no one has yet come up with a way to make online counseling profitable. Of the four large-scale commercial providers that managed to launch their services, only one survives. The marketing materials of these former companies led therapists to believe that online counseling could be a lucrative addition to one's practice. We know of no one, however, who is making a full-time living as an online counselor. Even the most successful online counselors have only a handful of online patients.

This may seem to paint a fairly bleak picture of the economic viability of the online counseling field; and if online counseling were purely a business, it would. But the "bottom line" for online counselors is more than financial. Every day, counselors participate in helping relationships via the Internet with hundreds, maybe thousands of people. Consumers report that online counseling is effective. For most counselors, that is the real bottom line.

Even if online counseling never becomes financially profitable, it will continue. People will continue seeking help on the Internet, and counselors will continue to provide it and to be excited enough by its possibilities to continue whether or not it makes them rich.

While online counseling grapples for a foothold in the United States, counselors in Europe and Asia are making significant strides. For example, Kokoronomado.com, a Japanese online counseling provider, launched at the beginning of the 21st century with funding from NEC; the site is reportedly doing a robust business. Online counseling providers are doing well in the United Kingdom, Greece, Australia, and elsewhere. Mental health professionals in the United States would do well to observe continuing developments in online counseling in other countries.

Consumers who express interest in online counseling frequently want to know whether their health insurance will pay for it. So far, the answer to this question has almost uniformly been "no." While it is possible that this may change in the future, the federal government (which sets the rules for Medicare) and insurance companies have moved very slowly when incorporating telehealth into their reimbursement schedules. Medicare incorporated some reimbursement for telehealth in 1999, but the regulations limited reimbursement to "interactive" modes (e.g., videoconference, instant messaging, Internet phone, or chat), withholding reimbursement for the much more common "store and forward" technologies (e.g., email). Although it is less likely that insurers would make this particular distinction when consideration is given to actually reimbursing online counseling, we should expect to see barriers erected. Insurance companies are cutting back coverage as overall medical costs continue to increase. It is unlikely that they will voluntarily cover this relatively new mode of delivering services.

LICENSURE ISSUES

Regulatory and licensure issues may represent the most crucial intersection in the future of online counseling. The global reach of the Internet has raised many legal boundary issues affecting not only health care but also commerce, copyright, and more. Many nations are wrestling with these issues, but for our purposes we will focus on developments in the United States, where lawmakers are considering legislation that could have a profound effect on online counseling, either enabling its further development in this nation or setting strict limits that could create a significant barrier to development.

One of the inherent qualities of the Internet is the way that it dissolves geographical boundaries. The physical distance between two persons is irrelevant to Internet communication. The Internet makes it possible for counselors to reach underserved populations who might otherwise have little or no access to care. It potentially allows everyone access to mental health care, regardless of his or her geographical location or that of the provider. A psychologist in Maryland can treat a depressed patient above the Arctic Circle. An isolated Nebraska farmer can talk to a therapist in New York City. An American in Kuwait can get help from a counselor back home. These are exciting possibilities, but existing licensure laws were not designed to account for such global interactions.

At present, most mental health professionals in the United States practice under a government-issued license that authorizes them to practice in a specific state. They may not practice in another state unless they also become licensed in that state (generally an expensive and burdensome prospect), because states typically do not recognize mental health licenses issued by other states. To help us consider the future, it will be useful to examine the reasons for the current system of state-based licensure.

The U.S. Constitution reserves to the states the power to adopt laws to protect the health, safety, and general welfare of their citizens. Licensing of health care providers enables the states to establish standards that reduce the risk of harm to their citizens from inadequate care. When these laws were written, health care was always a local, in-person activity. Now that global Internet technology allows health care professionals to diagnose and treat patients at any distance, many telehealth advocates believe that patients should have access to the highest quality of advice and treatment possible—even if it is in a different state.

Although much of the relevant legislation is not specifically related to mental health, the precedents it sets will eventually affect mental health professionals who are interested in online counseling. Most current legislation addresses "telemedicine," including telepsychiatry, which differs from online counseling in scale. Online counseling is based on consumer technology and is essentially operated by individual entrepreneurs at the e-commerce level. By contrast, telepsychiatry programs can require tens of thousands of dollars worth of sophisticated videoconferencing equipment and connectivity, and are usually pursued by hospitals, clinics, and large institutions that have financial resources to secure government funding. These large institutions are typically the ones paying for the attorneys, advisers, and lobbyists who work to secure the passage of supporting legislation. The mental health professions have mounted no similar efforts on their own behalf; yet those aspects of telemedicine legislation concerning licensure for physicians may be generalized to apply to mental health professionals.

Struggles over telemedicine law are marked by tension between the states in their role as protectors, physicians and patients who believe in the promise of telemedicine, and professional organizations protecting economic interests of their members from out-of-state competition. Most U.S. telemedicine advocates tend to favor either national licensure or mutual recognition as a method of resolving interstate licensing questions. *National licensure*, in which health care licensing would be handled by the federal government rather than the states (as, for instance, with airline pilots), would depend on all states agreeing on the same qualifications. If the considerable political and economic considerations were no barrier, this might be feasible for health care professions where licensing requirements are already similar from state to state (not typically true for mental health professions). The American Telemedicine Association (http://www.americantelemed.org) supports a national licensure scheme (American Telemedicine Association, 1998).

Mutual recognition refers to a reciprocity plan in which states would recognize licenses issued by other states. This is done now with drivers' licenses; if you are licensed to drive in one state, you may drive in any state. Mutual recognition is used within U.S. government agencies such as the Department of Veterans Affairs to enable physicians to practice across jurisdictions. The most successful example of mutual recognition to date is being promoted by the National Council of State Boards of Nursing. The Nursing Licensure Interstate Compact grants nursing licensure privileges in all participating states provided the nurse already has a valid license in at least one state. As of this writing, 18 states have agreed to this compact (National Council of State Boards of Nursing, 2002).

Some health care professional organizations oppose interstate licensing for economic reasons. In Florida, the radiologist lobby was nearly successful in getting a law passed that would have required *full licensure* in Florida for all physicians from another state who practice medicine in Florida (Telemedicine Information Exchange, 2000). The bill was eventually shelved, as it was thought to promote professional protectionism and to limit the health care choices of Florida consumers.

Although political action prevented the passage of that particular bill, the majority of states considering legislation on this issue have adopted a similarly restrictive approach. Full state licensure is firmly supported by the American Medical Association (AMA), which lobbies against bills that would enable interstate licensure. The AMA successfully lobbied against federal legislation that would have prohibited interstate commerce restrictions in telemedicine (American Medical Association, 1997). The Young Physicians Section of the AMA recently issued its own policy supporting uniform interstate licensure (Young Physicians Section, American Medical Association, 2002).

Other proposed schemes to regulate the practice of medicine across state lines, including limited licensure and registration, are favored by various organizations including the Center for Telemedicine Law (http://www.ctl.org) and the Federation of State Medical Boards (http://www.fsmb.org). The Association of State and Provincial Psychology Boards (http://www.asppb.org) has drafted a Model Act for Licensure for Psychologists that addresses interjurisdictional practice for psychologists. As of this writing no states have adopted it.

The American Telemedicine Association (ATA) asserts that because telemedicine is inherently national rather than local in scope, legislation that erects barriers against it violates the Commerce Clause of the U.S. Constitution by restricting interstate commerce (American Telemedicine Association, 1998). The ATA further notes that in legal challenges, activities that protect local economic interests at the expense of interstate commerce exceed the scope of state regulatory authority and are generally found unconstitutional. This may prove an effective argument for interstate licensing; however, the current Supreme Court appears unlikely to be swayed by it (D. Nickelson, personal communication, September 2002).

One important issue in interstate licensure is the question of where the treatment takes place. When a therapist and a patient in different states interact via the Internet, which state has jurisdiction, the patient's state or the therapist's state? Some online counselors have used contracts to attempt to define their own state as the location of the online counseling interaction. Licensing boards may not agree with this interpretation. Internet gambling sites that make the same argument still face legislation that restricts their activities in certain jurisdictions (although that has not shut these sites down).

Clinicians interested in online counseling are advised to stay abreast of developments in telemedicine legislation. One convenient source of news is the Telemedicine Information Exchange (http://tie.telemed.org), which tracks state and federal legislation concerning telemedicine.

As you see, professional associations have been effective in influencing telemedicine law—whether they support interstate licensure (National Council of State Boards of Nursing) or wish to restrict it (American Medical Association). The future of telemedicine is being determined in large part by those organizations that dedicate resources and proactively work to enact legislation to support their agendas. The future of online counseling in the United States could be determined by those who commit themselves to organized political action.

If online counseling is to flourish in the United States, those who practice it and believe in it will need to take organized political action on their own behalf to protect their own interests. Waiting for one's own professional organization to take up this cause may make it easier for those who support restrictive licensure requirements to accomplish their agendas, adversely affecting the development of online counseling. Traditional organizations such as the American Psychological Association and the American Psychiatric Association represent professions organized and regulated at the state level. When pressed to take a stand on the issue of interstate licensing they may choose a restrictive approach that protects local economic interests of their members against competition from counselors in other professions and in other states (like the American Medical Association has done), even if such a stance is not in the best interests of consumers. As of this writing, neither of these organizations has taken an official position regarding interstate practice (D. Nickelson, personal communication, September 2002).

Organizations such as the International Society for Mental Health Online (ISMHO) (http://www.ismho.org) have more at stake in these discussions. ISMHO is an independent, interdisciplinary organization founded in 1997 "to promote the understanding, use and development of online communication, information and technology for the international mental health community," and has quickly become the unofficial professional organization for online counselors. Independent organizations such as ISMHO might provide vehicles for online counselors to work together proactively toward passage of legislation that will solve the legal uncertainties surrounding the field.

Telehealth in general, and online counseling in particular, will only flourish in the United States if laws and regulations allow health professionals to practice across state lines. The promise of online counseling rests in part on the possibility of reaching people for whom traditional mental health care is not readily available. Online counseling can give someone in a sparsely populated area access to the same range of counselor options as someone living in New York City or Los Angeles. Restrictive licensure laws are viewed by many as limiting patient rights by denying them access to mental health care that is located in a different state.

Consumers accustomed to the immediacy, convenience, and global reach of e-commerce will have little patience for any restriction in their choice of online counselor. People often find it difficult to get up the courage to talk to a counselor. If their initial attempt doesn't work out, they may not try a second time. If a consumer is drawn to a particular therapist, works up the courage to make contact, and then discovers that he or she is restricted from communicating with that therapist, this consumer may choose to abandon the idea of counseling altogether, rather than to settle for a different counselor located in his or her own state. Restrictive licensure laws will not only create additional barriers to mental health care, they will seriously hamper the already challenged commercial viability of online counseling.

CONCLUSION

Like most worthwhile endeavors, online counseling faces a future filled with both risk and opportunity. We are cautiously optimistic as we consider the future of online counseling. Our optimism assumes that mental health professionals who are interested in online counseling will act on that interest. We have outlined some of the issues that will define the years ahead. The future of online counseling is largely up to you, the reader.

REFERENCES

Alter, J., & Gagnon, G. (2002). The future of New York. *Newsweek*, September 9, 51–52. Retrieved September 17, 2002, from http://www.msnbc.com/news/801471.asp.

American Medical Association (1997). H-275.973 State control of qualifications for medical licensure. Retrieved September 18, 2002, from http://www.ama-assn.org/apps/pf_online/pf_online?f_n=browse&doc=policyfiles/HOD/H-275.973.htm.

American Medical Association (2002). Legislation governing the practice of medicine across State lines. Retrieved September 14, 2002, from http://www.ama-assn.org/ama/pub/category/2378.html Alternatives.

American Telemedicine Association (1998). ATA policy regarding state medical licensure. Retrieved September 13, 2002, from http://www.atmeda.org/news/policy.html.

Association of State and Provincial Psychology Boards (2001). Model Act for Licensure for Psychologists.

Botella, C., Banos, R., Guillen, C., et al. (2000). Telepsychology: Public speaking fear treatment on the Internet. *CyberPsychology & Behavior*, 3(6):959–968.

Bouchard, S., Payeur, R., Rivard, V., et al. (2000). Cognitive behavior therapy for panic disorder with agoraphobia in videoconference: Preliminary results. *CyberPsychology & Behavior*, 3(6):999–1007.

Forster, E. M. "The Machine Stops." Reprinted in *Composing Cyberspace*, ed. Richard Holeton, 1998 (*The Oxford and Cambridge Review*, 1909), 187.

Heeter, C. (1999). Aspects of presence in telerelating. *CyberPsychology & Behavior*, 2(4): 325–335.

National Council of State Boards of Nursing (2002). Nurse Licensure Interstate Compact. Retrieved from September 15, 2002, from http://www.ncsbn.org/public/nurselicensure compact/nurselicensurecompact_index.htm.

Nickelson, D. (2002, September). Personal communication.

Pew Internet & American Life Project (2002). The broadband difference: How online Americans' behavior changes with high-speed Internet connections at home. Retrieved from September 17, 2002, from http://www.pewinternet.org/reports/toc.asp?Report=63.

Satel, S. (2002). New Yorkers don't need therapy. *Wall Street Journal*, July 26. Retrieved September 17, 2002, from http://www.sallysatelmd.com/html/a-wsj24.html.

Sealey, G. (2001). Fragile psyches: Mental health counselors gear up for potential crises in New York. *ABC News*, November 5. Retrieved September 10, 2002, from http://abcnews.go.com/sections/us/DailyNews/STRIKE_nypsyche011005.html.

Telemedicine Information Exchange (2000). Telemedicine legislative issues summary. Retrieved September 17, 2002, from http://tie2.telemed.org/legal.

U.S. Department of Health and Human Services (2002). National Standards to Protect the Privacy of Personal Health Information. Retrieved September 18, 2002, from http://www.hhs.gov/ocr/hipaa.

INDEX